God Wants You to Prosper

Yearly Devotional

Written by
Dave and Bonnie Duell,
Mike Fehlauer, Bob Nichols,
Marshall Townsley,
Andrew Wommack, and Bob Yandian

DAVE AND BONNIE DUELL

D ave Duell and his wife, Bonnie, are the founders and senior pastors of Faith Ministries Church International, started in Denver, Colorado in 1993. They also founded Faith Ministries Christian Fellowship of Greeley, Colorado, in 1978 and helped plant several other churches. Dave is the president and founder of Faith Ministries International Network and travels the world extensively ministering in large crusades and churches. Through his apostolic call, Dave has visited 72 nations of the world. Thousands of people have been saved as a result of his ministry.

Dave ministers the encouragement of Jesus Christ wherever he goes with signs and wonders following. The lame walk, the blind see, the deaf hear. People are released from oppression, addiction, and spiritual, physical and emotional problems.

Dave is on the board of Rick Renner Ministries, AIMS (Associated International Missions Services) and Andrew Wommack Ministries. Dave received an Honorary Doctorate of Divinity from Bethel College in Riverside, California.

Bonnie is gifted to challenge women to excellence. She has accompanied Dave around the world ministering in church meetings and crusades. She received an Honorary Doctorate of Humane Letters from Bethel College in Riverside, California. Bonnie was co-director of Women Embracing the World, an international women's missions organization, for seven years. She is also the co-founder of Women Ministry Leaders. Her exemplary life in the community and throughout the world sets her apart as a woman full of wisdom.

The Duells have four married daughters and 17 grandchildren. Their example as Christian leaders inspires and challenges believers to live a life of excellence and victory. Together, Dave and Bonnie wrote two books: *Faith, Believe It—or Not* and *Faith, What a Deal!*

Dave Duell Ministries
PO Box 609
Littleton, CO 80160-0609
303-777-1113

MIKE FEHLAUER

Mike Fehlauer had the honor of becoming the Senior Pastor of Tree of Life Church on March 4, 2001. Mike is a graduate of Olivet Nazarene University with a bachelor degree in theology. Mike and Bonnie have been in ministry nearly 20 years. Before coming to New Braunfels, Pastor Mike was the Director of Foundation Ministries.

While Director of Foundation Ministries, he achieved considerable notability establishing a strong reputation as a mentor in relationship development and family issues. As founder of the non-profit organization, Foundation Ministries, Mike and his wife, Bonnie, traveled extensively throughout the United States, and the world, holding seminars and conferences on a variety of topics that provided foundational principles necessary to living a life of victory and strength. They now bring this same dedication of strong lives and families to Tree of Life Church.

Pastor Mike is the author of *Finding Freedom from the Shame of the Past, Life Without Fear* and *Exposing Spiritual Abuse*, published by Creation House. Mike is also a frequent contributor to <u>Charisma Magazine</u>, as well as <u>Ministries Today Magazine</u>, both publications of Strang Communications. He and his wife, Bonnie, live in New Braunfels, Texas. They have a son, Josiah, and a daughter and son-in-law, Janae and Justin.

Tree of Life
652 Loop 337
New Braunfels, TX 78130
(830) 625-6375

BOB NICHOLS

Bob Nichols has developed an interesting and colorful background during his more than 40 years in full-time ministry, 34 of those years of pastoring Calvary Cathedral International. In 1964 God called him to start a church where ALL FAITHS COULD GROW IN FAITH. With no financial backing or members, he started services in an abandoned US Post Office building. From that humble beginning the church purchased two city blocks, outgrew the building, and in 1976 moved into the 2,000 seat auditorium and facilities of the historical downtown First Baptist Church.

Calvary Cathedral International has an academic training center for K-12th grades; Calvary Learning Center (daycare); Calvary Cathedral International Bible School, with full and part-time students in day and evening classes; a daily radio program; jail and prison ministries; STITCHES, a program to take the Gospel, along with food and clothing, to the projects of the inner city of Fort Worth, and 24-hours a day of full power television programming in the nation of Uganda in East Africa.

Pastor Nichols has ministered in over 200 video Bible colleges around the world. His ministry includes travel to India, Lebanon, Iran, Australia, the Hawaiian Islands, Canada, Haiti, Mexico, Grenada, St. Lucia, South Africa, East Africa, Guatemala, England, France, and Israel. He has a unique ability to minister to pastors, and has shared his ability in seminars across America and in many parts of the world.

He is a pastor who is used mightily in teaching and evangelism—who loves the entire body of Christ, and strongly believes that in this hour we must unite to finish the job of evangelizing the world.

Calvary Cathedral
1600 West Fifth Street
Fort Worth, TX 76102
(817) 332-1247

MARSHALL TOWNSLEY

Recognized for over 20 years as an outstanding Bible teacher, Pastor Marshall Townsley ministers the Word of God in the power of the Holy Spirit with a strong prophetic anointing. With a real heart for the people of God, Pastor Marshall teaches with a special emphasis on the grace of God, encouraging believers to rest in His unchanging character.

In 1980, the Spirit of God led Marshall and his wife, Cindi, to establish and pastor the Believers Center of Albuquerque. With over 1,200 members, BCA is a growing, dynamic family church that is fulfilling God's call to impact its city, the nation and the world. In addition to his duties at BCA, Marshall has traveled throughout the world ministering at conferences, seminars and special meetings.

Pastor Marshall ministers the Word of Faith with grace, clarity and practical insight. You'll be challenged and blessed by his teaching ministry.

Believers Center of Albuquerque
320 Waterfall Drive SE
Albuquerque, NM 87123
(505) 292-5082

ANDREW WOMMACK

A ndrew Wommack's ministry is centered in a strong emphasis on God's grace and unconditional love. He believes in and teaches the victorious Christian life.

Andrew was raised in a Baptist family, and committed his life to the Lord as a young child. However, on March 23, 1968, he had a decisive experience with God's love and grace that changed his life forever.

Since then, He has spread the message of God's love far and wide—first, as a pastor of three churches, and now as an independent Bible teacher and speaker. He fulfills his ministry by traveling throughout the United States and the world, speaking in churches, seminars, retreats, and special events. He is heard on numerous radio stations across the country, and to date has distributed over 3,500,000 cassette teaching tapes free of charge.

With the main office in Colorado Springs, Colorado, Andrew Wommack Ministries also has a office in the UK, and has made outreaches into formerly communist Rumania, Hungary, and Poland. This year, he will be ministering in Australia, Portugal and France. Andrew has written five books—*Living in the Balance of Grace & Faith, Hardness of Heart, Harnessing Your Emotions, The Effects of Praise,* and *The True Nature of God.* He has published five study Bibles, *Life for Today—Gospels Edition, Life for Today—Acts Edition, Life for Today—Romans Edition, Life for Today—I & II Corinthians,* and *Life for Today—Galatians, Ephesians, Philippians,Colossians Edition.* He also has a six-hour marriage seminar on video cassette.

Today, Andrew Wommack Ministries continues to expand both at home and abroad. Wherever he travels, his powerful emphasis on God's Word continues to set people free from sin, self-righteousness, and religiosity—often with signs and wonders following. As it began, Andrew's ministry continues to embody the scripture, *"And ye shall know the truth, and the truth shall make you free"* (Jn. 8:32).

Andrew Wommack is also the founder of Colorado Bible College, based in Colorado Springs, Colorado. CBC opened its doors on September 18, 1994. This new era of ministry is the fulfillment of a vision that Andrew had to marry the knowledge of a school situation with the on-the-job training of a personal discipleship program. The college offers the very best instruction in the Word of God, with a special emphasis on the grace of God, providing a balanced approach to Biblical truths. CBC provides students with a ministry apprenticeship, foreign missions trips, and a complete sending, servicing, and training experience for ministry at home and abroad.

Andrew Wommack Ministries, Inc.
P.O. Box 3333
Colorado Springs, CO 80934
(719) 635-1111 • http://www.awmi.net

BOB
YANDIAN

B ob Yandian is a gifted teacher, pastor and author. He attended Trinity Bible College in Tulsa, Oklahoma, and studied with Charles Duncombe, associate of Smith Wigglesworth. He continued his studies at Southwestern College in Oklahoma, where he studied Greek.

He was the Dean of Instructors at Rhema Bible Training Center under Kenneth Hagin Ministries. Bob taught at the Word and Faith Satellite School for four years and has traveled throughout the world teaching in countries such as Canada, South Africa, Guatemala, Mexico, England and the Philippines. He founded the school of the Local Church (adult ministerial school) and Covenant Federal Credit Union.

Bob attended Grace Fellowship in Tulsa, Oklahoma, since its beginning with 50 people in 1972, and became pastor in 1980. He is still pastoring there and experiencing incredible growth. He lives in Oklahoma with his wife, Loretta, and two children.

In addition to his academic accomplishments, Bob has written 13 books including the popular *One Flesh* and *One Nation Under God*.

Bob Yandian Ministries
P.O. Box 55236
Tulsa, OK 74155-1236
(918) 252-1611

PROSPERITY PLEASES GOD
3 JOHN 1:2

3 John 1:2 "Beloved, I wish above all things that thou mayest prosper and be in health, even as thy soul prospereth."

The Apostle John, inspired by the Holy Spirit, wished above everything else that we prosper as our souls prosper. That is God's will for us. This should not be surprising. It just stands to reason that anyone who loved us enough to sacrifice His Son to purchase our freedom would do anything for our welfare (Rom. 8:32). Yet today, many people think that our heavenly Father, who gave His only begotten Son for us, either delights in or is apathetic about our poverty and sickness.

The English word "prosper" means, "to be successful; thrive" (NAHD). The Greek word used twice in this verse for "prosper" and "prospereth" is "EUODOO" and means, "to help on the road, i.e. succeed in reaching; fig. to succeed in business affairs" (Strong). Prosperity is not limited to, but certainly includes financial abundance. As King David put it, the Lord *"has pleasure in the prosperity of His servant"* (Ps. 35:27).

One of the purposes of this daily devotional is to open your heart to the love and provision of the Lord for prosperity in every area of your life: spiritual, emotional, mental, and physical. Not believing this truth has caused many people to see God as only relevant to their eternal needs. Yet our great salvation includes much more. As we believe, experience, and preach a full Gospel, we will bring the reality and power of God into this present life also.

Jesus died to deliver us from this present evil world too (Gal. 1:4). What Jesus died to accomplish should not be rejected by us for any reason. It glorifies God to let Him prosper us (Ps. 35:27). Bring pleasure to the Lord as you walk in a new level of prosperity. *(Written by Andrew Wommack)*

JANUARY 2
WE ARE WINNING
REVELATION 7:9

Revelation 7:9 "After these things I looked, and behold, a great multitude which no one could number . . . . "

Do you realize that Christians are winning in spreading the Good News? Here are the future results of God's evangelism program that we are all participating in:

After these things I looked, and behold, a great multitude which no one could number, of all nations, tribes, peoples, and tongues, standing before the throne and before the Lamb, clothed with white robes, with palm branches in their hands, and crying out with a loud voice, saying, "Salvation belongs to our God who sits on the throne, and to the Lamb!" (Revelation 7:9,10).

Where has this march of faith brought us today after many centuries? There were 20,000 unreached people groups in 1994. As of August 1997 there were less than 1,700 groups. Today there are less than 700.

Jesus is winning! In Nepal in 1963 there were 24 believers in the entire nation. Now there are nine denominations with 200,000 in one denomination alone. People are being saved so quickly up in the hills, they can't keep count. The government says there are over 700,000 Christians—and it's illegal to become one!

Thirty thousand are being saved daily in China. India has over 103 million believers now. In the 80s, Indonesia was the largest Muslim nation on earth. The government now reports that 19 million have switched from Islam to Christianity!

What has happened since the time of Christ? First there were 360 non-believers to one Christian. In the year 1000 AD there were 220 non-believers to one Christian. In Martin Luther's time, 1500 AD, every believer had 69 people to reach. In 1900, with a population of 1 1/2 billion, one out of 21 were believers. In 1980 one out of 11 were believers. In 1989 when the Berlin Wall fell, one out of seven were believers. Today, one out of five are believers! (Thanks to Loren Cunningham, Founder of Youth With A Mission and to Marriage Ministries International for this information.) My favorite scripture is Psalms 2:8, *"Ask of Me, and I will give you the nations for your inheritance, and the ends of the earth for your possession."* *(Written by Dave Duell)*

JANUARY 3
THE LAW OF THE FARM
MARK 4:26

Mark 4:26 "And He said, 'The kingdom of God is as if a man should scatter seed on the ground."

Jesus is describing how the kingdom of God and the Word of God work in our hearts. Notice, Jesus uses a "natural system" to explain this process. For example, have you ever crammed for an exam while you were in school? I have. Even though I received a passing grade, I honestly must say that I didn't really learn the material. It is possible for someone to go through his entire academic career cramming for tests, receiving passing grades, but not learning. Why? Because the school system is a *social system*. In other words, it is established and governed by the values and principles of men. As a result, it can be cheated, or manipulated. At the last minute you can cram for a test, not really learn anything, but still receive a passing grade.

Not so in God's kingdom. For example, let me ask you, can a farmer cram for a harvest? Of course not. Why? Because farming is based on a natural system, governed by the laws of an eternal God. Therefore, it is a system that can't be cheated or manipulated. That is why Jesus never used a social system to describe how the kingdom of God works. Whatever we sow, we reap. We cannot talk ourselves out of things we have behaved ourselves into. Either the Word of God has authority in our lives, or it doesn't. We can't fake this thing—not for very long anyway. All we can do is surrender to process. The seed of God's Word must be planted in our hearts and then we must surrender to the lordship of the Word. We may try to navigate around the laws of God and try to "work the system" to our benefit, but it can't be done. God and His Word stand supreme— unaltered and unchanged by us, or our opinions. Have you surrendered to His lordship today? *(Written by Mike Fehlauer)*

JANUARY 4
FAITHFUL IN SOWING, AGGRESSIVE IN RECEIVING
MATTHEW 25:14-30

Matthew 25:14 "For the kingdom of heaven is as a man travelling into a far country, who called his own servants, and delivered unto them his goods."

One thing we must understand about stewardship is that we are not the owners of the goods, but they are God's goods. Reading this portion of scripture we see that talents here are not abilities. These talents literally mean money. Faithful in your giving, aggressive in your receiving. That is my working definition of a steward. When we talk about stewardship, giving, or sowing, we are not limited to money. The master did not bless the men in this parable because of what they gave. They were blessed because of what they received. Some problems are not so much in the sowing as they are in the receiving. We cannot be like a farmer that scatters the seed and says, "I'll see you later. I'll come back in six months." If we do that, there isn't going to be anything there for us to harvest! Some say that they have been tithing and giving for six months, eight months, or a year but it doesn't seem to be "working." God's way always works. Are they aggressive in their receiving? We do not just sow into the Spirit, we reap from the Spirit. We don't just want to sow financially into the kingdom, we have to reap a harvest.

The one who is aggressive in his receiving is keeping some kind of a log that says, "God, here is the seed sown. I believe you for the harvest." An aggressive receiver has scriptural promises that he is praying and confessing over his seed sown. Water the seed that you have sown in faith with the Word. Take Luke 6:38 and pray like this: *"I give, so it shall be given unto me; good measure, pressed down, and shaken together, and running over, shall men give into my bosom!"* And Proverbs 11:24: *"I scatter, and yet I increase!"* Speak the Word over your seed.

This principle will enable the church to maintain and spread revival because the focus will not have to be on finances. We must get more radical in our receiving because there are projects that need to be funded. That's what being a steward is about. God always has more in store so that we can bring more people into the kingdom of God. It's about more than just sowing seed. It's about increase. It is about sowing seed, but it's also about reaping the harvest off of that seed. Seed from your harvest is going to produce your future harvests. So be faithful in your sowing, but you must also remember to be aggressive in your receiving. *(Written by Bob Nichols)*

JANUARY 5
HIS VICTORY IS OUR VICTORY
1 JOHN 5:5

1 John 5:5 "Who is he who overcomes the world, but he who believes that Jesus is the Son of God?" (New King James).
God's Word on any issue has a sanctifying quality to it if we just give heed to what it says. We should always hear God with the intent of becoming a doer of what He says. As we become doers, the Bible says we will be blessed in our deed! The end result will be a higher and better way of life lived to God's glory. God calls us up, His Word doing a sanctifying work in our lives, setting us apart from the world unto Himself. His ways, the Word says, are higher and better than ours and only good awaits those who walk where He leads.

Now that's not to say that everything is going to be smooth sailing for us while we're here on this earth. This is not heaven; and though heaven can't come soon enough for the believer, Jesus said in the world we would have tribulation, and we will. Light confronts darkness. Darkness will confront the light. But at the same time, Jesus said to be of good cheer—and for good reason. He said, *"I have overcome the world" (John 16:33).* Now His victory has become ours because by grace and through faith we are in Him. His victory over sin and death is now ours. We are more than conquerors through Him who loved us and gave His life for us. His love is greater than mere human love; His peace greater than what the world might offer and on and on and on. God is greater, stronger, wiser, you name it – God is above all. And greater, the Word says, Who is in us than he who is in the world. In all cases and under all circumstances, God's grace will fill every weakness, if we allow, causing us to grow and change and to rise up to meet every situation in His power and strength. *(Written by Marshall Townsley)*

JANUARY 6
MEEK NOT WEAK
JAMES 1:21

James 1:21 "Receive with meekness the engrafted word which is able to save your souls."
Where have we come up with the idea through the years that to be meek means to be *weak?* Maybe since the words rhyme we assume they mean the same thing. Dog and hog rhyme, but they are not the same. This misinterpretation has led us to envision a meek person as one without stamina, one who will not look you in the eye when he speaks, dresses shabbily, eats lettuce and birdseed and lets others walk over him. Jesus was called meek (Matthew 11:29) and He certainly never failed to look a person in the eye when He spoke. He also was far from being weak or letting others push Him around. He picked up the money changers and threw them out of the temple.

The Greek word for meek is "praus." The root of this word comes from a horse that can easily be controlled by the bit in his mouth, a horse that can be quickly trained. The word means to be *teachable.*

A meek person knows there is more to be learned. A teachable person will never have a problem with pride or arrogance. An arrogant person thinks he has arrived and is unteachable. This is a sure sign of coming destruction. A truly meek person knows the more he learns, the more there is to be learned. Knowledge is a two-edged sword. Learning reveals what you do not know.

James tells us we are to "receive with *meekness* the engrafted word" (1:21). We must always have a teachable attitude when we learn the Word of God. When sitting under the teaching ministry of others, we should not listen with a critical attitude, but a teachable one. There is much to be learned, even from those we disagree with.

Jesus told us "the *meek* shall inherit the earth" (Matthew 5:5). Teachable people understand God's message of prosperity and will inherit land, possessions and finances in the earth. It pays to be teachable. *(Written by Bob Yandian)*

JANUARY 7
RELUCTANT COMPLIANCE
LUKE 5:1-11

Luke 5:4-5 "Let down your nets . . . I will let down the net."
Jesus had just used Peter's boat, while preaching to the people. He wanted to bless Peter for the use of his boat and also to show Peter how He could meet all his needs. Jesus told Peter to let down his nets for a catch. At that moment, all the fish in the lake started swimming for Peter's boat.

Peter had been fishing all night and had caught nothing. He certainly was not going to have any better luck now. Jesus may have been a wonderful preacher, but what did He know about fishing? Peter was the expert there. It is to Peter's credit that he obeyed, but he didn't do it whole-heartedly. Jesus told him to cast his nets (plural) into the sea. Peter only threw in one net. Peter obeyed, but he wasn't expecting much.

The results were that all the fish that were intended to fill two or more nets, all jumped into Peter's one net. The net was not able to handle all the fish and it began to break. This was the biggest catch of Peter's life, yet it could have been even bigger. The fish were actually fighting to get into Peter's net but he wasn't prepared. No doubt, many fish that Jesus commanded to be caught were unable to comply because Peter wasn't prepared.

We often miss some of God's supply because of our own little faith. The widow in 2 Kings 4:6 could have had more oil, but she didn't have any more vessels to fill. Joash, the king of Israel, could have completely destroyed his enemies, but he wasn't aggressive enough (2 Ki. 13:18-19). Likewise, we often limit what God is wanting to do for us, through our little faith (Ps. 78:41).

What has God told you to do? Do it with all your heart and make plans for big results. The size of your faith determines God's supply. *(Written by Andrew Wommack)*

JANUARY 8
PEACE ON EARTH
LUKE 2:14

Luke 2:14 "Glory to God in the highest, and on earth peace, good will toward men."
Jesus came to establish peace. There was such joy in heaven at the announcement of the birth of our Lord and Savior that the angels shouted, "Glory to God in the highest, and on earth peace, good will toward men" (Luke 2:14). They were proclaiming that for the first time since Adam ran out of God's presence in the garden, there was going to be peace between God and man.

Through the Messiah, there was going to be reconciliation. Now having a loving relationship with God would be possible. God would deal with the sin problem through the cross. By receiving Jesus, we receive God's righteousness and He finds no fault with us because we have been washed clean by the blood of the Lamb. In this environment of peace and acceptance, we can come to God without fear. We can establish a real relationship with Him. We have no need to be afraid that He will reject or hurt us. We are at peace! God has good will towards us!

We know Satan is a defeated foe. The battle is over, yet we have a responsibility to believe and walk in the reality that Jesus purchased. What we believe comes into play. The struggle for self-worth has been the real battle the believer has lost. We were created in the likeness and image of God. That alone should give us a tremendous sense of self-worth. If I have no value for myself, I have no value for mankind. If I have no value for mankind I can murder, lie and work all kinds of destruction.

It is my belief that Satan fears and envies man beyond comprehension. He knows that if man ever accepts his true identity in Christ, he will have no more opportunity to work in this planet. So one of his greatest strategies revolves around keeping mankind ignorant of who he is in Jesus.

Let's come alive in Jesus and in our true identity. We can come boldly unto His throne of grace and receive what He has already given to us. God is not angry, and if we think He is angry we will do every thing we can to perform for an angry God. But praise God, He is our loving Heavenly Father. *(Written by Dave Duell)*

JANUARY 9
OBEY TO ABUNDANCE
MATTHEW 7:24

Matthew 7:24 "Therefore whoever hears these sayings of Mine, and does them, I will liken him to a wise man who built his house on the rock." (NKJV)
There is a greater force than the force of faith. It is the force of obedience. Actually, genuine faith always results in obedience. Let's look at 1 Peter 1:22. In verse 22 Paul says that it is through their obedience to the truth that their souls are purified. Their souls consist of their mind, emotions, and wills.

I know of someone who committed adultery. He had been caught in his sin and had not yet repented, but was experiencing depression. He sought help from a psychologist. After being examined by the psychologist he was labeled clinically depressed. This gave him an excuse to remain depressed. He was depressed because he had disobeyed God. The cure for his depression is to obey the truth and repent. It is through obedience that our souls are purified.

Jesus said that it is those who hear and do His sayings that experience His strength in life. Is there something He has asked you to do? Is there an area where He has challenged you to a place of obedience? The mistake is to look for His strength so you can obey. It is in obedience that you find His strength. Commitment always releases the dynamic of God in our lives. *(Written by Mike Fehlauer)*

JANUARY 10
FAITHFUL STEWARDS
1 CORINTHIANS 4:2

1 Corinthians 4:2 "Moreover it is required in stewards, that a man be found faithful."
As stewards, we are not owners, but we are entrusted with the oversight of everything we have. It all belongs to God (see Psalm 24:1-2). This applies to every person in the world. Everyone has something, even if it seems like they have nothing. If there was not another possession that you had, you are clothed and in your right mind. You can read. You have something to steward over.

When people separate just one little area of life and say, "Well, finances are everything we are stewards over," they leave room for the enemy to get glory from their life. If someone is a faithful steward over their ministry anointing, but are not faithful with finances, there are problems. Right now there are preachers in jail who have an anointing, but they weren't good stewards over finances. The law is the law whether you have a preacher's card or a union card. You cannot just steward over one area of your life and expect to get a "well done, thou good and faithful servant," because we are a package—spirit, soul and body. The financial and social realms are part of that package.

That's why it is important how you treat your car, your house, your cow, your wife or husband, because it all belongs to God. We have been entrusted with them. That's why we must take good care of the clothes we have. We wash them. If they need to be mended, we mend them. Why? Because they belong to God. We are being faithful stewards over what God has entrusted to us. If you want to see if someone has the heart of a steward, watch them in a rental car. Some people rent a car and suddenly, to them, speed bumps don't exist. God notices that. It's *His* car. It may say a rental company's name on the bumper, but Daddy God owns it. If you are living in an apartment and you want God to bless you with a house someday, don't tear up the apartment. Take good care of it. You are sowing seed when you are thankful for the old beat up car you may be driving. Wash it! If you have only one hubcap on it, shine that one hubcap. Believe God for the rest. Vacuum out the inside. You get in some people's cars and you have to move through five fast food bags and you feel like you need Lysol and a breather mask! That's not being a good steward.

I had an assistant that had a car with holes in the floorboards. When you were riding in it you could see the pavement zipping by. If it rained, you could get splashed right in the eye. He got a floor mat and praised God for what he had. I saw him awhile after he had stopped working with me. He was driving a brand new Honda. I remembered how he was with his old car and thought, *Now there goes somebody who has a hold of something.* Be thankful. Be a good steward over what you've been given. It may surprise you what the Lord will do for you. *(Written by Bob Nichols)*

JANUARY 11
MONEY WITH A MISSION
MARK 16:15

Mark 16:15 "And He said to them, 'Go into all the world and preach the gospel to every creature.'"
Jesus asked His followers to take His Message to all the nations of the world. Some of the people groups on this earth have yet to hear the Good News of God's love expressed for them through His Son. They live in total spiritual darkness because of this ignorance.

So many Christians think that if they have enough money to meet their own needs, they can be satisfied. They think only of taking care of themselves. That is a selfish attitude.

We who live in countries where there is abundance need to feel responsible to use that abundance to reach those who have not heard. As God told Abraham in Genesis 12:2-3, *"I will bless you . . . and you shall be a blessing . . . and in you all the families of the earth shall be blessed."* We should believe to prosper so that we can be a blessing to the nations of the world.

It takes money to travel to the world with the gospel. Prosperity is having enough of God's supply to accomplish God's instructions. Believe God to supply all your needs and give you enough to supply the needs of others. See your money as having a mission to accomplish. *(Written by Bonnie Duell)*

JANUARY 12
SEVEN SONS, ONE NAME
ACTS 19:15

Acts 19:15 "And the evil spirit answered and said, Jesus I know and Paul I know, but who are you?"
Paul has come to Ephesus at the leading of the Lord and a three-year revival has broken out. The power of God is so strong in his meetings that people are being set free of demons and sickness whether they are at the meetings or not. Some people are leaving the meetings with handkerchiefs and aprons taken from Paul's body. They are taking these to the oppressed in the city and demons and diseases are leaving infirm bodies. Revival has come to Ephesus.

A revival of this magnitude has never been seen by the people. The citizens of Ephesus were used to manifestations of the supernatural, but from Satan and demons, not God. A group of seven men, the sons of Sceva, had been around the area for years casting out devils for money. They were called "exorcists" because they worked in partnership with Satan to appear as if they were operating in God's power. Although they appeared to cast out devils, they only temporarily relieved the suffering. The demon took worse control at a later date and the men were called back to work their magic again and take more money from the suffering families.

Paul came to Ephesus and had permanent results without charge. He came in the name of Jesus. The sons of Sceva decided to try Paul's method along with theirs as well. They used their own magic formula along with this powerful name. "We adjure (exercise) you by Jesus whom Paul preacheth" (vs. 13). They were not expecting what happened.

The demon spoke back to them and informed them that he knew Paul and Jesus but *did not know them.* Isn't that interesting, Satan does not know his own. Sinners are unknown in their own kingdom. Here's the sad part, they are unknown in God's kingdom too. To those who one day try to claim eternal life through their works, Jesus will say "Depart from me, you workers of iniquity, *I never knew you.*" When you accept Jesus as your Lord, you are known in both kingdoms. "Paul I know, and Jesus I know." You can put your name in there too. *(Written by Bob Yandian)*

JANUARY 13
WILLING AND OBEDIENT
ISAIAH 1:16-20

Isaiah 1:19 "If ye be willing and obedient, ye shall eat the good of the land:"
One Sunday a little boy in church was playing with his toy cars during the pastor's sermon. He would stand up during the message and make car sounds right during the preacher's message. The minister had finally had enough and told the boy, in front of the whole church, to sit down and shut up. The boy complied, but he could be heard muttering under his breath, "I may be sitting down on the outside, but I'm standing up on the inside."

We all can relate to this story. Every one of us has been forced into obedience at times, but that doesn't mean we did it with a willing heart. Yet in the kingdom of God, it takes willingness and obedience to receive the goodness of God. First Corinthians 13:3 says that even if we make great sacrifices, but are not motivated by love, it profits us nothing. The attitude behind the action is as important as the action.

Certainly, every parent has experienced the sadness of his children obeying, but doing it with a bad attitude. It makes you want to say, "If that's the attitude you are going to do it in, just forget the whole thing." God is our heavenly Father. Obedience is important to Him, but a willing heart is what brings Him joy (2 Cor. 9:7). God's blessings flow abundantly when we get our hearts and actions lined up so that we not only do what is right, but we do it with the right attitude.

Check your attitude. If your motives are wrong, don't quit doing what is right, but spend some extra time with the Lord until you get your attitude straight. Jesus didn't die for us out of duty. He was motivated by love. We should live our lives for Him out of love also. *(Written by Andrew Wommack)*

JANUARY 14
DELIVERED FROM THE LAW
ROMANS 4:15

Romans 4:15 "Because the law works wrath, for where no law is,
there is no transgression."
Fear is a product of the law. *"Because the law works wrath, for where no law is, there is no transgression"* (Romans 4:15). The law does not empower righteousness, but it empowers sin. It cannot give a sense of righteousness; it only creates an awareness of shortcomings. *"Therefore by the deeds of the law there shall no flesh be justified in His sight for by the law is the knowledge of sin"* (Romans 3:20).

The law works condemnation and the expectation of judgment. If one has expectation of judgment from God, it will be impossible for him to believe God is for him. It will be impossible to look to Him as the loving Father who wants to meet every need. Condemnation returns us to the very root of the sin nature—fear.

When Adam sinned in the garden, who went looking for whom? God was reaching out for reconciliation. He was not there to punish, but to restore. God had never hurt Adam. Why was Adam afraid of God? His nature had changed. He now had a sin, fear nature. It was now his nature to fear instead of trust.

The first result of fear was to run from God. Adam was hiding in the trees fearing for his life. God had come to heal. Man was never designed to live in fear. Fear opposes and denies love. Love is built around trust. It is impossible to love or trust a God of whom we are afraid. Our doctrine of an angry God has driven man out of the arms of God and into the arms of the enemy.

Satan is not really our problem—man is. Lost man does what he does out of ignorance. The Church fails to do what it should out of unbelief. As we learn who we are in Jesus and Who He is in us, then we can rule and reign as God desires. *(Written by Dave Duell)*

JANUARY 15
THE VALUE OF THE UNSEEN
MARK 4:26-27

Mark 4:26-27 "And He said, 'The kingdom of God is as if a man should scatter seed on the ground, and should sleep by night and rise by day, and the seed should sprout and grow, he himself does not know how.'"
We previously talked about how the idea of farming is used to describe the kingdom of God. Within that idea we talked about the difference between a natural system and a social system. Once we begin to understand the natural system of God's kingdom, we then begin to learn several important lessons.

One powerful lesson is that there is something more important than what we can see. In other words, when it comes to God's kingdom, what we can't see carries more weight than what we can see. Once a farmer plants that seed, under the surface, in the darkness, a miracle begins to take place. The seed containing life within itself, begins to break open, developing a root system that will sustain the plant. God has always placed more value on what can't be seen than on what can be seen. We on the other hand, tend to place more importance on outward appearances. For example, we sometimes think that the only words that matter are the ones others can hear. Yet, it is the words spoken in secret that carry more weight than the ones spoken in public.

God has always done His work in secret. It was in the darkness of the womb of a woman named Mary that God's miracle was formed. Jesus spoke in parables. In Matthew we read that the kingdom of God comes not with observation. Paul talked about the mysteries of the kingdom, and in Proverbs 25:13 we read that it is the glory of God to conceal a matter.

In Matthew, Jesus taught that when we pray, fast, or give offerings, we must first enter the secret place—for that is where God is, and that is where He first rewards. Jesus is trying to get us to value the unseen. I want to encourage you today to place more value on the unseen power of His promises for you than on the circumstances in your life. Embrace the eternal! *(Written by Mike Fehlauer)*

JANUARY 16
AGGRESSIVE RECEIVERS ARE INVESTORS
PROVERBS 27:23-27

Proverbs 27:23 "Be thou diligent to know the state of thy flocks, and look well to thy herds."
Aggressive receivers don't quit. They are always looking for a new avenue into which they can sow. An investment always means money out before there's money back in. Romans 14:12 says that every one of us will give an account of himself to God. Meditate on that awhile and it will get you on your face! God will open that account book and say, "Okay, let's talk about your yard. I see here that when you didn't have time to mow your yard, you hired somebody to mow it. I appreciate that, because that's *My* property. And your boots—you kept your boots shined. That's an extra star for your crown." The difference between an aggressive receiver and other people is that other people refuse to take a scripture like Romans 14:12 literally. I want to have a good account when I get to heaven. I am laying up things in store. They say that you can't take it with you. No, but I'm sending it ahead! Why? Because I'm a steward over the anointing and the things God has given me. That's why in Colossians 3:23, Paul says that whatever you do, do it heartily as unto the Lord.

Stewardship is not God coming after your money. It's God coming after poverty! Proverbs 27:24-25 says, *"For riches are not for ever: and doth the crown endure to every generation? The hay appeareth, and the tender grass sheweth itself, and herbs of the mountains are gathered."* This shows that provision is coming. The condition is to be diligent to look well to the herds. Investing is another word for sowing. When you sow to the Spirit by being faithful in your tithes and offerings, you are operating on an entirely different economy than the world. The fruit will appear when you need fruit. The hay will appear when you need hay. Be faithful to sow. Sow in harvest and sow in famine; just keep sowing. Why? You cannot receive a harvest until you sow the seed. Until you loose what's in your hand, God cannot loose to you what is in His hand. Investing in the kingdom of God yields supernatural dividends. *(Written by Bob Nichols)*

JANUARY 17
IN JESUS' NAME
COLOSSIANS 3:17

Colossians 3:17 "And whatever you do in word or deed, do all in the name of the Lord Jesus, giving thanks to God the Father through Him" (New King James).
Have you ever wondered why we pray in Jesus' name? I mean why do we begin or end almost all prayer with that short little phrase "in Jesus' name"? We could use our own name; after all we're the ones doing the praying. Sounds irreverent doesn't it? In my name I pray. Amen. But in effect, even though many of us could never, or would never, do such a silly thing, we in effect do just that through either the content of our prayers and/or the motives our the heart.

Anytime we ask the Father to do something for us in prayer suggesting that He do it for us because of something we've done for Him, we have, in reality, asked in our own name.

First, it's horribly presumptuous to think that our deed or deeds might be good at all. Remember, we're dealing with God's holy standards and not our own definition of good. Jesus taught that there is none good but God. God embodies good. Something might be judged by others as good but God rejects it as bad or evil. Consider the offerings of Cain and Abel. We tend to forget that God's standards run *high above*, not *just above*, our own. We often lose perspective of His holy and righteous standard while we so generally compare ourselves among ourselves. We might just admit that we more often than not fall well short of His glory than achieve His good. Second, the whole idea that good works can add up or accumulate and be counted as righteousness is clearly condemned in scripture. Our good works, added up, pressed down, shaken together, and made to run over are still viewed as filthy rags not amounting to much at all when we attempt to exchange them for the right to stand before God as just or righteous. We are not made worthy to receive what we ask for in prayer by good works.

Paul makes it clear that works are *never* credited as righteousness. Faith is, but never good works. God recognizes good works, will not forget them, and eventually rewards the Christian for them, but will not justify him on that basis.

We pray in Jesus' name because He and He alone is our salvation and our righteousness. His name is the only name given whereby a man can be saved. His name is above every name. His work on our behalf represented by His name appears in the Greek as being perfectly perfect and completely complete. We can't, nor should we, attempt to add to it. *(Written by Marshall Townsley)*

JANUARY 18
YOUR BODY IS A SEED
1 CORINTHIANS 15:42-43

I Cor. 15:42-43 "So also is the resurrection of the dead. It is sown in corruption; it is raised in incorruption . . . sown in weakness . . . raised in power:"
Sowing and reaping is the foundational theme of the Word of God from Old Testament to New. Whether it be finances, love or friendship, you always reap what you sow. You also reap back more than you sow. Every seed has the one hundred fold potential, "good measure, pressed down, shaken together and running over . . . ."

The resurrection of the saints is no different. Our body "is *sown* in weakness, *raised* in power." We will have a resurrection body one day just like that of the Lord Jesus. As great as the human body of Jesus was in this earth, He received a greater body in resurrection. One day, we too will have a body like His. It will be a body that will last forever, never get sick, will not be tempted to sin and can exist in heaven or on earth. This body can appear and disappear just like Jesus could when He was with His disciples after the resurrection.

In this verse, our body is compared to a seed. When a seed is planted in the ground, only the shell of the seed dies. The heart is then released and the new sprout and eventual plant or tree grows. The tree does not come from the shell of the seed, but from the heart. The shell dies, the heart never dies. The heart of the seed carries the image of the plant or tree that will be formed.

When a Christian dies and is placed in the ground, only his body decays. The eternal heart goes on to be with the Father in heaven. One day a resurrection body will come out of the grave, but it will be a *spiritual* body (vs. 44). In other words, a body made of spirit. Our spirit, our inward man, carries the image of our resurrection body. The resurrection will be the great reaping day. That which was sown will be harvested.

We do not bury Christians: We plant them. (Written by Bob Yandian)

JANUARY 19
A WILLING SACRIFICE
GENESIS 22:1-18

Genesis 22:9 "And they came to the place which God had told him of; and Abraham built an altar there, and laid the wood in order, and bound Isaac his son, and laid him on the altar upon the wood."
This amazing account of Abraham offering his son Isaac to God as a sacrifice has inspired people through the ages. Yet Abraham wasn't the only one to express an amazing faithfulness. Isaac's actions were awesome.

Most scholars believe that Isaac was about 17 at this time. That would mean that Abraham was 117. Isaac probably could have overpowered Abraham. Certainly he could have outran his dad. But Isaac allowed his father to bind him and place him on the altar knowing full well that Abraham intended to make him a sacrifice. There is no indication that Isaac was screaming for help or that he resisted in any way. Either Isaac had complete trust in God, in his father, or both.

This is a perfect picture of how God sacrificed His Son Jesus for us. It was an astonishing act of love for us on God's part, but it was equally wonderful what Jesus did. The scriptures say, *"He was oppressed, and he was afflicted, yet he opened not his mouth: he is brought as a lamb to the slaughter, and as a sheep before her shearers is dumb, so he openeth not his mouth"* (Isa. 53:7). He could have called for legions of angels to deliver Him (Mt. 26:53), but He didn't. He yielded Himself to His Father just as Isaac did, even unto death.

Such love and sacrifice certainly had a purpose. If God gave His Son so freely for us, how could we ever doubt that He will supply our every need (Rom. 8:32)? God loves us and delights in our prosperity (Ps. 35:27). He has proven that beyond any reasonable doubt.
(Written by Andrew Wommack)

JANUARY 20
A BETTER COVENANT
HEBREWS 8:6

Hebrews 8:6 "But now has He obtained a more excellent ministry, by how much also He is a mediator of a better covenant, which was established upon better promises."
Under the Old Covenant, if a person fell short in any way he would rightfully look for the curse of the law on his life. He had a covenant with God that was based on his performance. The promises of that covenant were contingent upon a person's ability to obey.

The New Covenant was different. It is a better covenant. Hebrews 8:6 says, *"But now has He obtained a more excellent ministry, by how much also He is a mediator of a better covenant, which was established upon better promises."* We have a better covenant with better promises. Yet, unbelief in the New Covenant makes us continually look back to the Old Covenant.

In this New Covenant, God does not make a covenant with us individually. He made a covenant with Jesus. Galatians 3:16 says, *"Now to Abraham and his SEED were the promises made. He saith not, 'And to seeds,' as of many; but as of one, 'And to thy Seed,' which is Christ."*

The Old Covenant was based on each individual's ability to uphold his side of the Covenant. The New Covenant, however, is based on one man's ability to uphold the Covenant. That man is Jesus. He fulfilled all the righteous requirements of the law. He made the covenant sure. It has been sealed by His death. It cannot be changed.

God does not, therefore, uphold His covenant with us on the basis of our ability to always perform properly. We are in Christ. He has received the covenant and because we are in Him, we receive along with Him.

This is the Good News that Paul received from Jesus. Jesus taught Paul and told him in advance the things that he would have to suffer for preaching the right message: *"For I will show him how many things he must suffer for My name's sake"* (Acts 9:16). If Paul would have taught even one law with the message, he would not have ever spent time in jail or have been beaten. *(Written by Dave Duell)*

JANUARY 21
THE VALUE OF TIME
MARK 4:27

Mark 4:27 "And should sleep by night and rise by day, and the seed should sprout and grow, he himself does not know how."
Another lesson we learn when we look at this verse is that there is something more valuable than the immediate. The process of the kingdom in our hearts involves time. Time in and of itself carries very little value. I know that you have probably heard that time heals all wounds. Not necessarily so. It is when time is added to the foundation of the Word of God that miracles take place. Once the Word of God has been sown in our hearts, we must then understand the value of time.

There is a certain tree called the Chinese Bamboo tree. When it is first planted, all you see for the first four years is a small sprout and a bud. Then from year four to year five the tree will grow to 80 feet high! What is happening *over time* is an intricate root system is being developed. The roots are carving out places in the earth, extremely deep and wide. Deep and wide enough to sustain a tree of great magnitude and majesty. If one does not understand the process and nature of the seed of the Chinese Bamboo tree, he might dig up the seed and roots before the miracle of growth can take place.

We might have the tendency to do the same thing. If we don't understand the nature of the seed of God's Word *and* the value of time, we too will dig up the seed of the Word before the miracle of growth takes place in our hearts. No wonder James encouraged us to allow patience to have her perfect work in us. The result if we do, is that we will become mature, lacking nothing. Embrace time as a friend today. If you have sown the seed of the Word, a miracle is taking place. Resist the call of the immediate. Your fifth year is coming! *(Written by Mike Fehlauer)*

JANUARY 22
AGGRESSIVE RECEIVERS ARE RADICAL THANK-ERS
2 CORINTHIANS 9:11

2 Corinthians 9:11 "Being enriched in every thing to all bountifulness, which causeth through us thanksgiving to God."
People who know how to prosper in the Lord are radical in their thanksgiving. Every time you thank God for what He's already done, it is sowing seed for the next need, or the next miracle. It's like putting another baited hook in the water and getting ready to haul in "the big one." When you thank God, He can hardly stand it, and just loves to move on your behalf. It's as if He says, "They're thankful for what I've already given them. Send them something more. They're faithful people—faithful to give me praise and thanksgiving. Let's bless their socks off." Get radically thankful for what you've been given! It is sad that some people believe God for some big "thing" and when He does it, they run off and enjoy it without even stopping to say, "Thank you, Lord, for what you've done." Like the ten lepers in Luke 17; only one returned to thank Jesus, and he was made completely whole! I believe that all ten were cleansed—meaning the leprosy ceased—but I believe that the thankful one was completely restored by creative miracles! New fingers, new toes! Whatever he lost was restored.

Aggressively thankful people are ready to jump in and thank God, from their hearts, when others get blessed! If your blessing ship hasn't come in yet, start getting radically thankful any time anybody around you gets blessed. Then, just watch God notice you. Why? It raises up a memorial to God. The worst thing in the world would be for someone to gripe about the old clunker he is driving. That is the worst seed he can sow! Be thankful that things are as good as they are. Be thankful for what you <u>do</u> have. To receive aggressively, you must thank aggressively. Aggressive receivers are aggressive thank-ers! *(Written by Bob Nichols)*

JANUARY 23
PROSPEROUS THOUGHTS
PHILIPPIANS 4:8

Philippians 4:8 "Whatever things are true . . . noble . . . just . . . pure . . . lovely . . . of good report . . . any virtue . . . praiseworthy—meditate on these things."
It is said that the first seven minutes we're awake in the morning often controls our entire day. What we think about first thing can make for a good day or a bad one. It is your choice. Choose to think about the goodness of your Father God to you and spend time in thankfulness and praise to Him. Make it a good day! Think on what God has to say about you and your circumstances rather than what your brain can conjure up. Your brain can lie to you. Tell your mind what to think!

My husband is a great example of this. He decided years ago never to have a bad day. And he doesn't—no matter what might come against him.

Learn to appreciate the blessings and beauty God has placed in your life. Learn to appreciate and honor the people He has placed around you. Life will give you back exactly what you put into it. Smile at your future. God does!

Attitude is more important than reality because attitude can change reality! What happens to you isn't half as important as how you respond to what happens to you.

When you get squeezed by the pressures of life, what comes out of you is what you've been thinking—peace, joy and forgiveness or cursing, depression and negative comments. Make your thoughts prosperous by meditating on the Word and watch good things come out of you. *(Written by Bonnie Duell)*

JANUARY 24
A LITTLE SIN, A BIG STUMBLING BLOCK
HEBREWS 12:1, 3

Hebrews 12:1, 3 "Let us lay aside every weight and the sin which does so easily beset . . . consider Him . . . lest you become wearied and faint in your minds."
One day I looked at this verse more closely. The sin which does so easily beset is singular. Furthermore, that sin is defined in verse three, "fainting in your minds." The sin which does so easily beset us as believers is *discouragement*. Discouragement can be brought on by a number of circumstances in life.

1. Pressures of life: Every believer faces trouble; it is not only prophesied, but promised and guaranteed. "Many are the afflictions of the righteous, but the Lord delivers him out of them all"(Ps 34:19). God has given us weapons to handle Satan's attacks, but one thing we must not do is give up.

2. Satanic attack: Our troubles may not come by way of circumstances, but can come directly from demons. Whether they be "serpents or scorpions," God has given us authority over all of Satan's power. But we must not give up.

3. Personal failure: Everyone of us has failed as a Christian. We have promised the Lord our all and failed to come through on our promises. But again, we cannot let ourselves become discouraged and give up. We need to take heed to Hebrews 12:12 and "lift up the hands that hang down . . . make straight paths for our feet."

4. Doing right with little results. This can be one of the greatest areas of discouragement in our spiritual walk. Paul warns us to, "not to be weary in well doing for in due season we shall reap if we *faint not*" (Gal. 6:9).

In all cases, discouragement comes when we take our eyes off the Lord and put them onto ourselves or our circumstances. Self pity will bring on discouragement every time. Lay discouragement aside, set your eyes on God's Word again, and you will be back on the road to success. You will pull through very soon. *(Written by Bob Yandian)*

JANUARY 25
WHAT ARE YOU THINKING?
GENESIS 22:1-18

Genesis 22:5 "I and the lad will go yonder and worship, and come again unto you."

It is hard for most of us to relate to the story of Abraham offering his son, Isaac, to God as a sacrifice. Much of the reason is because we incorrectly imagine how hard this must have been on Abraham.

One movie about this incident depicts Abraham hitting his fist against a stone wall and crying out, "No God! Anything but Isaac!" It portrays Abraham wrestling with God all night and finally grudgingly giving in to the Lord and complying with His demand. But that is not what the Bible states. There is no hint of any resistance on Abraham's part. In fact, verse three shows Abraham rising early the next morning and heading to the place of sacrifice.

The reason we would be unable to sacrifice our own child is because we think about our son being dead and imagine our guilt from knowing that it happened at our own hand. Abraham didn't think that way. He told his servants, "*We will worship and then we will come back to you*" (Gen. 22:5 NIV).

In Hebrews 11:19, we find that Abraham was believing God to raise Isaac from the dead. You see, Abraham never saw Isaac dead and gone. He had a promise that God was going to give him a multitude of children through Isaac and Isaac did not have any children yet. Therefore, Isaac had to live. Abraham wasn't thinking on death. He was thinking about resurrection.

What are you thinking about? Are you looking at the sacrifice or the reward? What you think upon will determine your reaction. If you, like Abraham, think on the promise, you will have faith like Abraham to sacrifice anything. The choice is yours, and your choice will determine whether you rejoice or resist. *(Written by Andrew Wommack)*

JANUARY 26
WORKS RIGHTEOUSNESS
ROMANS 10:10

Romans 10:10 "For with the heart one believes unto righteousness, and with the mouth confession is made unto salvation."

The most enticing logic to the human mind is "works righteousness." It just makes sense to us because we can understand that. It appeals to the carnal, natural mind. If Paul had preached works righteousness, he could have tacked Jesus onto the end of the Law and he would never have been persecuted. The human mind cannot conceive of righteousness as a free gift. Rather than trusting the love of God, we trust our logic and we are cheated.

No one can live under the Law and qualify. The Jews tried it for a few thousand years and failed. The Law states that no one will ever be justified by keeping the Law. Yet, we foolishly cling to it, because it is logical to us.

While the Bible obviously supports good works and godly living, it does not support a works oriented belief system. It does not support a concept that our works righteousness can provide more for us than Jesus' righteousness.

Jesus called a man named Paul who knew all about the law, and in a moment of time on the road to Damascus, Jesus showed Paul what a sinner he was by keeping the law. Paul later on said that his righteousness was as filthy rags. Once you see what Jesus has done for us in giving us His righteousness as a free gift when we were born again, this message, will change your life and even cause a statue to shout.

We have been taught most of our lives that keeping the Law will make us righteous. But the truth is that there was not one person who was ever declared righteous by keeping the Law. Yet there are Christians who make studying the Law their lives work. That was the Galatians' problem. They heard the Good News and then the lawful people showed up and they went back under the law. Paul called them "foolish Galatians" in Galatians 3:1. *(Written by Dave Duell)*

JANUARY 27
THE WORK OF THE KINGDOM IS A PROCESS
MARK 4:28

Mark 4:28 "First the blade, then the head, then the full grain in the head."
The growth of the Word of God in our hearts is progressive. No one becomes a spiritual giant overnight. Instantaneous growth is rare and almost always ends in destruction. Progress is the key. God looks for movement forward.

Not only is growth progressive, but so is error. Sin doesn't conquer our lives overnight. It takes time for our hearts to be hardened and our consciences to be calloused. It is compromise in the small areas that make room for compromise in the larger areas.

In 1 Timothy 1:19 we read, *"holding faith and a good conscience; which some having put away concerning faith have made shipwreck."* Paul said that some have rejected a good conscience and as a result their faith suffered shipwreck. Their ability to relate to God on an intimate level suffered. This is a process. Systematic disobedience. Paul said later on in this letter that it is possible for a believer to harden his heart to the point where his conscience is seared.

Which direction are you traveling today? Are you moving closer to being conformed into His image? Or, have you been taking steps away from His lordship in your life? Maybe this devotional you are reading is the first time you have spent with God in a long time. If it is, make today the first in a habit of seeking His perfect will for your life. *(Written by Mike Fehlauer)*

JANUARY 28
BE PREPARED
LUKE 14:28

Luke 14:28 "For which of you, intending to build a tower, sitteth not down first, and counteth the cost, whether he have sufficient to finish it?"
That is not just a slogan for Boy Scouts. Stewardship is preparation. The word "budget" is not a bad word. Many times when we hear people in the world say "budget" they are really saying, "Well, things are tight. We had to get on a budget." No, the reason things are tight is because they don't have a budget. If someone is a good steward, he will have a budget. A budget is simply making preparation for needs that you know will occur. "Let's get back to the shouting stuff, brother." This will keep you shouting if you put it into practice. Satan will use everything he can to distract you from revival and more of God. If he can attack your finances successfully, it can affect your marriage, your health and how you pursue God. If he's successful, you are then focused on "God, I need this. God, I need that." It becomes, "I, I, I—me, me, me," rather than, "God, I praise you. God, I worship you." It will get your eyes off of God if you let it.

There are things that will wear out. Tires are a good example. It doesn't matter how much you plead the blood, how much you pray or read the Bible, the tires on your car will wear out. A good steward looks at his expected income, figures out how much new tires will cost, and then slices that big amount into one-month or one-week slices. He pulls that amount out each time he is paid and lays it up in store for when he needs it. It's the same thing for clothes and other expenses.

It's not God's fault that some Christians have to have a miracle every 30 days. They pay the rent, the light bill and buy some food, if they have any money left over—party time! They don't prepare and then all of a sudden they're calling everyone for prayer saying the devil's attacking them. To come out of that cycle of bondage, they're going to have to plan ahead. They cannot continue to do what they have been doing and be successful. They must do something different. A good steward will budget for upcoming needs. It has been well said that failing to plan is planning to fail. Start where you are, make a plan and stick to it. That way, you can shout the shout of victory and keep your sights where they're supposed to be—on God. *(Written by Bob Nichols)*

JANUARY 29
FAITHFUL TO THE FINISH
I THESSALONIANS 5:24

I Thessalonians 5:24 "Faithful is he that calleth you who also will do it."
God finishes what He begins. He is the Alpha and the Omega; the Beginning and the Ending; the Author and the Finisher of our faith. One translation indicates that He takes it to a fine finish! What God's grace initiates in us, God's grace finishes in us. If you initiate things on your own, you have no such guarantee. Again, the old hymn "Amazing Grace" says, "'Twas grace that brought us safe thus far and grace will lead us home."

So often, you and I start out knowing—I mean being absolutely persuaded—that we have grace on our lives to do this or to do that. But then along the way, for whatever reason, we lose sight of God's available grace to finish the project.

There is a rest in God that is indescribable for those who receive His grace to succeed. I encourage you to rest in His promise to you and His grace to finish what He has started in you. Even if you've quit—God hasn't. *(Written by Marshall Townsley)*

JANUARY 30
DON'T TRUST YOUR EYES OR EARS
2 PETER 1:19

2 Peter 1:19 "We have also a more sure word of prophecy . . . . "
In the beginning of this chapter, Peter is reflecting on his experience on the Mount of Transfiguration. He was part of a select group of three who saw Jesus transfigured, His face shine like lightning, and His clothing shine like the sun. He also witnessed Moses and Elijah appear and begin talking with Jesus. He emphasizes how He *heard* God speak to Jesus from the cloud and say, *"This is my beloved Son in whom I am well pleased."* He also emphasizes that he *saw* the transfiguration of Jesus with his own eyes (vv. 16,18).

I am sure Peter's congregation felt blessed to have one of the original 12 disciples as its pastor. They felt especially blessed to have one of the three men who formed the inner circle of Jesus' friends. Peter was a special man for another reason. He actually saw Jesus transfigured and heard God speak from heaven.

But Peter tells them there is something more powerful than having an open vision or hearing God speak from heaven. It is having the Word of God in front of you. The Word is a *more sure word.* Not everyone has had a vision or heard God speak audibly. But everyone can have the Word of God.

The Word has to be our final authority. If what we see contradicts the Word of God, we should go with the Word. If what we hear contradicts the Word, we should choose to go with the Word. Peter was simply reminding the people to place the Word of God as the highest priority of their life. God has placed His Word above His own name (Psalm 138:2).

Circumstances can never change the promises of God, but the promises of God can change circumstances. Heaven and earth will pass away, but God's Word will never change. *(Written by Bob Yandian)*

JANUARY 31
GOD IS GREATER
GENESIS: 22:1-18

Genesis 22:2 "And he said, Take now thy son, thine only son Isaac, whom thou lovest, and get thee into the land of Moriah; and offer him there for a burnt offering upon one of the mountains which I will tell thee of."
Consider how great a sacrifice God asked Abraham to make. Never before or after, did God ask this of anyone. God was always the giver. He used animal sacrifices to illustrate that there had to be shedding of blood for the forgiveness of sins (Heb. 9:22), but this was only foreshadowing His own sacrifice. Why would God ask this of a man?

This action isn't clearly explained in scripture, but no doubt that one of the purposes for God doing this was to give us assurance. He would never ask more of us than what He was willing to give. If Abraham could sacrifice his son, then certainly God would do no less.

Our Lord Jesus used this same reasoning. In Luke 11:11-13, Jesus asked, *"If a son shall ask bread of any of you that is a father, will he give him a stone? or if he ask a fish, will he for a fish give him a serpent? Or if he shall ask an egg, will he offer him a scorpion? If ye then, being evil, know how to give good gifts unto your children: how much more shall your heavenly Father give the Holy Spirit to them that ask him?"*

Our heavenly Father's love for us certainly surpasses any earthly man's love and devotion to Him. Therefore, if Abraham, a mere mortal, could find the strength to sacrifice his son, surely God could do the same. The Lord was assuring us that He would make the ultimate sacrifice for our sins. God so loved the world that He would sacrifice His only begotten Son to redeem us back to Himself. Think on that. *(Written by Andrew Wommack)*

FEBRUARY 1
THE POWER OF WORDS
MATTHEW 12:34

Matthew 12:34 "For out of the abundance of the heart the mouth speaks."
We all know how important words are to us. *Words are containers that carry destructive or creative power.* The words that we speak can help the devil bring destruction into our lives, or we can speak what God has said and bring great blessing into our lives.

It is possible to deceive ourselves about ourselves. We do good works and think we are good, but the true person is seen by his heart, and the heart is seen by words. Matthew 12:34 says, *"For out of the fullness (the overflow, the superabundance) of the heart the mouth speaks."* We can learn a lot about ourselves by listening to what we say.

The devil cannot do a thing to us unless we give him permission. He never speaks to you and says, "You are no good, you can't do anything right, you will not make it," and on and on. He gives you the thoughts and makes you put everything in the first person. "I'm no good, I can't do anything right, I will not make it."

The enemy gets us to say these words and then takes the power of those words and uses them against us. In doing this, we give him the position in our lives to control us. Deception occurs when a lie is believed.

We can be the enemy's mouthpiece or God's. David said that he would put his hand over his mouth so he wouldn't say the wrong things. We should be so smart. Paul said in 2 Corinthians 10:5, *"casting down arguments and every high thing that exalts itself against the knowledge of God, bringing every thought into captivity to the obedience of Christ" (emphasis added).*

If we agree with God, we will end up with His will in our lives. If we agree with Satan, we will have his will for us. So, who is using your mouth? *(Written by Dave Duell)*

FEBRUARY 2
RECEIVING THE WORD
MARK 4:16

Mark 4:16 "These likewise are the ones sown on stony ground who, when they hear the word, immediately receive it with gladness; and they have no root in themselves, and so endure only for a time . . . ."
These are the people who start out strong, with a good showing, but don't have what it takes to finish. The scriptures say that they received the Word of God with gladness. They heard the preaching. They got excited about the idea of God, but somehow missed His life-changing presence. The word "receive" in this verse means a "passive response." They took the word simply because it was offered. Obviously something in the message touched them emotionally. I am sure that they agreed with what they heard, but their lives were still unchanged by the Word. Why?

Only two out of the three aspects of their souls were touched. Their minds were affected by the message of God's Word. They mentally agreed with what they heard. They were moved emotionally by the Word of God as well. These two parts of the soul are not enough to produce permanent change. One vital aspect of their souls was left untouched—their wills.

The will is the most sacred part of a man's soul. God will not extend Himself beyond a man's will. He will invite, draw or appeal to our will, but God will never force us to accept Him. Therefore, all change is established and executed by the will. In Mark 4:20 we read, *"But these are the ones sown on good ground, those who hear the word, accept it, and bear fruit: some thirty, some sixty, and some a hundred."* The ones who produced the Word in abundance accepted the Word. The word "accept" means "to take to one's self." Like a man will take to himself a wife. It speaks of a deep commitment that involves the surrender of the will. The words "obedience" and "submission" are also part of the definition of the word "accept" in this verse. This is why they produced thirty, sixty and a hundred fold.

I want to encourage you to accept His Word today and not just receive it. Let the life of His Word conquer your will. May His desires override yours and His passions replace yours. *(Written by Mike Fehlauer)*

FEBRUARY 3
IT'S TIME TO CHANGE DENOMINATIONS!
EPHESIANS 3:20

Ephesians 3:20 "Now unto him that is able to do exceeding abundantly above all that we ask or think, according to the power that worketh in us."
There are more one hundred dollar bills in circulation than there are one dollar bills. I once heard someone ask, "Isn't it funny how one dollar looks so small when going to the grocery store, but so big when you take it to church?" Many Christians need to change denominations! God wants us to stretch our faith. He wants us to prove Him. You can't out give God! It is just not possible. I want increase in my growth with the Lord, so I also want to increase my giving. I have decided that I do not want to be limited to ten dollars or one hundred dollars. I do not want to limit God. I want to increase to one thousand dollars, ten thousand dollars and beyond. But that will not happen until I change denominations.

Pray about it and ask the Lord. If you've been giving one dollar offerings, bump it up to five dollars. If you've been giving ten dollars, bump it up to fifty. Beloved, it's time to change denominations! *(Written by Bob Nichols)*

FEBRUARY 4
DIVINE APPOINTMENTS AWAIT YOU
PHILIPPIANS 1:12

Philippians 1:12 "The things which happened to me have actually turned out for the furtherance of the gospel."

We were flying in a small plane with two other couples to preach to a group of people in a remote town in Montana. It was decided to first land in Great Falls and have lunch. We rented a car to go to the restaurant and on the way back to the airport we drove past a shopping mall. "Turn in here!" I shouted impulsively. We walked into the mall and found a clothing store going out of business with all items on sale for 90 percent off the regular price. God's desire to prosper us was at work! We women were ecstatic.

The men sat in the commons area patiently waiting. A stranger approached my husband, and asked, "Are you Dave Duell?" My husband was shocked that anyone would know him in Great Falls.

"My son goes to your church in Colorado," the man stated. "This morning I was in an ice cream store in this mall and I told the owner, who had a bad back, that I know a man from Colorado and if he was here, he would pray for you and you would be healed."

After we finished shopping, we all prayed for the ice cream store owner. He was healed and born again. We left that city excited that God had directed our steps to a Divine Appointment. And we filled the airplane with our bargains.

What Divine Appointments might God have for you today—to further His gospel?

(Written by Bonnie Duell)

FEBRUARY 5
WE DON'T GET WHAT WE DESERVE
1 CORINTHIANS 15:10

1 Corinthians 15:10 "By the grace of God, I am what I am . . . . "

Pastoring a church can be a very challenging occupation. There are wonderful people in the congregation, but there are also many others who try your patience.

One such lady approached me after one of the church services and told me she had seen me in public not living up to my own preaching. I do not remember exactly what the circumstance was, but I had said something or did something that was contrary to what I had preached in church. She let me know what a hypocrite I was for not living what I preached and she planned to go to another church that had a more spiritual preacher. She ended her reprimand by telling me, "You don't deserve to be in the pulpit."

I told her, "Yes, you're right, I don't deserve to be in the pulpit. And you don't deserve to sit in the congregation either." She was stunned. I continued to tell her, "If we hung a sign outside of the church that said, 'All Deserving May Enter,' no one could come. We are all here by the grace of God."

I am not called into the ministry because I am perfect. God called me as I am, because the call of God is by grace. *"But when it pleased God, who separated me from my mother's womb, and called me by his grace"* (Gal. 1:15). I also do not take advantage of God's grace by looking for every opportunity to sin. I strive with everything in me to live a life pleasing to God. But if you followed me every day you would probably find me sinning, not living up to God's Word.

I am not anointed to live it, I am anointed to teach it. When I leave the pulpit, I have to put the same effort into living the Christian life as everyone else does. I also do not have time to follow my congregation home to see if they are living the Christian life. I have a full time job looking after myself, as do they. Only One follows each one of us home, the Holy Spirit. The One who called us by grace, watches over us. *(Written by Bob Yandian)*

FEBRUARY 6
IT WILL BE WORTH IT ALL
ROMANS 8:1-20

Romans 8:18 "For I reckon that the sufferings of this present time are not worthy to be compared with the glory which shall be revealed in us."
There have been terrible sufferings in this world. Even a casual glance at history will reveal sufferings so unspeakable that it challenges our ability to understand how God will ever wipe the tears away from some people's eyes (Rev. 21:4). But this verse assures us that God's reimbursement will be much greater than our expenditures.

Many things in life come only through much effort and hardship. Take for instance childbirth. By anyone's evaluation, nine months of pregnancy isn't all fun. And the actual birth process involves pain and suffering. Yet Jesus said it was all soon forgotten because of the joy that the child brings to the new parents (Jn. 16:21). Look at the suffering that athletes put themselves through. But all the afflictions of training are swallowed up in the ecstasy of winning the gold. The end result makes all the effort more than worthwhile.

That's the way it will be with us when we see Jesus. The worst injustice that any person in history has suffered is not even worthy to be compared with the glory that awaits those who love the Lord. Anyone who doesn't see it that way is empathizing more with the suffering than with the reward. It is so easy to feel the pain, but most of us have never had a glimpse of the glory that awaits us. Certainly none of us have fully comprehended how wonderful that will be (1 Jn. 3:2). Yet God's Word assures us that God's provision is so infinitely greater than our need that there is no comparison between the two.

Take joy in that whatever you may be suffering today will someday fade into oblivion as you experience God's limitless supply. *(Written by Andrew Wommack)*

FEBRUARY 7
THE POWER OF THE TONGUE
PROVERBS 18:21

Proverbs 18:21 "Death and life are in the power of the tongue, and those who love it will eat its fruit."
Let's look at your giving. You can bless or curse it. You can say things like "I can't afford it" or "I'm broke" or "Every time I turn around something happens to take my money." We should water our giving with the water of the Word and expect an abundant harvest.

Sow your seed and speak prosperity scriptures over your finances. Say things such as, "I have given and it is given unto me, good measure pressed down and running over shall men give to me." "God delights in the prosperity of His children." "It is God Who gives me power to get wealth that He might establish His covenant in the earth."

We should water our seed with His Word and not curse our seed with our own mouth. We can make ourselves feel better or worse by the words of our mouth. Proverbs 18:21 says that *"Death and life are in the power of the tongue."* It goes on to say, *"they that love it shall eat the fruit there of."* We eat our words.

God showed me that the words coming out of my mouth are like a freeway that we walk upon. We walk on our words.

Life itself will bring negatives, but that does not say that we have to choose them. Choose to be positive no matter what. Be a person who can see good and not evil. Life is not fair, but God is good!

Christianity is awesome and there is nothing negative about it. God is not negative and we were never intended to be negative. The world can be very negative, but we need to look for the good. Don't be critical. Don't be a faultfinder. Be a visionary who can look in the spirit realm and find something good in everything. *(Written by Dave Duell)*

FEBRUARY 8
A FAMILY HERITAGE OF RIGHTEOUSNESS
HEBREWS 11:21

Hebrews 11:21 "By faith Jacob, when he was a dying, blessed both the sons of Joseph; and worshipped, leaning upon the top of his staff."
The family is the foundation of our society. Marriage is the cornerstone of that foundation. The health of our society is a direct reflection of the health of our families. As the moral fabric of our families unravels, so does the moral fabric of our nation. The tragedy at Columbine High School in Littleton, Colorado, is a perfect example of this. If we are going to live a life of abundance, it must first start in our homes. Today, more than ever, we need to establish a heritage of righteousness in our families.

What is a heritage? A heritage is the social, emotional and spiritual legacy that is passed on from parent to child—*good or bad.* In other words, we will leave a legacy. Another way of stating this is that we can not, not model. What is encouraging though, is that it doesn't ultimately matter how we started, but how we finish. Jacob is a great example of this. He started out as a deceiver, but finished as a patriarch of faith. Notice Hebrews 11:21 says, *"By faith Jacob, when he was a dying, blessed each of the sons of Joseph; and worshipped, leaning on the top of his staff."*

What kind of legacy are you passing down to your children? If you were to die this year, what kind of heritage would you leave? If you don't like the answer, it's not too late. Today you can begin to live your life for someone more than yourself. *(Written by Mike Fehlauer)*

FEBRUARY 9
LET'S JUST STICK TO *SPIRITUAL* THINGS
MATTHEW 6:21

Matthew 6:21 "For where your treasure is, there will your heart be also."
It has been said that there have been a lot of hot arguments over cold hard cash. Some people get offended when a preacher starts talking about money. They'll say or think "Money? I'm here to hear about *spiritual* things, about the *things of God.*" Well, if they are offended by men of God today, they'd certainly have been offended by Jesus! The New Testament speaks more about money than about both heaven and hell combined. Sixteen of the 38 parables Jesus spoke dealt with money. Some of these same folks would say, "Talk about sin or anything else, but leave my money alone." Please bear in mind that when we talk about money—it's not *your* money or *my* money; it all belongs to God. It is *His* money. Psalms 24:1 tells us that the earth is the Lord's and all it contains. That includes all the money. In 1 Chronicles 29:12 David prayed, *"Both riches and honor come of thee."* Even the Apostle Paul reminded the Colossians in Colossians 1:16, "*For by him were all things created*, that are in heaven, and that are in earth, visible and invisible, whether they be thrones, or dominions, or principalities, or powers: *all things were created by him, and for him*:" We cannot separate money, giving, and stewardship from our worship of God. It's part of us and who we are.

When you love, you give—and your expression of that love is something tangible. Talk about love, Jesus gave *Himself!* Jesus said no one can be His disciple who does not give up all he possesses (Luke 14:33). There is a definite link between a person's heart and his pocketbook. Jesus said that where you put your money, that is where your heart is. We can tell a lot about a person just by taking a look at their checkbook. A true gauge of whether we are being spiritual or not is in our giving. Focus today on being truly spiritual by putting God first in everything, including money. *(Written by Bob Nichols)*

FEBRUARY 10
A PROSPERING BODY
PSALM 127:1

Psalm 127:1 "Unless the Lord builds the house, They labor in vain who build it . . . . "
Jesus is building a church! One that He continues to labor for and to pray for. He intends for us to stand as His dwelling place and the tabernacle representing Him to our cities; indeed to the nations. He intends to make us so strong that we will be able to prevail against the very gates or authorities of hell itself. This is not a church that capitalism can build. It's not a church that can be assembled by the very best of man's ideas and efforts, though we try. Jesus is building His house, and one day His work will emerge as far superior to man's self-conceived version of this living masterpiece the Bible refers to as the Church.
Using the human body as an example, the Apostle Paul illustrates the thoughtfulness and care with which we have been set in the Church in I Corinthians 12:18 where He writes, *"But as it is, God has placed and arranged the limbs and organs in the body, each (particular one) of them, just as He wished and saw fit and with the best adaptation" (Amplified).* The Greek word used to describe this choice and process is the word "tithemi" which, again, indicates the careful and strategic placement of something as compared to, say, the random or even careless placement of something. The same word is used to describe the action of appointing Jesus as heir of all things in Hebrews 1:2. With that *very same* forethought and planning, God has graced us and set us in the church as it hath pleased Him.
Instead of worshipping at the Church of our choice as we're so often encouraged to do, we should seek His guidance, the guidance of the Holy Spirit, and discover His choice and obey His voice. Instead of being led by personality and program, pet doctrine and personal preference, we should allow God to help us find that special and strategic place in His Body. His blessing is on His setting. *(Written by Marshall Townsley)*

FEBRUARY 11
HOW DO WE HANDLE DISAGREEMENTS?
PHILIPPIANS 3:15

Philippians 3:15 "If in anything you be otherwise minded, God shall reveal even this unto you."
Paul was addressing his favorite congregation, the Philippians. This group of people supported him with prayer, love and finances when no one else would. As he is coming to the end of his prison sentence, he wants to see no one else but the Philippians. We might consider them as close to a perfect congregation as possible. But what is a perfect congregation? It is certainly not one that makes no mistakes. It is also not a group of people who agree on every teaching.
One Wednesday night as I was teaching, I asked the congregation how many of them disagreed with some things I had taught through the years. Every hand went up. I was a little disturbed. My ego was hurt. I thought maybe a few people might respond, but certainly not everyone.
A Spirit-filled church is unique. It is not united because of doctrine. The congregation is made up of Baptists, Methodists, Catholics, Presbyterians and more. We are all united by the new birth and the baptism in the Holy Spirit. We all brought our pet doctrines with us when we became filled with the Spirit. Many of these teachings will not be corrected until we stand before the Lord at the judgment seat of Christ, no matter how well the pastor preaches otherwise. We are all going to disagree on certain issues until we get to heaven. No one has the corner on the market on every doctrine.
So what does unite a church? What unites a church is not doctrine, but vision. The vision is winning souls and meeting the needs of the Body of Christ. Paul says, *"if in anything you be otherwise minded, God shall reveal it unto you"* (Phil. 3:15). When we disagree, we should turn it over to the Lord, who will one day settle every issue. In the meantime, we can disagree without being disagreeable. We do not need to strive to make everyone believe as we do. We should *"endeavor to keep the unity of the Spirit in the bond of peace"* (Eph. 4:3). *(Written by Bob Yandian)*

FEBRUARY 12
GOD'S WORD GIVES LIGHT
MARK 4:21-23

Mark 4:21 "And he said unto them, Is a candle brought to be put under a bushel, or under a bed? and not to be set on a candlestick?"
Jesus had just given the parable of the sower sowing the seed. Then He interpreted it to His disciples. This teaching stressed the importance of God's Word in our lives. We can't bear fruit without putting God's Word in our hearts any more than a farmer can have a harvest without planting seeds. Then Jesus said that a candle must be put on a candlestick to shed its light. Jesus was still speaking about the importance of God's Word.

"Thy word is a lamp unto my feet and a light unto my path" (Ps. 119:105). Jesus was saying that God's Word is how He sheds light on all our situations. Without the illumination of God's Word we will stumble around in the dark. What's the purpose of having a light if we aren't going to use it? Why would anyone place a light under his bed or under a basket that would block the light? That doesn't make sense. But that's exactly what we often do with the light that God has given us.

How many times have we neglected meditating on God's Word because of our busy schedules and just stumbled blindly through our day? The influence of God's Word in our lives is not a luxury that we can do without. It is as essential as light in the midst of darkness. Light in the darkness enables us to function as if it were day, as long as the light is in a prominent place.

The candlestick that we need to set the light of God's Word on is the focus of our hearts. As we meditate on God's Word day and night, there is no circumstance or secret that will not be clearly revealed to us through the light of God's Word (v. 22). *(Written by Andrew Wommack)*

FEBRUARY 13
BUSY ABOUT OUR FATHER'S BUSINESS
JOHN 9:4

John 9:4 "I must work the works of Him who sent Me while it is day; the night is coming when no one can work."
We have been busy with our Father's business. One of my favorite scriptures is John 9:4 where Jesus says, *"I must work the works of Him who sent Me while it is day; the night is coming when no man can work."* In Strong's concordance the word "works" means "energy" and "urge." In other words we have an unction to function. When we are about the Father's business we have an energy and an urge that won't quit. What Bonnie and I do would kill the average person without that energy or urge. Someone said to me that they should call me, "Dave Duracell."

The Word goes on to say that it is His occupation, enterprise, deed, task, accomplishment, employment, performance, work, labor, course of action. As I look at this verse, I can see that is exactly where we are. People have asked me how I got into full-time ministry from ranching. I just got so busy working for Jesus that I did not have time to do anything else.

Jesus studied for 30 years for three and one half years of ministry. Jesus was our prototype. He showed us how to live, work, and love by His life. He said in John 20:21 *"Peace to you! As the Father has sent me, I also send you."* The word "sent" means to be set apart for a special service, sent out with a mission to fulfill, equip and dispatch one with the full backing and authority of the sender.

This was Jesus' vision and assignment on this earth. He worked in a carpenter shop for many years until His time to fulfill what was assigned to Him. Each one of us has a different makeup and job description. My life is energized with this verse. The more I work the vision that God has given to us, the bigger it gets. We are seeing activation and fulfillment of the vision that God has given to us. Our greatest hour is now! *(Written by Dave Duell)*

FEBRUARY 14
THE HERITAGE OF GOD
JOEL 2:17

Joel 2:17 "O Lord, and give not thine heritage to reproach, that the heathen should rule over them: wherefore should they say among the people, where is their God."
According to the scriptures, we are God's heritage. In the general sense, we are His only expression of His reality and relevancy on the earth. There are basically four stages to our lives or families—survival, stability, success, significance.

The first level is survival. These families and marriages are literally fighting for survival. They are in a crises situation: economically, mentally and most important, spiritually. Their lives are filled with uncertainty, often feeling like they are victims of circumstance.

The second level is stability. These folks are surviving. They have stabilized their lives. Most of their communication though, is about the most pressing issues of life. They rarely talk about how to get their families and marriages to a place of greater strength. They generally find their satisfaction away from the home. The sense of independence is greater than interdependence with no sense of shared accomplishments.

The third stage is success. Family matters to them. They genuinely enjoy being together. There is a sense of excitement concerning their lives. Their homes are marked by family activities. They are determined to live better and love better. Yet, there is a dimension that is missing—making a difference in the lives of others.

Significance is the level where a heritage is truly established. This is where the family is involved in something other than themselves. This is where a family embraces a unified vision to live beyond their own lives and invest in the lives of others. This is a heritage. What stage is your family in? As God's people we are to express His reality to this earth. What does that mean for you and your family? What specifically is His purpose for your home? What is your family mission statement? I want to challenge you to discover His purpose for your family today. He does have one for you. Your life matters to someone else and so does your family. *(Written by Mike Fehlauer)*

FEBRUARY 15
NOAH GAVE WHAT HE NEEDED THE MOST
GENESIS 8:20-22

Genesis 8:20 "And Noah builded an altar unto the LORD; and took of every clean beast, and of every clean fowl, and offered burnt offerings on the altar."
As a result of sin, the whole earth was flooded. All of humanity, as well as the vegetation and animals, were all destroyed. There were precious few animals that were spared in order to repopulate the earth. Noah could have said, "Wow. God gave us the beasts for food now, and we don't have very many left. I'd better ration them and make sure we'll have enough. They're all the food we have." But he didn't say that. He gave. He knew that God kept them, and that He was able to continually keep them. So, he sacrificed burnt offerings to God.

For Noah to look at what he had as his *provision* when it was only a *seed* would have been a fatal mistake. A mistake that would not only have affected him, but his family and the whole human race! The fate of the human race really did rest in Noah's hands! (No pressure.) But Noah sowed what he needed the most. God only asks you to give what he wants you to have more of. You need to give the most when you have the least. He is no fool who gives what he cannot keep to gain what he cannot lose.

Second Chronicles 16:9, *"For the eyes of the LORD run to and fro throughout the whole earth, to shew himself strong in the behalf of them whose heart is perfect toward him."* God is just waiting for you to release your faith and give as He leads without worry or fear. Then He can show Himself strong on your behalf.

If what you have is not enough to meet your need, understand that it is just your seed. *(Written by Bob Nichols)*

FEBRUARY 16
SICKNESS AND POVERTY OR HEALTH AND PROSPERITY?
3 JOHN 2

3 John 2 "Beloved, I pray that you may prosper in all things . . . ."
Do you still wonder if God really wants you to prosper in all things? I struggled with this concept for a long time because of religious thinking. I finally had this revelation: when someone is sick, who does he think about? When someone is poor, who does he think about?

A sick person is able to concentrate only on the pain in his body. A poor person is able to think only of where to get money to pay his rent or buy his next meal for himself and his family. The sick and the poor are unable to think about being a blessing to someone else.

That is one of the reasons the enemy desires you to be sick and poor. He knows he can then put you out of commission as far as being a light in the world. You'll be too busy worrying about yourself to be able to think about loving your neighbor.

Therefore, God provided health and prosperity for you in Jesus. His great love for you desires the best for you. He wants you to prosper in all things so that you can reach out beyond yourself and influence others for His kingdom. Opt for His best for you—health and prosperity! Tell Father God you're willing to receive everything He has provided for you. *(Written by Bonnie Duell)*

FEBRUARY 17
THE BLESSINGS OF UNITY
PSALM 133:1-3

Psalm 133:1-3 "Behold how good and how pleasant it is for brethren to dwell together in unity. It is like the precious ointment upon the head, that ran down upon the beard, even Aaron's beard: that went down to the skirts of his garments; As the dew of Hermon, and as the dew that descended upon the mountains of Zion: for there the LORD commanded the blessing, even life for evermore."
Only Christians (brethren) can truly dwell in unity. The world can come together, but they cannot be unified. True unity is supernatural. It comes from the Holy Spirit. When two sinners come together, one plus one equals two. When two Christians come together, one plus one equals ten thousand (Deut. 32:30). The world adds but the Holy Spirit multiplies.

David spoke of the goodness and pleasantness of Christian unity in verse one and the blessings of unity in verses two and three. The blessings are twofold: *power and refreshment.*

It is first like the oil that ran down the beard of Aaron to the skirts of his garment. Oil represents the *power* of the Holy Spirit. Aaron was the high priest. When the anointing oil was placed on his head, it ran onto his beard and down his garments to the bottom tassels. This is a type of the baptism of the Holy Spirit. On the day of Pentecost, the oil of the Holy Spirit was poured upon our great High Priest, Jesus (Heb. 1:9). It then ran down to the garments, the 120 waiting in the upper room on that day. It has continued to flow throughout the Church age and will one day reach the last tassel on the hem of the garment when the final person is born again. Jesus will then come back for His body, His church.

Second, unity is like the dew that descended on Mount Hermon. Dew speaks of supernatural *refreshment* that comes from the Holy Spirit. The Spirit not only comes to bring us power, but as Isaiah tells us, *"this is the rest . . . this is the refreshing"* He was referring to, *"stammering lips and another tongue"* (Isa. 28:11,12).

In an atmosphere of spiritual unity, there is power and refreshing. It is also in this moment of unity that the Lord commands blessings. No wonder we should *"strive to keep the unity of the Spirit in the bond of peace"* (Eph. 4:3). *(Written by Bob Yandian)*

FEBRUARY 18
PHYSICAL HEALING
ISAIAH 53:1-5 & MATTHEW 8:16-17

Isaiah 53:4 "Surely he hath borne our griefs, and carried our sorrows: yet we did esteem him stricken, smitten of God, and afflicted."
Physical healing is so prominent in scripture, especially the New Testament, that there should be no debate about it, but there is. Many people interpret the promises concerning our healing to apply only in a spiritual sense. They believe scriptures such as Isaiah 53:4-5 are speaking of being healed spiritually.

The best way to interpret scripture is by scripture. If a passage is quoted and applied in another passage of scripture, then we have a very clear understanding of exactly what the Lord is saying. This happened with Isaiah's prophecy concerning the Messiah bringing us healing.

In Matthew 8:16, multitudes came to Jesus for healing and He physically healed every one of them. Then in verse 17, the gospel writer said this happened, *"That it might be fulfilled which was spoken by Esaias the prophet, saying, Himself took our infirmities, and bare our sicknesses."* This emphatically states that Isaiah's promise of healing was for our physical bodies. Praise the Lord!

Healing is just as much a part of the atoning work of Christ as is the forgiveness of sins. The Greek word that was used for salvation hundreds of times in the New Testament is "sozo" and it was also translated in reference to physical healing in Matthew 9:22; Mark 5:33; Luke 8:48 and James 5:15.

All faith for physical healing has to begin at the place of believing that it is God's will to heal us. The truth that this was part of the atoning work of Christ as prophesied in scripture, provides us with that foundation. *(Written by Andrew Wommack)*

FEBRUARY 19
YOU ARE WHAT YOU THINK
PHILIPPIANS 2:5

Philippians 2:5 "Let this mind be in you which was also in Christ Jesus."
We live in a very negative world. From every angle of life our minds are attacked by words that are just the opposite of the Word of God. It seems like an endless process for control over what we hear. We always become who we associate with or what we hear. But praise God, God has given us His answers in the Bible.

Philippians 2:5 says, *"Let this mind, attitude, be in you which was also in Christ Jesus."* We are either the masters or victims of our attitudes. It is a matter of personal choice. Who we are today is the result of choices made yesterday. Tomorrow we will become what we choose today.

There is a power in negative thinking. Why is it so hard for us to take the Bible at face value in the areas of healing, prosperity and deliverance? Why do we have so much trouble accepting that His promises written in the Bible are for us?

The answer is negativism. It is all around us and affects our faith. We are programmed from childhood to think negatively, to expect bad instead of good. As a result, we limit ourselves on what we can accomplish in life. How easy it is to fall into the trap of confessing the Word with our mouths but wavering in our hearts. Negativism attacks and ultimately destroys our faith and hope until our dreams are abandoned in an atmosphere of frustration and despair.

In Psalm 78 the story is told about the children of Israel. It's amazing to see how people can experience the power of God and by their attitude so easily turn from His blessings. In verse 41 it says, *"Yes, again and again they tempted God. And limited the Holy One of Israel."* Sorry to say, but the Body of Christ is guilty today of the very same attitude and sin. *(Written by Dave Duell)*

FEBRUARY 20
ESTABLISHING A GODLY HERITAGE FOR YOUR FAMILY
JOSHUA 24:15

Joshua 24:15 "But as for me and my house, we will serve the Lord." There are several elements necessary in establishing a heritage of righteousness. One primary element is a clear vision and sense of purpose. If we don't have a sense of destiny for our homes, we will not be able to navigate through the difficult times in life. As a matter of fact, a sense of destiny is the difference between a healthy family and an unhealthy family.

Because of my travels, I fly thousands of miles a year. I try to stick with one airline to accumulate miles and upgrades. The airline I mostly fly leaves one of their audio channels open so it is possible to hear the communication between air traffic control and the pilots. As a result, I have heard hours of air traffic chatter. One of the things that I have realized is that we rarely fly from one city to the next in a straight line. There are usually course adjustments made throughout the trip. We often adjust altitude. Or, we change our flight pattern to avoid storm fronts or inclement weather. Even though all these changes take place, we still end up in the correct city. Why? Because the pilots knew their destination.

If we know what our destination is, we will know when we are off course. As a result, we will know when a course correction is necessary. Otherwise we will find ourselves caught up in the jet stream of society, which today, can prove to be family fatal!

This is the time to establish a clear vision and sense of destiny for you and your family. *(Written by Mike Fehlauer)*

FEBRUARY 21
THANK GOD THAT THINGS ARE AS GOOD AS THEY ARE
PHILIPPIANS 4:6

Philippians 4:6 "Be careful for nothing; but in every thing by prayer and supplication <u>*with thanksgiving*</u> *let your requests be made known unto God." (Emphasis added.)*
I know of a gentleman in Fort Worth who found himself going through some tough times financially. He had two luxury cars and a nice home, but then he lost his job. During that time he was able to keep his house, but unfortunately he lost both cars. Many people who found themselves in that situation would throw up their hands in discouragement or blame God, their job, or everyone else around them. "Why me? I'm supposed to be a child of God. How could this happen?" Not this man. Although the man had no car, he had a bicycle. Just before his car was repossessed, refusing to give the devil the victory by blaming God, he took the garage door opener out of his car and attached it to his bicycle. Every morning he would go out to the garage and get on his bike. He'd push the garage door button to open the door, ride out of the garage, push the button to close the door and off he'd peddle that bike to work. Every day he peddled that bike and every day he thanked God he had a bike to get to work. He kept tithing, he kept giving and he kept thanking God for what he <u>did</u> have instead of complaining about what he didn't have. He went to work praising God that God was going to restore. He kept a P.F.A.: Positive Faith Attitude. It wasn't very long before that man did not have to peddle to work anymore. He believed, "new car cometh," and it did!

What do you need? Are you thankful for what you already have? Keep your switch of faith turned on and thank Him that things are as good as they are. Be a faithful steward with what you have and be faithful in giving your tithes and offerings. Sow in faith believing and you will see your harvest come in. Throughout the day today, practice thanking Him for what you have and for what He has done in your life. Thanksgiving gets God's attention showing that we know <u>all</u> our needs are met in Him! *(Written by Bob Nichols)*

FEBRUARY 22
OUR GIVING GOD
JAMES 1:5

James 1:5 "If any of you lacks wisdom, let him ask of God, who gives to all liberally, and without reproach, and it will be given to him" (New King James).
From this statement by James, the Lord's brother, we can extract two important and foundational truths. First, we see that the Lord is a giving God. The eternal creator is the possessor of heaven and earth. He owns all things but desires to give to His people. To give is God's nature. Just as it is God's nature to always speak the truth, so it is God's nature to give.

Notice the different characteristics of His giving. One, He gives continually. In verse five, the participle translated "who gives" has the meaning of continual giving. God never, for one moment, ceases to give. He gives continually because it is His nature to give. God doesn't just have love—He is love. And genuine love must give.

Two, He gives to all men. James echoes many of the sayings of Jesus, and here, is repeating what he must have heard Jesus say in His Sermon on the Mount. *"Ask, and it will be given to you . . . for everyone who asks receives" (Matthew 7:7,8).* Let no one think that others are more privileged or more acceptable than himself, *"for there is no respect of persons with God" (Romans 2:11, King James).* God is no more interested in someone else than He is in you. God loves no one as much or any more than He does you. *(Written by Marshall Townsley)*

FEBRUARY 23
ANOTHER REASON YOU NEED A PASTOR
DEUTERONOMY 1:38

Deuteronomy 1:38 "Joshua the son of Nun . . . shall cause you to inherit it (Canaan)."
Stop and think of as many things as you can that cause prosperity to come into your life. I am sure you will think of meditating on God's Word first. Next you will remember to be a doer of the Word, walk uprightly before Him (sanctification), and finally, be a giver. All of these are found in God's Word and a part of the plan of supernatural prosperity, but here's one you might not have thought of: *being a committed member of a church.*

Just as in Joshua's day, being submitted to a pastor, a leader, *causes you* to inherit the promised land of prosperity and blessing. A good pastor represents the leadership of Jesus in your life. Like following the Apostle Paul, to follow a good pastor is to follow Christ. Just like Jesus watches over His flock, the Church, a pastor watches over the sheep given to him. He is responsible for many areas of your personal life.

"Obey them that have the rule over you, and submit yourselves: for they watch for your souls, as they that must give account" (Heb. 13:17). First, a pastor watches out for your soul. He teaches God's Word so you will be able to take authority over every thought that does not line up with God's will for your life. The care of your soul is not left with you alone, but also with a shepherd, your pastor. He prays for you *". . . that you may stand perfect and complete in all the will of God"* (Col. 4:12). Second, your pastor will one day give an account to God, not only for his teaching, but for your spiritual growth. He is benefited by your submission to his teaching, but you are also. You will be rewarded in heaven for your obedience to his revelations of the Word.

You will not only be rewarded in heaven one day, but also prospered right here on earth. Your pastor will *cause* you to inherit the blessings of God. *(Written by Bob Yandian)*

FEBRUARY 24
IT'S A DONE DEAL
1 PETER 2:21-25

1 Peter 2:24 "Who his own self bare our sins in his own body on the tree, that we, being dead to sins, should live unto righteousness: by whose stripes ye were healed."
The last phrase of this verse is the same as Isaiah 53:4, with one important exception: It places our healing in the past tense. We have already been healed. This is a hard concept for some people to grasp. They cannot understand how they could already be healed if there is sickness in their bodies. So, one way to get around this is to say that this is speaking of spiritual healing. However, Matthew 8:17 made it very clear that the healing Isaiah was speaking of was physical, not spiritual.

The key to understanding this concept is relating it to the forgiveness of our sins. When were our sins forgiven? According to scripture, they were forgiven when Christ died, long before we ever received it. Our prayers only enable us to receive what was already accomplished in the spiritual realm and bring it into physical reality. That's the way it is with healing.

Jesus has already accomplished our healing. The same virtue that raised Jesus from the dead is resident within every believer (Eph. 1:19-20). It's a done deal. All we have to do is believe and give physical substance (Heb. 11:1) to what is already true in our born again spirits. It is infinitely easier to release something that we already have than to try to get something that we don't have.

Start releasing your healing by confessing and acting on your faith instead of trying to use your faith to ask God to heal you. He's already done it. *(Written by Andrew Wommack)*

FEBRUARY 25
THE DESTRUCTIVE POWER OF NEGATIVE THINKING
PHILIPPIANS 4:8

Philippians 4:8 "Finally, brethren, whatever things are true, whatever things are noble, whatever things are just, whatever things are pure, whatever things are lovely, whatever things are of good report, if there is any virtue and if there is anything praiseworthy—meditate on these things."
Hope is an essential element of faith. I do not mean the kind of hope that says, "Someday God might do something for me." The word translated hope in the New Testament means "confident expectation of good." Bible hope is the breeding ground of faith. Without a confident expectation of good, we will never be able to work real faith.

Once hope, the confident expectation for good, is destroyed, fear takes over. Fear is the opposite of biblical hope—it confidently expects the worst. Fear is the breeding ground for unbelief which always leads to disobedience. This process of fear and unbelief starts in childhood and often lasts a lifetime.

In Matthew 18:3 Jesus tells us that we must become as little children. Young children possess a quality that is essential to achieving their dreams. They know no limits. They do not know what they can't do, so they dream big dreams. They are limited only by their imagination. Research has shown that few adults can be classified as highly creative, whereas 95 percent of all four-year-olds studied were considered creative, and only four percent of all seven-year-olds studied, retain their creativity. What happened to these children? The answer is obvious. They started school and began to learn what they couldn't do.

The only limitations that God has are those in your mind. When we get saved we have to renew our minds so that we may know what is that good and acceptable and perfect will of God (Romans 12:1,2).

When you received Jesus, you became a new creation. All the old has gone and the new has come. To live this new life to the fullest of your potential, you must change your thinking. Otherwise, you will always limit what God can do in your life by negative thinking. As for me, I cannot meditate on one negative thought. If I do, I would wind up in a white jacket. That's how powerful it is to me. *(Written by Dave Duell)*

FEBRUARY 26
THE JOY OF PERSEVERANCE
ROMANS 5:3-4

Romans 5:3-4 "And not only that, but we also glory in tribulations, knowing that tribulation produces perseverance; and perseverance, character; and character, hope."
Being able to live a life of abundance requires perseverance in times of tribulation. In our scripture today we see that we can glory in tribulation. Notice the Apostle Paul did not say that we glory *for* tribulation. We know that God is not the author of tribulation, crises or tragedy. If He was, we would glory for it. Since we know that Satan is the author of tribulation we glory in it. Paul realized that even though God did not cause tribulation, if we have the right attitude, it will set into motion a divine chain reaction.

The kind of perseverance we are talking about is not the determination shown for the sake of our own affairs, but for the sake of others. Involved in the idea of perseverance is the spiritual force of patience. Patience is emotional diligence. It is the willingness to bear inward pain for the sake of others.

Perseverance then produces character. Character comes as a result of a history of making decisions that place the welfare of others above ourselves. Character is achieved from making choices out of conviction rather than convenience. This results in the forging of tempered steel of virtue.

Character always produces hope. I am not talking about a wish mixed with uncertainty. Hope is an assurance cemented not in the somethings of life, but in the Someone of life. These forces are sustained by the power of God's love.

I don't know what trials you may be facing. Whatever it is, you can glory in it. His love will empower you to persevere, forging His tempered steel in your life, flooding your heart with eternal hope. Trust Him today. *(Written by Mike Fehlauer)*

FEBRUARY 27
YOU CAN'T TAKE IT WITH YOU, BUT YOU CAN SEND IT AHEAD
MATTHEW 6:19-21

Matthew 6:19-21, "Lay not up for yourselves treasures upon earth, where moth and rust doth corrupt, and where thieves break through and steal: But lay up for yourselves treasures in heaven, where neither moth nor rust doth corrupt, and where thieves do not break through nor steal: For where your treasure is, there will your heart be also."
We live in a society that is concerned about things: buying the biggest and best house, having the best car, having the latest gadget. But that is not the primary focus of the Lord, nor should it be for any believer. The Lord does not object to *us having things*; what He does object to is *things having us*. God didn't say that money was the root of all evil. He said the *love* of money was. That means putting money first in our lives above everything else.

The psalmist wrote, *"Delight thyself also in the LORD; and he shall give thee the desires of thine heart"* (Psalms 37:4). Jesus tells us to *"seek first the kingdom of God, and His righteousness; and all these things shall be added unto you"* (Matthew 6:33). The Apostle Paul told the Colossians *"Set your affection on things above, not on things on the earth"* (Colossians 3:2). Our focus should be furthering the kingdom of God. If our bottom-line, heart motivation, isn't souls, we're not focusing on the right thing.

There is a record in heaven where we will have to give an account of everything that we do and say (Romans 14:12). Matthew, chapter six, verse 20, says we are to lay up treasures in heaven. So, every time we give to the Lord out of a pure heart, we are laying up a heavenly bank account and increasing our balance. Giving is making another deposit for eternity. And just like with an earthly bank account, we can make withdrawals.

Consider giving as an opportunity to advance God's kingdom and enhance your heavenly bank account. Who knows you better: the teller at the bank, or the recording angel of the bank of heaven? *(Written by Bob Nichols)*

FEBRUARY 28
A YELLOW CADILLAC
3 JOHN 2

3 John 2 "Beloved, I pray that you may prosper in all things . . . . "
"I will never ride in that car! What will people think?" I cried to my husband when he came home and excitedly told me that some businessmen wanted to give us a brand-new yellow Cadillac. I knew that we needed a new car. You could see the ground as you drove in our old, dilapidated vehicle. And we were going to be traveling hundreds of miles to a Bible school in another state.

After three days of feeling sick to my stomach about the new car, I came up with a plan. "Dave, why don't you ask the pastor of our church what he thinks about this?" My kind husband made an appointment. "Pastor, what should I do?"

The wise gentleman told Dave something that changed my attitude: "Tell your wife, if she doesn't want the car, I'll take it." If the Presbyterian pastor was willing to drive that car, I decided I could ride in it too.

Now I know that my Father God desires to bless me with good things and I receive them thankfully. God wants to prosper you and give you good things. Don't resist Him with foolish pride, but cultivate a thankful heart. Raise your hands to Him and say, "Father, I thank you for all the good things you want to lavish on me!" *(Written by Bonnie Duell)*

FEBRUARY 29
WE ARE UNITED BY BLOOD
ACTS 17:26

Acts 17:26 "And hath made of one blood all nations of men for to dwell on the face of the earth . . . . "
Suppose you are dying, in need of a blood transfusion and the hospital is out of your blood type. They decide they have enough time to rush blood from another hospital and it arrives just in time to save your life. Before the doctors hook you up you ask them about the blood. "Is the blood from a black person, oriental or white person? Is this female or male blood? Was this blood taken from a poor or rich person? Is this person educated or not?" These are stupid questions and you could die in your prejudice. Blood unites all people. Nationality, social status, gender and skin color may be dividing points, but not blood. I can take blood from you, but I cannot take your nationality, your gender or skin.

Jesus did not shed His skin for us, but His blood. He gave the part of Him that unites us all, not a part that divides us. His blood has made us a brand-new race where there is no male or female, rich or poor, Jew or Gentile.

The world is in Adam, spiritually dead: therefore headed for eternal death. The world's thinking comes from the nature of death; therefore it is filled with prejudice toward anyone different than them. Why should we who are born again, a part of the kingdom of God, a chosen generation and a holy nation, be taken in by the world's way of thinking? The book of Philippians tells us we should let the mind that was in Jesus Christ be in us, and esteem others better than ourselves.

All mankind is united by natural blood. The family of God is united by supernatural blood. *"And they sung a new song, saying, Thou art worthy to take the book, and to open the seals thereof: for thou wast slain, and hast redeemed us to God by thy blood out of every kindred, and tongue, and people, and nation"* (Rev. 5:9). *(Written by Bob Yandian)*

MARCH 1
VOICE ACTIVATED FAITH
HEBREWS 11:1-6

Hebrews 11:3 "Through faith we understand that the worlds were framed by the word of God, so that things which are seen were not made of things which do appear."
God created the world and the universe by faith. And that faith was released by the words He spoke. There are eight times in the first chapter of Genesis that God spoke things into existence. Everything physical that we see around us was formed by words. Faith is always voice activated.

King David said in Psalm 116:10, "*I believed, therefore have I spoken.*" Paul quoted this statement of David in 2 Corinthians 4:13 and referred to it as a "*spirit of faith.*" Therefore we can see that the true spirit of faith speaks.

Jesus spoke to the fig tree in Mark 11:13-24 and it obeyed Him. His disciples were amazed, and He explained to them that anyone with faith could do the same thing. Three times in verse 23, Jesus linked our operating in faith to the words we speak. Most people say what they have and continue to have more of the same. Instead, we can say what we are believing for and it will come to pass when we speak in faith. We can say what we already have, or have what we say. The choice is ours.

You may think your words don't matter so much, but they do. Jesus said that what is in your heart in abundance, will come out of your mouth (Mt. 12:34). You can tell what you really believe by the words you speak. If you are pessimistic, your words will reveal that. If you are full of faith and hope, your speech will certainly coincide.

What words are you speaking? If you realize that your words aren't filled with faith, don't just change your words, change your heart and your words will follow suit. Words are the gauge of the heart. *(Written by Andrew Wommack)*

MARCH 2
THE POWER OF VISION OR DREAM, PART 1
ACTS 9:15-16

Acts 9:15-16 "But the Lord said to him, "Go, for he [Paul] is a chosen vessel of Mine to bear My name before Gentiles, kings, and the children of Israel. For I will show him how many things he must suffer for My name's sake."
I want to share with you a teaching on the power of a dream or vision. In Acts 9:15-16 we see the call on Paul's life. *"But the Lord said to him, 'Go, for he (Paul) is a chosen vessel of Mine to bear My name before Gentiles, kings, and the children of Israel. For I will show him how many things he must suffer for My name's sake.'"*

There is persecution that comes in following Jesus. Situations will come against you because of God's vision for your life. They help prepare you for all that God is doing and will do through you. What the enemy means for evil will be used by God for your good, for your benefit. Just remember—you are God's chosen vessel.

Your dream or vision for your life acts as a compass, giving you the direction you should travel. In my own life, a vision I received when I was sixteen years old, has given me lasting direction for my life. I knelt down by a hay bale and asked God for the privilege to support 500 missionaries. It wasn't until a few months ago that I was free to share what God said to me at that time.

As I was praying, I knew God was going to make me a very wealthy man. He told me this part of the dream would cost me a lot of money and friends. He also said it would be worth it all because of the eternal results that would happen because I believed Him. He told me that the walk of faith is not easy, but it would be the only way to see the completion of my vision.

A dream gives you hope for today and for the future. It helps you prioritize everything you do. When you have a dream, you are not just a spectator sitting back hoping everything will turn out right. You are taking an active part in shaping the purpose and meaning of your life.

You can pursue your dream no matter where you are today. What happened in the past is not as important as what lies ahead in the future. "No matter what a person's past may have been, his future is spotless." *(Written by Dave Duell)*

MARCH 3
THE POWER OF A VISION OR DREAM, PART 2
GENESIS 37:5

Genesis 37:5 "Now Joseph had a dream . . . . "
Before anything else, getting ready is the secret to success, but few want to pay the price. Whether you know it or not, your life has been preparing you for your dream. Mike Wallace interviewed a Sherpa guide and asked, "Why would you help someone do what they couldn't do in their own power? There are so many risks and dangers to your own life. Why do you insist on taking people to the top of Mt. Everest?" The Sherpa guide answered without hesitation, "It's obvious you have never been on top." No dream grows out of a vacuum but out of a life.

I. Believe in your ability to succeed.
No person can consistently perform in a manner that is inconsistent with the way he sees himself. You must believe you can succeed if you are to succeed. The best way to predict your future is to create it.

II. Get rid of pride.
People full of themselves usually don't have much room left over for a life-changing dream. Pride can keep you from trying new things or asking questions because you are afraid of looking stupid. It makes you want to stay in your comfort zone instead of striving for the end zone. Pride puts your focus on appearance instead of potential. It prevents you from taking risks—something you must do to discover your dream.

III. Cultivate constructive discontent.
Discontent is the driving force that makes people search for their dreams. Every invention registered in the United States Patent Office is the result of creative discontent. Complacency never brings success. You must desire positive change.

IV. Escape from habit.
A habit can be defined as something you do without thinking. Habits can kill a dream because when you stop thinking, you stop questioning and dreaming. Habits can cause you to go through the motions rather than think about the possibilities. They slowly close the door on potential. Be creative. One person can make a difference. *(Written by Dave Duell)*

MARCH 4
THE POWER OF A VISION OR DREAM, PART 3
ACTS 11:5

Acts 11:5 "I was in the city of Joppa praying: and in a trance I saw a vision, an object descending like a great sheet: let down from heaven by four corners: and it came to me."
Let's continue with the previous teaching on developing your vision and dreams. The previous points are: believe in your ability to succeed, get rid of pride, cultivate constructive discontent and escape from habit. (Thanks to John Maxwell and his book, *Leadership*, for some of these thoughts.)

V. Balance creativity with character.
Releasing your creativity to get yourself out of a rut and think about your dream is important, but nothing will come of it if you don't have the character to follow through with action. All the dreaming in the world won't do a bit of good unless you're ready to go to work and put it into action. With all I have been through in life, God told me that He was more interested in building my character than my ministry.

VI. Seeing it.
An old Italian proverb says, "Between saying and doing, many a pair of shoes are worn out." What separates the developer of a successful dream from a mere daydreamer is committed action. Dreams don't die, they just fade away. It takes tenacity and commitment to see a dream become reality. God told me audibly in a meeting one night, "Don't you dare give up! If you don't pursue it, the people won't get it." Your mind has much to do with your success. Even athletes are taught to see themselves making a basket, or throwing a touchdown pass, or jumping over the bar. If you can see it, you can have it.

VII. Dreams are fragile.
When a seedling oak tree is only a year old, a child can tear it out by the roots. But once it's had some time to become firmly established, even the force of a hurricane can't knock it down. Dreams can be shot down by close friends or family members, because they may be the only ones who know about them. We are so proud of our family who has remained supportive in all we do and only gives encouraging words to us. *(Written by Dave Duell)*

MARCH 5
THE POWER OF A VISION OR DREAM, PART 4
ACTS 26:19

Acts 26:19 "Therefore, King Agrippa, I was not disobedient to the heavenly vision."

Let me give you some more nuggets that will help you in what God has called you to do. The nuggets will give you insight into what you may be going through at the present time.

VIII.   Some will fight it.

Unfortunately, not everyone will want to celebrate with you when your dream comes to pass. There are two groups of people: Fire Fighters and Fire Lighters. Fire Fighters want to put out the fire that you have for your dream. No matter what you're for, they are against it. The way they criticize everything, you would think they get paid for it. Fire Lighters want to help you and are willing to do what they can to stoke the flames of your success even higher. Everyone needs a few of those people around to encourage them. No matter how people criticize you, don't let them take your focus off your dream.

IX.   Teach it.

Any dream worth living is worth sharing with others. The synergy of shared ideas often takes the dream to a whole new level. The dream becomes greater than the person launching it ever imagined it could be. When you are willing to share the dream by including others, there is almost no limit to what you can accomplish. When Mary was pregnant with Jesus, people got on their camels thousands of miles away and headed for the vision.

X.   Attitude determines your altitude.

Your attitude, not intelligence, talent, education, technical ability, opportunity, or even hard work, is the main factor that determines whether you will live out your dream. Attitude determines how far you can go on the success journey. If you have a positive attitude and are a positive thinker who likes challenges and difficult situations, then you have half of your success achieved. Your attitude determines your action and your action determines your accomplishment.

It is not what happens to you, but what happens in you that counts. Your attitude cannot be based on circumstances, upbringing, so-called limitations or other people. One of the greatest discoveries you can ever make is that you can change. What lies behind you and what lies before you are tiny matters, compared to what lies within you. *(Written by Dave Duell)*

MARCH 6
FAITH AND RELATIONSHIP
HEBREWS 11:6

Hebrews 11:6 "He who comes to God must believe that He is, and that He is a rewarder of those who diligently seek Him."

We must understand that without faith it is impossible to please God. A moment's thought will tell you that it's impossible to carry on business or have any successful human relationship in this world without the presence of faith. All business in the world would come to a standstill if men did not have faith in one another. The first inquiry of every businessman before he considers a business deal is, "Can the man be trusted?"

Unless you believe in a man, you cannot have any relationship with him. If you lose confidence in your doctor, you send for another. If you suspect that your merchant is taking advantage of you, you trade elsewhere.

This is a universal law that God has established regarding relationship. The reasons are not hard to find; the most obvious being that only through faith can we give God His rightful place as absolute Sovereign in our own lives. Unbelief in one way or another is a denial of God's truthfulness and authority. *(Written by Marshall Townsley)*

MARCH 7
DEATH OR LIFE?
PROVERBS 18:16-24

Proverbs 18:21 "Death and life are in the power of the tongue: and they that love it shall eat the fruit thereof." This verse says that the tongue has the power of death or life. Notice that it did not say there was also a multitude of nonproductive or vain words. No! Every word we speak either releases life or death. There is no middle ground. Jesus said in Matthew 12:36, *"But I say unto you, That every idle word that men shall speak, they shall give account thereof in the day of judgment."* We need to watch our words.

The Apostle James said that our tongue is like a bit in a horse's mouth or a rudder on a ship that steers the vessel (Jam. 3:3-4). We wouldn't get in a vehicle that we didn't have the ability to steer. That's suicide. Likewise, a person who has no control over his words is headed for destruction.

There are many distinguishing characteristics between man and the animal creation. Certainly, one of the most important differences that sets us apart is our ability to speak. That gives us creative power like God. God spoke the world and the universe into existence. We speak our own environment into existence by the words that we speak.

With this creative power comes responsibility. Our words have the power to bless or curse, to give life or release death. Sadly, the majority of people are using the negative power of their tongues instead of the positive power. We need to pray the prayer of David that says, *"Set a watch, O LORD, before my mouth; keep the door of my lips"* (Ps. 141:3).

Ask the Lord to show you the power of your words today and then use that power to bless God and man. *(Written by Andrew Wommack)*

MARCH 8
TITHING OPENS THE WINDOWS OF HEAVEN
MALACHI 3:10

Malachi 3:10 "Bring ye all the tithes into the storehouse, that there may be meat in mine house, and prove me now herewith, saith the LORD of hosts, if I will not open you the windows of heaven, and pour you out a blessing, that there shall not be room enough to receive it."
Here is the only place found in scripture where God tells us to prove Him. He says that if we act according to His command by bringing Him all our tithes, we can expect Him to follow through by opening up the windows of heaven and pouring out a blessing. Have you ever thought about opening up a window? What comes through windows? Light comes through windows. Except for electricity, if we didn't have windows in our homes or offices, they would be pretty dark. In the same way, light will come to us: revelation light, God ideas. Breezes also come through open windows. There is nothing as refreshing as the wind of the Holy Ghost. There's power in the wind of the Holy Ghost. Jesus said in Acts 1:8, *"But ye shall receive power, after that the Holy Ghost is come upon you: and ye shall be witnesses unto me both in Jerusalem, and in all Judaea, and in Samaria, and unto the uttermost part of the earth."* It was fulfilled in Acts 2:2. *The rushing mighty wind of the Holy Ghost filled the room where the disciples were gathered together.* And, it is still being fulfilled today because " . . . the promise is unto you, and to your children, and to all that are afar off, even as many as the Lord our God shall call" (Acts 2:39).

Every time we are obedient to God by faithfully bringing in our tithes and offerings, we give Him the opportunity to open up windows to shower down the unlimited resources of heaven. Give and it shall be given. Let us give saying, "On earth, as it is in heaven for my life!" *(Written by Bob Nichols)*

MARCH 9
THE DECEITFULNESS OF RICHES
MARK 4:19

Mark 4:19 "And the cares of this world, and the deceitfulness of riches, and the lusts of other things entering in, choke the word, and it becometh unfruitful."
The deceitfulness of riches is one of the most effective ways Satan chokes out the Word of God in our lives. Wealth carries with it a tangible power—an influence. This kind of power runs parallel to the anointing. Because of this, a carnal believer will respond to a person of wealth the same way he responds to a person who has a strong anointing on his life. This is why the Apostle James warned the church not to show favoritism to those of financial resources. Even though the power that comes with earthly wealth looks and feels similar to the anointing of the Spirit, it carries no power to cause eternal change in a person's heart.
The problem is not in prospering. The deceitfulness of riches comes when we begin to equate our spirituality with how much stuff we have. When we begin to think that because one drives a Mercedes, he is more spiritual than one who drives a Honda, this is when the deceit of riches has entered our hearts. Prosperity is not a right, but rather a privilege. It is a by-product of our relationship with Jesus, not a standard by which we measure our relationship with Him. Does God then desire us to live in poverty? No! He desires us to live in His abundance in every area of our lives. When it comes to finances, He wants us to understand His purpose. Finances is one of the means to making disciples, not the end in determining the value of a disciple. *(Written by Mike Fehlauer)*

MARCH 10
SOW WHERE YOU WANT TO GO
1 KINGS 19:19-21

1 Kings 19:21, "And he returned back from him, and took a yoke of oxen, and slew them, and boiled their flesh with the instruments of the oxen, and gave unto the people, and they did eat. Then he arose, and went after Elijah, and ministered unto him."
I've often said that a lot of people are waiting for their ship to come in, but they have never even sent out a rowboat. All things don't happen overnight; some things are long-range. Certain seeds take longer to grow than other seeds.
In this passage of scripture, the man of God—Elijah—came to Elisha and cast his mantle upon him. Elijah was beckoning Elisha to join him. By sacrificing his oxen, Elisha was sowing his livelihood. He then sowed his very life, ministering to Elijah. He was sowing where he wanted to go. When Elijah was taken up to heaven in a chariot of fire, his mantle was passed on to Elisha (2 Kings 2:11-14) who then also had a ministry of miracles. He was granted the double portion of Elijah's anointing (2 Kings 2:9-10). You go where you sow.
My wife and I have invested in other ministers' housing. Through the years, we've helped ministers make house payments. Then God gave us our home at 50 cents on the dollar. Ultimately, the home was supernaturally paid for. All of that was a result of sowing. It's line upon line, precept upon precept.
Giving is a way of life. I like the way missionary evangelist, Wayne Myers, said it, "I live to give." He's the first one I ever heard say that, and he does live to give. He made a large pledge to a Bible school and paid that pledge. Then he later pledged double that amount and paid that pledge as well. He is the first missionary that ever fought me for the lunch ticket. He and his wife are blessed because they are a blessing.
Giving is not just in finances alone, although it certainly is that, too. You invest in other people's children. You bless them, you encourage them, you love them. You get the same seeds back. Again, you sow where you go, and you go where you sow. If you have a prodigal son, pray for someone else's prodigal son. God will recognize your seed and meet your need. Mark 4:24, *"Take heed what ye hear: with what measure ye mete, it shall be measured to you: and unto you that hear shall more be given."* *(Written by Bob Nichols)*

MARCH 11
A PROSPEROUS SOUL
ROMANS 12:2

Romans 12:2 "Be transformed by the renewing of your mind . . . . "
Your soul consists of your mind, will and emotions. God wants your soul to prosper. To have soul prosperity you must renew your mind with the Word. This is the main part of repentance—to have an inner change or transformation take place as you change your way of thinking. By meditating on the Word of God you will not be conformed or molded by the world's system.

Spiritual warfare mainly deals with your mind and flesh rather than the devil. Your mind is the strategic control center for your entire life. As long as you believe the thoughts running through your mind are yours, you'll never be free. You'll never succeed. Second Corinthians 10:4-5 tells us that we are in warfare to pull down strongholds by bringing *"every thought into captivity to the obedience of Christ."* I used to have many strongholds in my soul, wrong thought patterns that caused 'uncontrollable' sexual thoughts, fear, unforgiveness, and so forth. I didn't know that there was anything I could do about them. I finally saw in the Word that I was being controlled by the enemy because I had allowed my thoughts to get out of control. I called out to God. He delivered me and gave me the freedom to think thoughts that lined up with His Word.

Use the replacement principle. Replace your wrong, negative thoughts with thoughts that are lovely, pure and of good report. Your wrong thought patterns or strongholds will soon give way to thoughts of God and His Word. Your soul will enjoy prosperity! *(Written by Bonnie Duell)*

MARCH 12
EVERYTHING HAS A VOICE
JOHN 3:6

John 3:6 "That which is born of flesh is flesh, and that which is born of the Spirit is spirit."
The spiritual law of Genesis is *everything produces after its own kind* (Genesis 1:12). This is true in the spiritual as well as the natural kingdom. Love produces love, turnips produce turnips, cats produce cats, people produce people and God produces spirits.

Every living thing passes on attributes. Cats have whiskers, dogs have tails and people have hands and feet. Those attributes come with birth. Hands and feet are not added later—the original ones grow with the rest of the body. I received all of God's attributes when I was born of Him.

My outward man was born of man, but my inward man was born of God. I have feet and hands because I was born of man. I have love, joy and faith because I was born of God.

Every creature has a voice. Cats meow, dogs bark and babies cry. These are voices that are handed down through birth. Babies cry because this is the voice handed down by the parents. The voice of the new creation, the spirit man *"calls those things which be not as though they were"* (Romans 4:17). This is the voice of God given to each one of us at the point of the new birth. It is just as natural for a Christian to call those things which be not as though they were as it is for a cat to meow, a dog to bark or a baby to cry.

Your mind may tell you the Word of God cannot be believed. The word says, "You need to look at the circumstances with your *eyes*. You need to listen to the reports of men with your *ears*. You need to figure out an answer with your *mind*." Your eyes, ears and mind came from the first birth. They came from men. Your eyes are made to see with, not believe with. Your ears are made to hear with, not believe with. Your mind is made to think with, not believe with. You believe with your heart. The heart was created by God. It came with the new birth. *(Written by Bob Yandian)*

MARCH 13
THE FIG TREE
MARK 11:13-24

Mark 11:14 "And Jesus answered and said unto it, No man eat fruit of thee hereafter for ever. And his disciples heard it." This is an amazing story. Jesus was hungry and He saw a fig tree that already had leaves which led Him to believe it had figs. But that wasn't the case. There were no figs. In response, Jesus cursed the fig tree with His words saying, *"No man eat fruit of thee hereafter, forever."*

Jesus talked to the fig tree. This verse says, *"Jesus answered and said unto it."* That means the fig tree had been talking to Him. Some people think this is weird, but things talk to us all the time. Your checkbook tells you that you don't have enough money to make it. Your body tells you that you are sick. Situations speak negative things to us without saying a word. Most of us pick up on those negative comments and speak them right out of our mouth, thereby giving them power over our lives.

Jesus did the right thing. He used His words to silence the hypocrisy of this fig tree. It professed fruit by having leaves, but it didn't possess it. It had spoken something to Him that it couldn't deliver. Jesus said that it would never yield fruit to anyone ever again. And it didn't. It immediately died at its roots (Mk. 11:20), and its death was visible the next day.

His disciples were overwhelmed with this miracle and questioned Him about it. He said that this was the power of words. Anyone who speaks in faith, without doubting in his heart will have whatsoever he says. This works in the positive or negative.

Whenever a negative circumstance starts speaking to you today, talk back to it in faith and watch the situation change. *(Written by Andrew Wommack)*

MARCH 14
FEAR NOT
I JOHN 4:18

I John 4:18 "There is no fear in love, but perfect love casts out fear, because fear involves torment. But he who fears has not been made perfect in love." The two greatest deterrents in life are fear and failure. The Bible tells us 365 times to "fear not." One for each day of the year. Also in 1 John 4:28, it says, *"There is no fear in love, but perfect love casts out fear because fear involves torment. But he who fears has not been made perfect in love."*

All people experience fear, and it is a part of life. Fear can keep you from doing what God wants you to do. If allowed to control our lives, it can keep us from making any progress. Fear breeds inaction; inaction leads to lack of experience. Lack of experience fosters ignorance and ignorance breeds fear. The bottom line is that if you can overcome your fear, you can break the cycle and live to see the death of your ignorance and the birth of your vision.

Fear also causes procrastination. It divides your focus and weakens you. It can even make you feel isolated. Fear is the darkroom where your negatives are developed. Fear robs you of your potential and prevents you from moving forward toward your purpose in life.

Most of the fears that we face are not based on facts. They are generated by our feelings. Sixty percent of our fears are totally unwarranted, and they never come to pass. Twenty percent of our fears are focused on our past, which is completely out of our control. Ten percent of our fears are based on things so petty that they make no difference in our lives. Of the remaining ten percent, only four or five percent could be considered justifiable.

As we recognize what fear can do to us we can take these evil thoughts captive. How do we do that? Let's take Paul's advice in 2 Corinthians 10:5 where he says, *"casting down arguments and every high thing that exalts itself against the knowledge of God, bringing every thought into captivity to the obedience of Christ."* *(Written by Dave Duell)*

MARCH 15
WITH HIM
GALATIANS 2:20

Galatians 2:20 "I have been crucufired with Christ . . . . "
God desires us to walk and live in His prosperity—in every area of our lives.
For us to experience His fullness, we must dare to believe in our identity in Him.
Notice that Paul says that he was crucified with Christ. In Romans it says that we are
buried with Him in baptism. There are two aspects of us being one with Jesus. The
first is His oneness with our sin on the cross. The second is our oneness with Him in
His glory. Simply put—He became as we were so we could become as He is! He
became one with our death so that we could experience His fullness of life. He
became sickness so that we could experience His health. He shared in our weakness so we could live in His strength.

As you begin your day, remember that you have been crucified with Him. Because
He completely identified with you, you can live in His glory. Everything that He has, you
have. Everything He is, is available to you. Keep in mind as you face the challenges of life
this day, that "as He is, so you are in this world." He died to make us live. He became weak
to make us strong. He suffered shame to give us glory. *(Written by Mike Fehlauer)*

MARCH 16
YOU'VE MILKED THIS COW LONG ENOUGH
GALATIANS 6:9

*Galatians 6:9, "And let us not be weary in well doing: for in due season we shall reap, if we
faint not."*
Many years ago, we started a little church in an old Post Office building on Berry Street in Fort
Worth, Texas. Those were days of small beginnings for us. I was the pastor, youth minister, singles'
minister, janitor and yard man. We bought an old building and fixed it up to be a nice little chapel
all by the grace of God. I was hungry for God and crying out, "Lord, as long as it's right and as long
as it works, I'll do whatever it takes, but we've got to have a move of God." God answered that
prayer and sent a group of young hippies to spring us into a revival that totally turned our church
around. Praise God! We grew and finally we were using everything we could get our hands on.
Then God opened up the opportunity for a beautiful building in downtown Fort Worth.

As impossible as it seemed, in 1976 we came downtown, but we assumed someone else's
indebtedness with the purpose of buying the building. We left Berry street with 300 people, and got
downtown with about 200. When we left, we sowed our church to a young congregation who
never could have purchased even that small church. After 12 years, we just walked away and
blessed them with our equity and stayed on the bank note. We let them have a break that we didn't
have to begin with, so that they could just take over a beautiful little chapel out on Berry Street. You
know, when I look back and see some of the steps we've taken, it scares me. But God is faithful. At
that time, I think we would have charged hell with a dry water pistol! When you have a word from
God, you don't sweat the small stuff.

Then the balloon note on our beautiful downtown church property was coming due. It had
to be paid or we would forfeit the whole property. A gentleman in our congregation came forward
one Sunday morning and asked what he could do to help me. I told him our situation. That
gentleman went to the bank where we had our account, put his cowboy hat on the desk, shook
hands with the bank president and said, "This preacher needs a loan. You've milked this cow long
enough, it's time to feed it a little bit." The banker laughed and asked how much money we
needed. We got our loan. It was God. It wasn't me, it wasn't the man in the cowboy hat and it
wasn't the banker. It was God.

All of our life is sowing seeds. Everything we do is sowing seeds—our words, our actions, our
smiles, our finances. We may not have money, but we can give something that helps somebody.
Tithe is what God said to do, but our giving is where we get into the blessing and the return. *(Written
by Bob Nichols)*

MARCH 17
HEARING FROM GOD
LUKE 8:8

Luke 8:8 "He who has ears to hear, let him hear."
How we hear is an urgent matter. We have all too often assumed that the message is what controls the hearer. But there is a sense in which the hearer controls the message. In Proverbs 4:20-22, we are given three steps on how to hear God's Word. Step one, is to *attend.* The word attend means to focus the mind, the total consciousness, on what God says. Our attitude in hearing must be one of individual attention so that we may understand what God means by what He says. Furthermore, it implies that all human opinions, tradition, circumstances, and even our own experiences must not be allowed to take the place of God's Word. Personal experience or the experiences of others must not be allowed to define truth. Truth should be exercised to interpret and define the nature of our experiences. Never the opposite.

The second step is to *incline.* The word "incline" means to bow down or to submit. We are to be submissive to its teachings and allow them to be the determining factor of both thought and deed.

And, finally, step three is to *keep.* We must be diligent to hold to what we hear from God. We must, therefore, hear with a continuing diligence. God, through Moses, set forth a command for the priority of His Word: *"And these words which I command you today, shall be in your heart; you shall teach them diligently to your children, and shall talk of them when you sit in your house, when you walk by the way, when you lie down, and when you rise up. You shall bind them as a sign on your hand, and they shall be as frontlets between your eyes. You shall write them on the doorposts of your house and on your gates" (Deuteronomy 6:6-9).*

It is in attending to God's Word that we come to understand it. In inclining to it, we come to receive it, and in keeping God's Word we will retain it. These three steps, if followed, can lead to the kind of mountain-moving faith that Jesus spoke of Himself in His own teachings on this subject. So let the Word of Christ dwell in you richly. *(Written by Marshall Townsley)*

MARCH 18
NO CHILD OF GOD IS BETTER THAN ANOTHER
1 CORINTHIANS 12:15

1 Corinthians 12:15 "If the foot shall say, because I am not the hand I am not of the body . . . . "
This verse comes from an interesting part of 1 Corinthians chapter 12. We have body parts talking to each other. Not only does the foot speak to the hand, the ear talks to the eye (v. 16). What we have is hidden parts speaking to visible parts. The foot and ear are not as readily visible to others as is the eye and hand.

If one part of your body could complain, it would be the foot to the hand: "I carry the weight all day. This man puts me into a sock, crams me into a shoe, and no one sees me. The hand is seen all day long. When is the last time this man bought me a ring or watch?" The ear could also complain about the eye. "I am under this hair and no one can see me. The eye is right around the corner and everyone looks deep into it. When is the last time this woman washed back here? She buys eye makeup, but never ear makeup."

This may all sound silly, but the body parts speak of the offices we all have in the body of Christ. Often times we complain, because someone else is being shown all of the attention. "I serve in children's church and no one knows I am back here. The music director is seen by everyone. The ushers get more attention than I do." Because you are not as visible in your ministry does not mean you are less important or not needed.

Would you rather lose your hand or your foot? Would you rather lose your sight or your hearing? When it comes to function, all of your body parts are equally important. The same is true with God. God would not want to lose the children's worker over the pastor. Both are equally important. Your ministry is just as important to the body of Christ as the best known evangelist, pastor or teacher. *(Written by Bob Yandian)*

MARCH 19
GOD'S WAY OF TALKING
ROMANS 4:16-25

Romans 4:17 "(As it is written, I have made thee a father of many nations,) before him whom he believed, even God, who quickeneth the dead, and calleth those things which be not as though they were."
Paul was speaking about God's dealings with Abram. The Lord appeared to Abram and told him that he would give him children and they would become so numerous that they would number as the sand on the seashore or the stars in the heavens (Gen. 15:1-6). Then years later, the Lord reassured Abram of His promise, and as a token, changed his name to Abraham which means "father of a multitude."

God called Abram the father of a multitude when he didn't even have the promised son yet. That's what Paul was referring to when he said, *"God . . . calleth those things which be not as though they were."* God speaks what He believes, not just what He sees.

In Genesis 1:3, God said, *"Let there be light; and there was light."* But it wasn't until the fourth day of creation that God created the sun, moon and stars (Gen. 1:14-19). He spoke light into existence before He created the sun. That's not the way we do things, but that's how God operates.

If we want godly results, we need to learn to talk like God. Instead of speaking about what you have, use your faith to speak about what you are believing. There is creative power in your words. Speak about the things that aren't manifest in the physical yet as though they were, and if you are speaking in faith, they will come to be. *(Written by Andrew Wommack)*

MARCH 20
GOD HAS NOT GIVEN US A SPIRIT OF FEAR
2 TIMOTHY 1:7

2 Timothy 1:7 "For God has not given us a spirit of fear, but of power and of love and of a sound mind."
Most of the fear we face is generated by our feelings. Statistics show that any time or energy you give to fear is totally wasted and counterproductive 95 percent of the time. Fear is interest paid on a debt you do not owe. Acknowledge your fears, deal with them and keep moving on. What God has called you to do is the most effective antidote for fear. It can fuel the flames of the desire within you until you are willing to confront and overcome your fear.

The bottom line is that you have a choice. You can feed your fears or you can starve fear. Both fear and faith will be with you every minute of every day. But the emotion that you continually act upon, the one you feed, dominates your life. Action on the right emotion can lead to victory.

The irony is that the successful person who keeps growing, taking risks, and moving forward feels the same feeling of fear as the one who allows fear to stop him. The difference comes because one doesn't let fear dominate while the other does.

Unsuccessful people are often so afraid of failure and rejection that they spend their whole lives avoiding risks or decisions that could lead to failure. They don't realize that success is based on their ability to fail and continue trying. When you have the right attitude, failure is neither fatal or final. It can even be your springboard to success.

"For God has not given us a spirit of fear, but of power and of love and of a sound mind" (II Timothy 1:7). A sound mind means to have good judgment, disciplined thought patterns and the ability to understand and make right decisions. It includes the qualities of self-control and self-discipline. *(Written by Dave Duell)*

MARCH 21
CAPTURING YOUR TEENAGER'S HEART WITH LOVE
1 CORINTHIANS 13:13

1 Corinthians 13:13 "And now abide faith, hope, love, these three; but the greatest of these is love."
The most important factor is creating an atmosphere where your teenager can experience God's unconditional love. Three important characteristics of God's love are acceptance, understanding and commitment. The opposite of these is judgment, rejection and manipulation. Manipulation loves the end result—the behavior, more than the person. In other words, the ultimate goal in *conditional love* is seeing our teens conduct change instead of seeing them changed. If our teenagers are displaying unhealthy attitudes or destructive behavior, it is far too easy to reject and judge them for their actions. Although there are times when discipline and punishment are necessary, we need to differentiate our children from their actions.

When we love conditionally, our hope is that their desire for our acceptance will be strong enough to cause them to change their behavior. If this approach does cause some change in them, it is usually short-lived. We are also inadvertently training them to live for the acceptance of others, and not for the honor of God. When our teens know that our commitment and acceptance of them is not based on their actions, then they are free from the need to defend themselves. This is the point where our prayers become effective because love has freed them to hear and respond to the voice of God. Be encouraged today. God's wisdom is with you. Allow His love to flow freely to your teen, and believe that He is working in him His will and good pleasure. *(Written by Mike Fehlauer)*

MARCH 22
TALK TO GOD ABOUT YOUR NEED, HE'LL TELL YOU TO PLANT A SEED
PROVERBS 11:24-25

Proverbs 11:24-25 "There is that scattereth, and yet increaseth; and there is that withholdeth more than is meet, but it tendeth to poverty. The liberal soul shall be made fat: and he that watereth shall be watered also himself."
During a challenging time in our ministry, when God worked out our financing for our church facility, the bank said, "We'll handle the financing on the upper part of the property for you if you'll sell the lower part." I thought it was like checkers or chess. What do you do? You survive. We bought it for $600,000 and we sold it for $850,000 with the stipulation that we had guaranteed parking rights for the church and that they would make it into a parking lot with improvements. Little did I know that that one stipulation cost them contracts with major hotel chains and a few others. Every other year or so, we would try to buy it back. One day we went over to Dallas to see what they would sell the parking lot for, and they said at that point it would be seven million dollars! Oh, but God was working.

For almost 13 years, every time I'd turn the corner to come to the church, that property would laugh at me, but I'd say, "In the name of Jesus, Isaac, you're on the altar, but you're coming up off that altar!" I had remembered the faithfulness of God and how God had miraculously brought us from tiny beginnings to that church while we stood on faith in His word to us in Isaiah 41:10.

We were in a meeting down in Florida, and that church desperately needed to buy some property. We pledged $5,000 and it was a hard $5,000, but we paid it. Listen, we've discovered something—what you make happen for someone else, God will make happen for you. We invested in another church's property when we desperately needed it. But thank God for the power of planting seed. God answered our need.

One day the bank set up a meeting with us, and the real estate agent said, "I'm Jewish and I don't know if you understand this, but this property has been like a Jonah to us." I told him I thoroughly understood. He continued, "Would you make us an offer?" I thought a while and then with a boldness from the heart of God, I said, "I'll tell you what we'll give you: $100,000 and we'll close any time you want to close." They looked at each other, gathered their papers and walked out. Thirty days later they called back and said, "We've been in this business for a long time and don't understand this." Hallelujah! We bought back Isaac off the altar for $100,000 and still have him today! Remember, when you go to God to talk about a need, He'll talk to you about planting a seed. *(Written by Bob Nichols)*

MARCH 23
CAN GOD SUPPLY?
2 CORINTHIANS 1:20

2 Corinthians 1:20 "For all the promises of God in Him are Yes, and in Him Amen, to the glory of God through us."

"Mom, I believe God wants me to go to Oral Roberts University," our daughter, Juli, informed me as she neared her high school graduation. "We can't afford that!" was my first response. "God will provide if I'm supposed to go there," Juli countered.

Finally, we agreed to give our daughter the money for the application fee. Juli was accepted into the university and we decided to agree with her that God would provide her needs as He promised in His Word. We didn't realize, though, that we would have to write a substantial check to the school before they would allow us to move her into her dorm room. It was a hot check.

"God, you know we cannot cover this check in the natural. Please provide for us." When we arrived home in Colorado there was a check in our mailbox from a church where my husband had preached two years before, for the exact amount of the check we had written to the school. We were praising God for His supply.

How would we continue to cover the cost of the schooling? God would receive the glory. He spoke to a farmer friend to make monthly payments to the university for the first year. Then Juli's years of practice on the violin paid off. She auditioned for the TV orchestra and that job paid for all of her tuition, board and books for the next two years. There, she was destined to meet her future husband.

Can God supply? Our daughter taught us that God's promises are yes and amen!
(Written by Bonnie Duell)

MARCH 24
GOD HAS ALREADY GIVEN EVERYTHING
2 PETER 1:3

2 Peter 1:3 "According as his divine power hath given unto us all things that pertain unto life and godliness . . . . "

This simple verse can change your entire life. The revelation given here is simple yet profound. God has already given us everything we need for our natural and spiritual lives. He will not make anything else. His divine power looked through the ages, saw everything we would need for life (natural life) and godliness (spiritual life) and made it ahead of time. When you received Jesus as your Savior, a storehouse was opened containing all you would ever need. It is almost blasphemous to think that we can face a need that will take God by surprise.

Our faith does not move God to supply, He has already supplied. Our study, prayer, faith and trust in God moves us into a better position to receive what God has already given. God is never the problem, we are.

When the thief on the cross received salvation, Jesus told him they would be together in paradise that day. Adam and Eve were removed from paradise; through Jesus we are brought back into the garden. The angels that kept Adam and Eve out have welcomed us back. God put Adam and Eve into Eden after he finished the garden. Everything was created, then the man and woman were placed into it. God did not create a tree when the couple had a need. The trees were already made for every need they could have.

God has done the same for us with our paradise, the garden of the New Birth. We were placed into this new life after God created everything we would need. We just need to wander through and find out what God has provided. Every tree is good. Because Adam and Eve sinned, they could not eat of the Tree of Life. Because we are born again, we are invited to eat of it. The Tree of Life is the Word of God (Proverbs 3:18). Everything that pertains to life and godliness is made available to us through His Word, *"through the knowledge of Him that hath called us to glory and virtue . . . "* through the *"exceeding great and precious promises . . . "* (2 Peter 1:3,4). *(Written by Bob Yandian)*

MARCH 25
YOUR RESOURCES OR GOD'S?
2 KINGS 4:1-8

2 Kings 4:2 "And Elisha said unto her, What shall I do for thee? tell me, what hast thou in the house? And she said, Thine handmaid hath not any thing in the house, save a pot of oil."
This woman was in a desperate situation. Her husband had died and she was unable to meet her financial obligations. The way these situations were handled back then was that if you couldn't pay your debts, you became the slave of the person to whom you owed money. The creditor was coming to take her two sons as slaves.

This woman's husband had been one of the prophets in association with Elisha. She made an appeal to Elisha for help. Elisha had been her husband's friend and mentor. She was looking to Elisha for aid. However, Elisha refused to take responsibility for this woman's prosperity and put the issue back in her court. It wasn't a matter of what he had, but what did she have?

Many people would think this showed a lack of compassion on Elisha's part. Why didn't he just give her money out of his own pocket? There could be many answers to that question but certainly one of the reasons was that Elisha's resources were limited. Even if he could have met this woman's need, there were others and their needs exceeded his ability. He was correct in pointing her to the Lord to get her needs met.

It is true that we should do what we can with what we have, but we will never be able to meet the needs of everyone. It is actually doing others a disservice to make them dependent on us for their supply. God should be everyone's source. Instead of Elisha helping her temporarily, he gave her a permanent solution to her problem. He taught her to use what she had and trust God to bless it. *(Written by Andrew Wommack)*

MARCH 26
FAITH RIGHTEOUSNESS
PHILIPPIANS 3:8-9

Philippians 3:8-9 "Yet indeed I also count all things loss for the excellence of the knowledge of Christ Jesus my Lord, for whom I have suffered the loss of all things, and count them as rubbish, that I may gain Christ and be found in Him, not having my own righteousness, which is from the law, but that which is through faith in Christ, the righteousness which is from God by faith."
We grew up in a church that taught or came to understand that our performance is how we relate to God. If we did everything right, God loved us and if we didn't, God was angry.

The way I see the Gospel is that God, Jesus and the Holy Spirit got together in Heaven and had a meeting. They came to the agreement that if they were to save the people on earth they would have to do it themselves. By this they made the New Covenant with themselves that cannot be broken. Jesus did it all by His life, death, and resurrection. He became sin, sickness, and poverty for us that we can become righteous, healed, and live in prosperity. All we have to do is believe what has already been done.

As we look at Paul's life and calling, we see that he was called as an apostle to the Gentiles. Jesus was his teacher and he was given special insight into our identity in Jesus. He was called to a people who had no knowledge of the law. God did not want them under the law. He did not want them to try to mix law and grace.

Paul knew more than anyone else, the futility of works-righteousness. All that we have and all we can do is the result of the finished work of the Lord Jesus at the cross. It is not our good works. Paul knew, that the secret of God's power was faith-righteousness, a message that still confuses the carnal minded. Faith-righteousness is a message that is only understood by revelation, yet the message is essential to every believer's victory. Without the absolute confidence of right standing before God, there cannot be an absolute assurance of his promises. *(Written by Dave Duell)*

MARCH 27
TAKING THE PAIN OUT OF PRAYER
1 THESSALONIANS 5:17

1 Thessalonians 5:17 "Pray without ceasing."
I can't think of three words that intimidate a believer more than these. Because of our tradi-tional views concerning prayer, these three words have discouraged more Christians from praying than probably any other three words. We know that the scriptures are true. There is not much room to adjust the interpretation of these verses. What does it mean to pray without ceasing? If it means being locked up in a room somewhere, on your knees, can you do this and keep a job? If you are a mother with small children, how can you spend hours a day in private prayer and still keep your home sane?

Have you ever worried without ceasing? Well, the same part of you that worries is the same part of your soul that prays. In other words, if we have the ability to carry around in our hearts and souls thoughts of concern all day, then we can direct our hearts in communion with God—without ceasing. This is not to say that there are never times where we separate ourselves for prayer. But, we really need to understand the essence of prayer—which is communion with Him. We have been created in a way to carry on that communion anywhere and anytime. Actually, the season we are in many times dictates the method of praying.

I want to encourage you to direct your thoughts and hearts toward Him today. Instead of trying to press into His presence, I want to encourage you to begin to simply *enjoy* His presence. *(Written by Mike Fehlauer)*

MARCH 28
START WHERE YOU ARE WITH WHAT YOU HAVE
MATTHEW 25:21

Matthew 25:21 "His lord said unto him, Well done, thou good and faithful servant: thou hast been faithful over a few things, I will make thee ruler over many things: enter thou into the joy of thy lord."
Tithing, which is giving God ten percent of all your increase, is the foundational basic to living a prosperous life. It is a starting point. We also need to give above just the tithe. An important thing to remember is to start where you are and give, stretching a little bit mixed with faith. This is a faith situation that is based on the Word of God. It is not a gimmick or a multilevel type of thing. It is God's promise, and it receives God's blessing—every time.

The only time in my life when I didn't tithe was in the early days when my wife, Joy, and I were just married. The bills were high and money was scarce. Once when I was an associate minister, I took a night job to try to catch up, but I just couldn't get caught up. I was getting further behind. One day, Joy said, "Bob, are we tithing?" Thank God for a godly wife. I wasn't trying to withhold my tithe; I intended to make it up, but it seemed like there was no way. That's where we learned that you start where you are and be faithful. Thank God, He brought us back out.

I remember one week recently that we *gave* more in one week than we *made*. The key thing is to start where you are and mix it with faith. Not too long ago, I was going through some old, old financial records. I'm surprised that we still had them. It was really interesting to me to see that there was a time when we were just married that my wife and I gave one dollar offerings. A dollar fifty would be like five or ten dollars today. That's all we could do at that time. It was also interesting to see the progression over the years of offerings going up to four dollars, and then five dollars. That was a lot to us. I think of how one hundred dollars would have been a week's salary when we were associate ministers.

Can you see the progression? Do what you can where you are, and stretch a little. It takes a little while sometimes, but put some seed in the ground. Some seed comes up real quick, but some seed take more time. We have some seed coming up now that we planted 20 years ago.

Be diligent. Start where you are with what you have. If you can't give money, give your time, give love, give clothes, whatever; just get some seed in the ground and watch God's Word work in your life. *(Written by Bob Nichols)*

MARCH 29
THE LIVING WORD
JOSHUA 1:8

Joshua 1:8 "This Book of the Law shall not depart from your mouth, but you shall meditate in it day and night, that you may observe to do according to all that is written in it. For then you will make your way prosperous, and then you will have good success" (New King James).

When God's Word is in the heart, it's like a seed planted in soil. It will produce results according to the condition of the heart. If the soil is rich and well prepared it will bring forth a strong and pure faith and you will no longer be trying to believe, or struggling to trust what God has said. This is very important to understand. In order for faith to receive the promise of God, the Word must become a vital part of your heart.

If you are trying to believe certain promises, such as those regarding your physical healing or the financial supply of your needs; if you are still struggling over them and reasoning about them, it's because they have not yet taken root in your heart. Now, you can allow yourself to become condemned over this issue, or you can diligently apply yourself to correcting it. The choice is yours.

To have the Scriptures in the mind in an academic way so that you just give mental assent to them is one thing. To actually step out on those promises and appropriate them in a time of crisis is another thing altogether. There is a distinct difference between mental assent, or merely giving credence to something, and genuine Bible-saving faith. And that difference is determined by whether or not God's Word has been truly planted and then rooted in your heart. What's in your heart in abundance you can't help but believe! *(Written by Marshall Townsley)*

MARCH 30
HOW DOES FAITH REST?
HEBREWS 4:10

Hebrews 4:10 "He who has entered into His rest has himself also ceased from his work as God did from His."

Resting does not mean to sit down and do nothing. God's idea of resting in our faith is not to sit in front of the television, eat a few chips and do nothing. God's idea of resting includes being busy.

Rest in the Christian life is freedom from worry, anxiety and stress. It is a relaxed enjoyment of each day as we work for the Lord.

Neither does resting mean to relax because you are tired. God does not want us to wear ourselves down working for Him, and then need time off. There is not a day off in the kingdom of God.

Our rest is compared to God. Can you imagine God sitting down in front of a television eating chips? Does God need to rest because He is tired? No, God is never tired though His responsibilities are never finished.

God rested on the seventh day because the work of creation was completed. His rest is an example to us. We rest because everything has been created or made for us. God has not failed to make anything we need or will ever need. Man and woman were placed into a garden that was complete. Adam could toil and dress the garden without a worry in the world. He could enjoy his labors. So can we enjoy our work in the garden of the New Birth.

Jesus entered a boat and commanded the disciples to "go to the other side." He then laid down and went to sleep in the midst of a storm. The disciples worried, fretted and even woke up Jesus, blaming Him for a lack of care for them. Jesus rebuked the storm and then rebuked the disciples. If Jesus could sleep through a storm, why couldn't they? The word was spoken and would come to pass. They would make it to the other side. We can rest in God's promises.

With the promises of God given to us, we will make it through every trial in life. We can rest as Jesus did knowing we are headed to the other side to set the captives free. True faith demands an attitude of peace. *(Written by Bob Yandian)*

MARCH 31
LITTLE IS MUCH WHEN GOD IS IN IT
2 KINGS 4:1-8

2 Kings 4:2 "And Elisha said unto her, What shall I do for thee? tell me, what hast thou in the house? And she said, Thine handmaid hath not any thing in the house, save a pot of oil."

By anyone's evaluation except God's, this poor widow's resources were woefully inadequate to meet her needs. Her tiny bit of oil was worth only a pittance and certainly not enough to get her out of debt and the impending slavery of her children. Reason would say her situation was hopeless. But faith said, *"With God all things are possible"* (Mt. 19:26).

The widow knew she had this oil. She's the one who told Elisha about it. No doubt, she had taken a complete inventory of all her assets and had dismissed them as insufficient to meet the need. *But little is much when God is in it.* She had failed to factor into her equation what God could do with what she had. The man of God opened her eyes to the possibility of what God could do with what she had and she acted in faith. She met not only her present need, but had enough left over to live off the rest of her life.

Like this widow, we often fail to see the potential of what God has given us. We look at ourselves and what we have in only human terms. We fail to factor in the anointing. With God's blessing, a few fish and a couple of pieces of bread can feed thousands. But we have to take that step of faith first.

This woman's oil didn't multiply until she had borrowed the vessels and began to pour out what she had. She prepared for increase and then began to give. As she gave of what she had the power of God multiplied it back to her abundantly.

Everyone has something. What do you have? It may seem too small to do any good, but give what you have to God in faith and watch it grow. *(Written by Andrew Wommack)*

APRIL 1
WHAT LOOKED LIKE THE GREATEST DEFEAT WAS THE GREATEST VICTORY!
2 CORINTHIANS 5:21

2 Corinthians 5:21 "For He made Him who know no sin to be sin for us, that we might become the righteousness of God in Him."

Isn't it great to know that we can celebrate Jesus' resurrection every day! Everything changed on that day. It was one of the greatest days ever on earth for mankind.

Once a man is delivered from unrighteousness, he can have peace with God. Because there is peace, there can be fellowship. Fellowship can only happen when enmity is resolved. "Therefore being justified by faith, we have peace with God through our Lord Jesus Christ" (Romans 5:1). The word "justified" has the same root as righteous. It could read, "Therefore, being made righteous by faith, we have peace with God." If one knows he is righteous, he will be at peace with God. More importantly, God will be at peace with him. He will no longer live in fear of judgment and death.

At the cross, God made peace with man through a New Covenant. This covenant was not secured by the blood of an animal, but by the sinless blood of the Lord Jesus Christ. This covenant was established in His blood. But what does that really mean? In 2 Corinthians 5:21, the Bible says, *"For He hath made Him to be sin for us, who knew no sin . . . "* [KJV]. *"Him who knew no sin, He made to be sin on our behalf."* [AMV] *"For God caused . . . actually to be sin"* [Phillips]. Jesus literally became sin! He was not a mere offering. He literally BECAME sin.

Now we begin to understand why Jesus had to become a man. A man brought sin into the world; only a man could bring righteousness into the world. A man brought death. Only a man could free us from death. Man sinned, so man had to die. In Jesus, the sins of all men were met and in Him they were all judged. *(Written by Dave Duell)*

APRIL 2
THE POWER OF HONESTY
EPHESIANS 4:25

Ephesians 4:25 "Wherefore putting away lying, speak every man truth with his neighbour: for we are members one of another."
One of the things that we tried to do when our children were growing up was to reward honesty. We often made it clear that when they confessed their wrongdoing to us or told us the truth when confronted, their punishment would not result in pain. I believe that this approach resulted in two things: First, it helped them see the benefit of truth and honesty; second, it facilitated open communication between us. As they became convinced that they could tell us anything without being judged or condemned, they began to share their sins and temptations. This has carried over into their teen years. Even to this day we have open and honest communication.

Another thing that has helped in our communication with our children is to admit to them when we are wrong. As long as we try to project the image that we always have it together, our children will not be open with us about their struggles or sins. It is imperative that we keep the lines of communication open during every season of their lives.

In the same way, the only way to maintain a healthy relationship with Jesus is through living a life of transparency. It is when we attempt to fool God as well as others, that we polarize ourselves from the power of God's grace in our lives. That is why Paul stressed the importance of the way he lived his life before the Corinth church. Choose today to live a life of transparency. Not only before others, but more importantly before God. As we value honesty, then we tap into a life empowered by wisdom and strength. *(Written by Mike Fehlauer)*

APRIL 3
"DON'T YOU BELIEVE WHAT YOU PREACH?"
JOHN 6:29

John 6:29 "Jesus answered and said unto them, This is the work of God, that ye believe on him whom he hath sent."
One time, in an emergency situation, a widow came forward and said that God told her to empty her savings out. I was so hesitant to receive that offering, but then she piped up and said, "What's the matter? Don't you believe what you preach?" Ouch. That was some of the hardest money to receive that I ever experienced. Yet, in a matter of 30 days, she came right back up to the platform, shook her finger in my face, and said, "Let me tell you what God did for me!"

Before he was deceased, her husband had been working with the railroad. A former co-worker of her husband came by and asked her if she had heard about the new benefits the railroad had. He further explained that the railroad was not telling people unless they knew how to look for those benefits. She told him that she had not heard about the benefits. The man checked into it and as a result, her benefit package increased by $400 a month as long as she lived, plus she received a $5,000 lump sum in cash. Her little meager savings that she'd emptied out was more than doubled in return. She knew that if she took care of God's house, He'd take care of her house. She believed God at His Word.

There is a valuable lesson in this. God's Word works—every time. Isaiah 55:11 says, *"So shall my word be that goeth forth out of my mouth: it shall not return unto me void, but it shall accomplish that which I please, and it shall prosper in the thing whereto I sent it."* God has done His part. The answer to the difficult is in the simple. He has given us His Word so that we may prosper and be in health (3 John 2). Our part is to simply believe Him and act on that faith in His Word. *(Written by Bob Nichols)*

APRIL 4
HOW DOES GOD SEE YOU?
EPHESIANS 2:10

Ephesians 2:10 "For we are His workmanship . . . . "
Someone once said, "It's not the person you believe in who influences you the most, but the person who believes in you." That could also apply to Father God and you. God believes in you. In order for you to live a prosperous life, He wants you to see yourself as He sees you. He wants you to have His view and opinion about you.

When your heart is established in grace, God's favor, and ability, you can view yourself as He does. *"For it is good that the heart be established by grace . . . "* (Hebrews 13:9). Know that God loves you unconditionally and He has forgiven you through His Son.

God says you are His workmanship, His handiwork, His divine creation. You are His greatest achievement.

You are wonderfully created. He has made you unique and has gifted you for an important function in His Body. He says that you are accepted by Him. He has adopted you as His son by Jesus Christ and this is all *"To the praise of the glory of His grace . . . "* (Ephesians 1:5-6).

What does it matter what others may think about you? What God thinks about you is what you need to concentrate on. He wants His view and opinion of you to be the determining influence in your life.   *(Written by Bonnie Duell)*

APRIL 5
THE TRUTH AND THE FACTS
JOHN 17:17

John 17:17 "Thy word is truth."
Do you remember Sergeant Friday on <u>Dragnet</u>? "Just the facts ma'am." God would rather hear from you, "Just the truth." There is a great difference between the truth and the facts.

Many Christians want to confess God's Word, but they are afraid they are lying. How can I say I am healed when my body is still sick? Isn't that lying?

We live in two worlds, the natural as well as the spiritual. We are in the world, but not of it. We are residing in the earth, but we are citizens of heaven. We are standing presently on the earth, but we are seated spiritually in heavenly places with Christ Jesus. We are an outward man and we are also an inward man. The earthly kingdom will not change the kingdom of God. But the kingdom of God can change this earthly kingdom.

Even in this natural world, circumstances change. The rain is falling, but the clouds will clear away. The night is dark, but the sun will shine tomorrow. We even have a greater hope in God's promises.

If our body is sick, that is a *fact*. The Word says we are healed. That is the *truth*. The facts will never change the truth, but the truth will change the facts. Facts can change, but the truth will never change. Whether you are sick or well, the Word will always say, *"by whose stripes ye were healed"* (1 Peter 2:24). Whether you are in abundance or lack, God's Word will always say, *"Beloved, I wish above all things thou mayest prosper . . . "* (3 John 2).

It is quite acceptable with God to look at and address the facts of your life, as long as the truth remains preeminent. Moses, David, Paul and others spoke of problems, sickness and the trials of life, but they did not allow these to cause shipwreck to their faith. You too can continue to trust in God's word and your circumstances will change. The truth will change your facts.   *(Written by Bob Yandian)*

APRIL 6
MIRACLES SPROUT FROM SEEDS
2 KINGS 4:8-37

2 Kings 4:10 "Let us make a little chamber, I pray thee, on the wall; and let us set for him there a bed, and a table, and a stool, and a candlestick: and it shall be, when he cometh to us, that he shall turn in thither."
The raising of this widow's son from the dead is one of the greatest miracles recorded in the Bible. Everyone would love to see God's miracle working power displayed in his life like this. Yet miracles don't just happen. There are reasons why God performs miracles for some and doesn't for others.

If it was only up to God, then all of us would have miracles. God loves the whole world and His power is extended to us in grace. Few experience the miraculous power of God because few cooperate with God. Electricity doesn't flow through wood and miracles don't come to those who don't plant seeds for them.

This woman recognized God's anointing on Elisha and she blessed him. This was not just her desire, it was God working through her to bless His servant, Elisha. This woman yielded to God's leading and thereby sowed a seed into her future. She gave what she wasn't obligated to give, and that put her in a position to receive a blessing by being a blessing.

This is not to say that she earned this miracle. No! None of us at our best deserve God's favor. Our unbelief can stop God's blessings and our yielding can allow God's blessings to flow. There's a reason why this woman's acts of kindness toward Elisha were recorded. It's because they were the seeds of the miracle she received.

Are you planting seeds today for the miracles you will need tomorrow? Tomorrow will come. Your need for God's intervention in your life will also come. Get ready today and plant seeds of God's love in someone's life. *(Written by Andrew Wommack)*

APRIL 7
GOD'S LOVE MESSAGE AT THE CROSS
JOHN 12:31-32

John 12:31-32 "Now is the judgment of this world: now the ruler of this world will be cast out. And I, if I am lifted up from the earth, will draw all peoples to Myself."
Because we have every kind of communication such as TV, radio and computers for e-mail, we have messages coming to us all the time. We hear the Gospel preached to us according to each one's belief and understanding. We hear daily that God is angry and is about to destroy the earth and us along with it. You must know what the Good News of the Gospel says to us here and now.

In John 12:31, 32, Jesus declared, *"Now is the judgment of this world."* The judgment of the world, for sin, took place two thousand years ago. He went on to say, *"If I be lifted up, I will draw all men unto Me."* The cross is at the heart of the church's mission and message, which draws all people to Jesus.

Not all men have been drawn to Jesus. All men will never be drawn to Jesus. But one thing did happen—all men's sin and all men's judgment was drawn to Him on the cross. He became sin for us and then He endured the punishment for us.

Until this time, the world was an enemy of God. Our sinful nature kept us bound to sin. Then our consciences made us run from God. Similarly, God was obligated to judge sin in man. However, praise God, that situation was changed in Jesus. 1 John 2:2 says of Jesus, *"And He is the propitiation for our sins . . . "* The word *"propitiation"* is best understood as appeasement. Jesus is the appeasement for our sin. To appease something means to satisfy. What was it that Jesus appeased? He appeased the wrath of God, which is the righteous penalty of the Law. Wrath has been satisfied in Jesus. Romans 5:9 says *"being now justified by His blood, we shall be saved from wrath through Him."* In Jesus, we are made righteous or justified. In Him, the wrath of God is satisfied. He suffered the wrath that we deserve.

Because the price has been paid for your specific sins, you have no reason to fear the judgment of God. You have no reason to fear rejection. The chastisement for you to have peace with God was fulfilled in the Lord Jesus. Faith believes this and enters into fellowship with the Father. And since we have no fear of an angry God chastening us in wrath, we can have peace in our hearts. Everything is all right between you and God. *(Written by Dave Duell)*

APRIL 8
RAISING CHAMPIONS
GOD'S ABUNDANCE IN THE HOME
PSALM 127:3-5

Psalm 127:3-5 "Behold, children are a heritage from the Lord. The fruit of the womb is a reward. Like arrows in the hand of a warrior, so are the children of one's youth. Happy is the man who has a quiver full of them; they shall not be ashamed, but shall speak with their enemies in the gate."

It may seem strange to devote several devotions to raising children. Yet, many of you who read these devotions are parents. One of the greatest privileges and responsibilities is the stewardship of raising children. It can be challenging, disappointing and even scary at times. Nonetheless, the Word says that they are a blessing (even when they don't act like it). Our children will experience trials and temptations. The challenge we face is raising them with a sense of purpose and passion for God.

In the above scripture we see that children are more than an obligation—they are meant to be a joy. I know that there are times in parenting when it is difficult to rejoice. Yet the Bible doesn't say that we rejoice *about* them, but that we rejoice *over* them. When we truly understand that our children have intrinsic worth simply because God loves and values them, then we too can learn to truly enjoy and value them. This takes us beyond a sense of duty and causes God's love to be the motivating force as we coach them through the issues of life. That's when we parent with joy. Malachi 4:6 says that as the hearts of the fathers are turned toward their children, then the hearts of the children are turned toward their fathers.

Spend time today focusing on what is right about your child. Meditate on his or her potential rather than their problems. Highlight in your mind those traits that make your child unique. As you do, you will find God's wisdom to guide them through life, and you will discover His patience during the difficult times. *(Written by Mike Fehlauer)*

APRIL 9
WE DON'T THROW MONEY, WE SOW MONEY
HEBREWS 11:4

Hebrews 11:4 "By faith Abel offered unto God a more excellent sacrifice than Cain, by which he obtained witness that he was righteous, God testifying of his gifts: and by it he being dead yet speaketh."

God testified of Abel's gifts. Why? Because Abel offered his sacrifice by faith. He did not give by faith in himself or faith in his gift, but by faith in God. This is a powerful principle that I've learned. It's something that needs to be stressed for living in the abundance of God. We are to be givers, but we must give in faith based on God's Word. We hear all kinds of appeals, but we should have the mind of God on where and how much we are to sow. You don't ever throw money—you sow money. You sow it on purpose, in faith, believing.

It's not just a minister's thing. The widow woman in 1 Kings 17 who gave the last little meal that she had was blessed; it wasn't just the prophet who got blessed. She was blessed until the famine was over. Her obedience blessed the prophet, but her obedience brought blessing to her own house and her own family.

No, it is not just a preacher thing. I watch children who really catch the concept of giving. It is amazing what you see God do for a child. When you tell young children something, they believe it. They do not weigh out the pros and cons or analyze the variables. They simply believe. They have faith. Years ago, when one of our church member's children were smaller, they agreed for the Lord to give them a van for the family. That is not what their parents really had in mind. But, in the process of looking for a car, the salesman said, "I don't believe I have the car you want, but I have a van over here." Out of curiosity, they looked at the van, and they decided that they liked it. Instead of buying the car, they bought the van. As they were driving down the road, the children were all rejoicing that God had answered their prayer.

Don't just throw your money. Keep your faith active and operative every time you give. *(Written by Bob Nichols)*

APRIL 10
RISE UP!
EPHESIANS 3:20-21

*Ephesians 3:20-21 "Now to Him who is able to do exceedingly abundantly above
all that we ask or think, according to the power that works in us, to Him be
glory in the church by Christ Jesus to all generations, forever and ever"
(New King James).*
Throughout the centuries of human history, from one generation to the next,
God has remained committed to lifting His people out of the limits of their own ways
into the limitlessness of His own great ability.

The word "grace" is used primarily in two different ways. First, it is central to the
heart attitude of God which moves Him toward people; which makes people His greatest
concern. It is because of His grace, by and through His grace, that He is willing to be
involved with you and me. He yields up His love and resources freely, not on the basis of
performance.

His love is not swayed by what you do or do not do. He loves you regardless of your
actions because you are His child. Again, that's not to say that He finds pleasure in all you
do or can condone all you do; He may absolutely hate what you're doing but still loves you
because of who He is. God doesn't just have love—He is love. It is because of who God is
that He can be gracious, offering Himself to the undeserving—even criminal!

Second, grace is the power, active within the heart of the believer, that works in him
and empowers him to do the will of God; to rise up to go well beyond the call of duty; to
turn the other cheek; to go the extra mile; and to give his best coat away in addition to his
shirt.

It is grace at work that helps us to stay married when divorce seems to be the only
solution; to keep running the race of life instead of giving up and giving in to our critics. It
is the grace of God that keeps a Pastor before his congregation, leading them to greener
pastures when he enjoys no vote of confidence from them. It is grace at work that refuses
to allow us to be conformed to this world and presses us from within to be more like
Jesus. *(Written by Marshall Townsley)*

APRIL 11
WHAT'S UNDER YOUR CLOTHES?
2 SAMUEL 6:14

*2 Samuel 6:14 "David danced before the Lord . . . and was girded in
a linen ephod."*
King David personally brought back the ark of the covenant to it's rightful
home in Jerusalem among the people of God. David not only walked ahead of the
ark, he danced in front of all of Jerusalem's citizens. His wife watched from a window and was filled with wrath as her husband, *the king*, took off his prestigious robe
and was dressed as a common priest. There were many priests, but only one king.
How could her husband be so callous toward her feelings to dress and act as a
common priest? David could not be recognized among the priests. He no longer
looked like a king. He left the throne and joined the people.

When we come to church we are meeting the family of God, joining the royal priesthood. We need to take off our kingly robes and look and act like the priests that we are. We
need to shed the attitude of our worldly positions. Leave your banker's clothing at home.
You are not an attorney or investment counselor when you come to church. Neither are
you a waiter at a restaurant or a janitor. Every person who is a child of God is dressed in a
linen ephod. When we come to church we all look alike to God. The banker is standing
beside the janitor, worshipping God together. This is the place where we worship God with
all our might, song, shout and dance.

Church on earth is a type of the throne room in heaven. One day we will all stand
before God as the redeemed of the ages and praise the Lamb of God forever. There will be
no white or blue collar section, no rich or poor, but all priests rejoicing before the Great
High Priest, Jesus. Why wait until then? Let's start now. *(Written by Bob Yandian)*

APRIL 12
WHAT'S YOUR MOTIVE?
2 KINGS 4:8-37

2 Kings 4:13 "And he said unto him, Say now unto her, Behold, thou hast been careful for us with all this care; what is to be done for thee? wouldest thou be spoken for to the king, or to the captain of the host? And she answered, I dwell among mine own people."

Have you ever noticed that giving to others causes them to want to give back to you. Buy a friend's lunch sometime. I am confident that he will say something to the effect of, "I'll get it next time." This is just a law of God.

This woman had built an extra room on her house and furnished it just for Elisha. He appreciated it and wanted to bless her back. When she was asked what could be done for her, she didn't have any request. Elisha offered her favor with the king or the top general in the land, but she didn't accept it. She never did make a request. This says volumes.

This woman wasn't kind to Elisha just so she could get something from God. She didn't give to get. However, she also wasn't so religious that when God wanted to bless her she refused His blessing out of false humility. She accepted His gift. But the motive behind her gift was totally unselfish. She gave expecting nothing in return. There's a lesson for all of us here.

Our giving should be with pure hearts of love for God and those to whom we give. We shouldn't be giving just to get something in return. Our giving should be selfless. Yet the law of God says that when we give, it will be given back to us good measure, pressed down, shaken together and running over (Lk. 6:38). Our seeds of giving will produce increase and we should receive it so that we can give even more. But our motives must always be pure.

Give like this woman gave—with a pure heart of love for others. *(Written by Andrew Wommack)*

APRIL 13
A KINGLY GIFT
PROVERBS 18:16

Proverbs 18:16 "A man's gift makes room for him and brings him before great men."

A little food for thought. When the Queen of Sheba came to visit King Solomon, along with the other gifts she brought to him, she gave him four tons of gold. At nine billion dollars a ton that would be 36 billion dollars. That's what you would call a kingly gift. She did all of that to come and sit with the wisest man on earth, and her gift made room for her. As the Bible says in Proverbs 18:16, *"A man's gift makes room for him and brings him before great men."*

The story does not end there; In 2 Chronicles 9:12 you can read the rest. The queen went home with more than she gave. It kind of sounds like what happens to us when we give into the Gospel.

I read of a study done by some theologians on the monetary system that was present when Jesus was on the earth. There were two kinds of giving: One was like the kingly giving that the Queen of Sheba gave to Solomon, and the other was when average people gave to each other.

Just think, when Jesus was born, the kings that came to Jesus knew that He was "The King of Kings." Do you think that they came with just a few gold coins to give to "The King"? I believe they came with a fortune for Jesus. The theologians believed that Joseph put the fortune in a bank to gather interest until Jesus came of age to receive it.

I thought for years that Jesus was poor on this earth until I got the revelation that it was on the cross that He became poor so that we could become rich. Just like Jesus became sin that we would be made righteous—Jesus came from Heaven. By coming down here to earth he became poor compared to Heaven. He had a staff which traveled with him and that involves finances. Jesus was not poor! *(Written by Dave Duell)*

APRIL 14
THE PAST IS NOT YOUR FUTURE
PHILIPPIANS 3:13

Philippians 3:13 "But one thing I do, forgetting those things which are behind and reaching forward to those things which are ahead."
Again, one of the primary responsibilities we have as parents is to raise our children to love and serve God. In trying to strengthen our influence over their lives, we may be tempted to remind them of their past failures to make, what we think, is a much needed point. When we bring up the past in order to drive home a point, we are poisoning our children's hearts with shame. This communicates to our children that we define who they are by what they have done. Despair is the result. Our children find themselves working against a ledger that they can never erase.

Our heavenly Father never uses the past shame to draw us into the future. The Bible says that God has taken our sins and thrown them into the sea of His forgetfulness where He chooses not to remember them or hold them against us. This does not mean that God literally forgets our past sins. It means that he refuses to relate to us according to the failures of the past.

Dwelling on the past celebrates defeat over victory. The past chains us to the paralyzing emotions of fear and guilt. The past keeps a ledger of failure. Forgiveness declares that mercy is greater than the mistake. Forgiveness expresses that the value of a person is greater than the importance of the sin.

Today, you are forgiven. You can attack this day with a fresh start. You are not what you have done . . . or what has been done to you. His mercies are new every morning and His blood is alive. It is that same blood that washes you not only from the power of sin, but from the guilt of sin as well. *(Written by Mike Fehlauer)*

APRIL 15
IT'S ALL DIRT
LUKE 16:13-15

Luke 16:15 "And he said unto them, Ye are they which justify yourselves before men; but God knoweth your hearts: for that which is highly esteemed among men is abomination in the sight of God."
Everything man desires comes from the dirt. Jewelry is and always has been a big business. Lots of people like to wear fine jewelry. We even buy jewelry as special gifts for loved ones or to commemorate and celebrate special events. But think about it, gold is from the earth, it's dirt. The gold that men prize so highly on earth is used for road metal in heaven. And did you ever notice those stones that we set in the gold? Diamonds are rocks—old, compacted dirt. It's all dirt. You've heard the saying, "not worth the paper it's printed on." Well, contrary to popular belief, money is made of cloth, not paper. It is actually called "rag" and is made from a form of cotton. At any rate, money comes from cotton, which grows out of where? The dirt. Food comes from the earth too. There are a lot of people driving cars today, aren't there? I know I drive a car. Almost everyone I know drives a car. Well, cars are from the iron ore, which is taken from the dirt. What about the seats in those cars? Many people like leather interiors. Those leather seats are the skins off a dead cow! Are you partial to furs? Minks are rodent hair coats. Oh, don't forget houses, they are totally made of dirt. They are just bigger, better mud huts. Are you seeing a pattern here? It's all dirt.

All these things are great, but let's keep them in proper perspective. There's nothing wrong with having nice things, but God knows the heart and these physical things that are highly esteemed and sought after by men are just dirt. Before you pass up a chance to sow into the Kingdom of God in exchange for some "thing," just remember and say to yourself, "*It's all dirt.*" *(Written by Bob Nichols)*

APRIL 16
YOU ARE CHOSEN
EPHESIANS 1:4

Ephesians 1:4 "He chose us in Him before the foundation of the world . . . . "
Can you see how prosperous your life can be when you renew your mind to see God's view and opinion of you? No one will be able to put you down. Nothing will be able to stop you from fulfilling God's specific plan for your life. You will be unstoppable!

God says He chose you! He wanted you to be a part of His family. He sent His mighty Holy Spirit to draw you to Him. And now that you have received what His Son did for you in His death, burial and resurrection, you have God's very life inside of you. Wow! What could be better than that? You should not spend your time trying to get more from God. Spend your time meditating on what He has already placed inside of you!

As He says in I Peter 2:9, *"But you are a chosen generation, a royal priesthood, a holy nation, His own special people . . . . "* The word "chosen" designates one picked out from among the larger group for special service or privileges. It describes you as a recipient of God's favor or grace. The scripture goes on to say one of the reasons you are chosen: *"that you may proclaim the praises of Him who called you out of darkness into His marvelous light."*

God chose you to let the dark world see His light in you as you proclaim His praises!
(Written by Bonnie Duell)

APRIL 17
WHAT ARE YOU WAITING FOR?
PSALM 1:1-3

Psalm 1:3 "Whatsoever he doeth shall prosper."
A few conditions are laid out before this verse is given. God will allow us to make our own decisions when we meet the guidelines of verses one and two. First we are not to walk in the counsel of the ungodly. God's children have been redeemed from the world and the advice of it. We are in a new kingdom with a new level of counsel—God's Word. God knows our problems and the source of them. He can give counsel that will always work.

Second, we are not to stand in the way of sinners. This means a life free from sin. How can we win sinners to the Lord if we live and act as they do? They know they are having problems. They are looking for answers to bring them out. Our life should be a louder witness than our voice.

Third, we are not to sit in the seat of the scornful. Bitterness and anger are not luxuries we can afford. Joy is a choice we are to make and walk in daily. To rejoice in the Lord is a command. Therefore it must be a choice, not a feeling that comes and goes.

Our delight must be in the law of the Lord and we must meditate in God's Word day and night. This will cause our roots to grow deep, our leaf to never wither and our fruit to remain.

Now God says, *"whatever you do will prosper."* What a remarkable thought— *God trusts you.* If your life is pleasing to the Lord and you have prayed for direction, but got nothing, perhaps God is telling you, *"you decide what is best and I will back it."* Many times you do not need a green light or a red one. No light at all means proceed. God will be there if you make a mistake. *(Written by Bob Yandian)*

APRIL 18
SHUT THE DOOR
2 KINGS 4:8-37

2 Kings 4:21 "And she went up, and laid him on the bed of the man of God, and shut the door upon him, and went out."

This woman was in a terrible situation. Her only son had just died a tragic death. All of us have experienced enough tragedy that we can imagine what she must have felt. This was a special child too; a direct miracle of God. That made the loss even greater.

What do you do in a crisis like that? Sadly, most of us tend to nurse our problems. We indulge our grief and rehearse the tragedy over and over in our minds. We don't let go. We don't cast the care of the situation over on the Lord as He commanded us to do (1 Pet. 5:7). We become dominated by our affliction.

To this woman's credit, she carried her son up to the man of God's room and left him there. She shut the door on him. That's hard to do. But there was really nothing better that she could have done. It wasn't going to change anything for her to sit there holding her dead son. She did what she had to do. She left the dead behind and went for help.

Have you experienced some hurt that still controls you? Are the thoughts of your tragedy never really out of your thoughts regardless of what you are doing? You need to take that pain to God and leave it there. Shut the door on it and then get on with what you have to do. Don't let grief paralyze you.

If this woman wouldn't have torn herself away from her son, she would have lost him forever. She had to travel 20 miles one way to reach the man of God and get her miracle. She couldn't have done that carrying a dead body with her. She had to let go to take hold of her miracle.

Make sure that all your care is cast on the Lord today. Shut the door on it and get on with what you have to do to believe God. *(Written by Andrew Wommack)*

APRIL 19
TIMING OF THE HOLY SPIRIT
ACTS 1:7

Acts 1:7 "It is not for you to know times or seasons which the Father has put in His own authority."

God has really put on my heart the importance of your positioning by the Holy Spirit. The Holy Spirit wants you to fulfill all He has created you to do. The devil, on the other hand, does everything he can to keep you from accomplishing what God has for you. It is a lot like the saying, "It's not what you know, it's who you know." It is arriving at the right place with the right people at the right time. Time is a big element in fulfilling what God has assigned you to do. Jesus arrived at the right time, or due season, to fulfill what God had given Him to do.

I believe God has been positioning you all your life for this moment of time. All of the training you have been through and all of the people who have come into your life have positioned you.

The enemy will try many things to distract you from your vision. Jesus had to focus on His ministry and life to make sure He was on track to accomplish everything He had to do in the short amount of time He had to do it.

Here are a few things to watch out for in your life so the devil cannot knock you out of your position. Be careful of what you hear and what you agree with. A little discontentment comes, usually very small, and then strife-filled words are spoken. Words that are spoken in secret return as a megaphone sounding in your ears. Don't let the devil use you as an instrument for his work. What started out as a small issue will become the one that will take you out of the race or vision.

I believe the reason God is having me tell you this today is that the enemy could be trying to get you out of position and blessing in your life. It takes faith to stand in the position that God has given to you. *(Written by Dave Duell)*

APRIL 20
THE JOY OF A FAMILY MISSION STATEMENT
HABAKKUK 2:2

Habakkuk 2:2 "And the LORD answered me, and said, Write the vision, and make it plain upon tables, that he may run that readeth it."
Most corporations have a vision or mission statement. The reason is so that as they are making decisions throughout the year, they will not violate their core values as an organization. Understanding God's purpose and vision for our lives is crucial as well. I also believe that it is important as a family, to have a clear sense of purpose.

That is why I think it is a good idea for every family to have a mission statement. This helps to keep families on course, especially during times of turbulence. It doesn't need to be long. Our family's mission statement is just three words: "we are leaders."

This doesn't mean that we don't understand the importance of following. As a matter of fact, good leaders are good followers. But leaders just don't flow with the current. Leaders just don't follow the direction of the masses because "everybody else is doing it." For example, leaders make decisions based on conviction, not convenience. Leaders do the right thing simply because it is the right thing. These are just some of the dynamics we have taught our children concerning leadership. This is our mission statement. This is who we are. Our children have been raised with that understanding. It doesn't mean that they have been perfect, but this sense of identity has helped us at times to coach our children through times of difficulties and temptations. Consequently, when there are times that I feel I need to say, "Remember, we are leaders," they know exactly what I mean.

A family mission statement creates a "we" mentality instead of an "I" mentality. A "we" mentality reminds us that the decisions we make affect not only our lives, but also the lives of others. The same is true for you and me as individuals. We are not an island. We affect others either toward God or away from Him. *(Written by Mike Fehlauer)*

APRIL 21
TRUE LIVING IS A LIFESTYLE OF GIVING
ACTS 20:35

Acts 20:35 "I have shewed you all things, how that so labouring ye ought to support the weak, and to remember the words of the Lord Jesus, how he said,
It is more blessed to give than to receive."
We must catch the concept that giving is all about our lifestyle. I've seen people who live to take. Takers are miserable people. The real joy is when you've sown and you see that seed coming up. Not all of giving is money. We have to remember what God saves us from having to spend. You begin to see that everything you do is planting a seed. In due season, we reap.

I watched my mother. She was a tither all of her life. My father's health declined and his hospitalization was terminated, leaving her with several thousand dollars worth of medical bills when he died. I watched mother take her Bible and say to God, "I've always been a tither and a giver." Every medical bill was paid when my mother died, and she had money in the bank. I've watched that principle of giving. We're setting an example for our own family and our own children. My mother taught me that if you will tithe, God will always take care of you. *If you put God first, you'll have God's best.* That is the greatest inheritance a person can have. She didn't leave me a lot of money, but she left me a gold mine of truth. *(Written by Bob Nichols)*

APRIL 22
GENETICALLY ENCODED
2 CORINTHIANS 5:17

2 Corinthians 5:17 "Therefore, if anyone is in Christ, he is a new creation . . . all things have become new."
Because of Jesus, God made you a new creation. You are a three-part being: spirit, soul (your mind, will and emotions), and body. When you received Jesus into your life, the part that God made new is your spirit. Your spirit man is fully matured. You have been given all the faith you'll ever need, all the anointing, all the fruit of the Spirit, wisdom, righteousness, and so forth. It's all in your spirit man.

Now it is your job to renew your mind to what you have been given and then operate in it by faith. You are genetically encoded with everything that God has because you received His nature. You received the life of God Himself inside you. God is love. God's love is in you. You are already prosperous and successful. That is why God can call you an overcomer and more than a conqueror through Jesus Christ.

The Word says you are complete in Him (Colossians 2:10). Don't let anyone cheat you "through philosophy and empty deceit, according to the tradition of men, according to the basic principles of the world, and not according to Christ" (Colossians 2:8). You are genetically encoded to be just like Jesus! Talk about prosperous! *(Written by Bonnie Duell)*

APRIL 23
WHEN GOD ROLLED UP HIS SLEEVE
ISAIAH 53:1

Isaiah 53:1 "Who hath believed our report and to whom is the arm of the Lord revealed?"
In many places God is compared to us as human beings. He is said to have feet, eyes and ears. After all, spiritually and physically, we are made in His image.

In Psalm 8:3 we are told, that God created the universe with His fingers. What an incredible thought. Your fingers are not known for much strength. Yet, with little effort, God used His fingers and created galaxies, planets and star systems without number.

In Hebrews 1:10 the writer tells us that God created the earth with His hands. There is more strength in your hands than in your fingers. It took more power for God to create the earth than it did the universe. God took time to mold the earth, shape it and prepare it for His crowning creation—man. This tells me, next to heaven, the greatest place in the universe is earth. Heaven and earth continually work together.

Yet, in Isaiah 53:1 it says, *"the work of redemption took the arm of the Lord."* This verse begins an entire chapter on the redemptive work of Jesus on the cross. It took more power to redeem one sinner than it did to create the universe and the earth. God had to roll up His sleeve to redeem us from Satan's curse and Adam's fall. Ephesians 1:19 tells us that when God raised Jesus from the dead it took *"the exceeding greatness of His power."*

Anyone can look into the sky at night and see the work of the fingers of God. The stars and planets are visible to all. Anyone also can look at the earth, the mountains, oceans and animals that live here and see the work of God's hands.

But only those who put their trust in the work of Jesus on the cross can see the work of God's arm. *The arm of the Lord is revealed to those who believe the report. (Written by Bob Yandian)*

APRIL 24
IS IT WELL WITH YOU?
2 KINGS 4:8-37

2 Kings 4:26 "Run now, I pray thee, to meet her, and say unto her, Is it well with thee? is it well with thy husband? is it well with the child? And she answered, It is well."
This was a great woman of faith. Her only son had just died and yet when Elisha asked how it was with her, her husband, and her son, she said, *"It is well."* That is awesome!

What if you had just lost your only son and someone asked you how you were doing. How would you answer? Would you praise God and say all is well or would you speak forth all your hurt? Your answer to that question is the reason you receive from God the way you do.

This woman had shut the door on her problem and she was believing for a miracle. She hadn't let the grief of her situation swallow her because she hadn't accepted it as being final. Faith gave her a different perspective on her problem than what other people would have had. Because of her faith, all was well.

Some people look at confessions of faith like this as lies. They see it as denying reality. That's not it at all. People of faith don't deny what exists, they just aren't limited to only physical truth. They realize the potential available through God and speak forth their faith. They supersede natural truth with greater spiritual truths.

What have you been speaking? Open up your spiritual eyes and see what God has promised you and then speak that into reality. If you are focused on what God says, then regardless of what may happen, it really is well with you. *(Written by Andrew Wommack)*

APRIL 25
GOD'S LOVE LETTER
GALATIANS 3:13

Galatians 3:13 "Christ has redeemed us from the curse of the law, having become a curse for us (for it is written, 'Cursed is everyone who hangs on a tree.')"
God's Word has been coming alive to us over the past years and I want to share some more exciting truths with you. We need to see God as He is. We have the tendency to see God in the light of our own actions. For example, the less giving we do, the harder it is for us to see God as generous. If we are to emerge from the negative thinking and unbelief in which we have been steeped, we must begin by seeing God as He really is.

As you read the Bible, mix it with prayer. Remember, you are not reading to find a list of "do's and don't's," you are reading to have a personal encounter with God. You are getting to know a Person, not a legal system. Read with your heart open and pray with your Bible open. God will reveal Himself to you.

As you read, remind yourself of some basics. First of all, you are a New Covenant believer. Do not try to relate to God through works-righteousness. It will always force you into legalism or self-righteousness. The only thing from the Old Covenant that belongs to you are the promises. You are qualified to receive the promises because you are in Jesus.

You must have an absolute grasp of the truth that Jesus set you free from all the curses of the law. Galatians 3:13 tells us that Christ has redeemed us from the curse of the law by becoming a curse for us. We are delivered from the wrath of God. 1 Thessalonians 5:9 says, *"For God did not appoint us to wrath, but to obtain salvation through our Lord Jesus Christ."*

That is good news. This Gospel that we all get to preach is so awesome that it is very hard on a carnal mind. God is not angry and we need to tell the world about that, because for so long the wrong message has been taught. People have been running from God because they know that they are not right with Him, but don't know that God is standing with open arms to receive them into His family. *(Written by Dave Duell)*

APRIL 26
CRUCIFIED WITH CHRIST
GALATIANS 2:20

Galatians 2:20 "I have been crucified with Christ; it is no longer I who live, but Christ lives in me . . . ."
In Paul's heart, being crucified meant being judged, condemned, cast out, stripped naked and nailed to a cross. Paul recognized his identification with Christ in His crucifixion. Crucifixion didn't mean death. It meant union with Christ in His disgrace and suffering, but also in Christ's attitude concerning the world. Crucifixion always points the way to death: death of the old man, of the sin nature. When we received Him, we were crucified with Him. This means that our old man, the hidden man of the heart who was filled with spiritual death, was nailed to the cross of Christ. In Romans 6:6 we read, *"Knowing this, that our old man was crucified with Him, that the body of sin might be done away with, that we should no longer be slaves of sin."*

If you and I are to live in His fullness, we need to see ourselves crucified with Him and raised with Him in His strength and abundance. The world holds no power over our lives. Our flesh and emotions are subject to the power of His Spirit. We no longer live in our strength or resources, but it is the One who conquered death, sickness, poverty, fear and shame that lives in us. He lives in you today! *(Written by Mike Fehlauer)*

APRIL 27
GIVE SACRIFICIALLY—RECEIVE SUPERNATURALLY
2 SAMUEL 24:24

2 Samuel 24:24 "And the king said unto Araunah, Nay; but I will surely buy it of thee at a price: neither will I offer burnt offerings unto the LORD my God of that which doth cost me nothing. So David bought the threshingfloor and the oxen for fifty shekels of silver."
David refused to offer a sacrifice to God that didn't cost him something. He wanted it to be meaningful—dear to him. There is a time for sacrificial giving. A sacrifice is giving something highly valued for the sake of one considered to have a greater value. In Genesis 26:1 and 12 we see that Isaac sowed in the year of famine and that same year he reaped a hundredfold. For Isaac to reap a hundredfold was a miracle! Giving sacrificially shows our complete trust in God as our Provider and the One who prospers us.

It is supernatural and the mind cannot grasp it. The natural mind cannot receive it and will fight you. To the natural mind, how can you give more when you seemingly are already in lack and come out ahead? Romans 8:7 tells us, *"Because the carnal mind is enmity against God: for it is not subject to the law of God, neither indeed can be"* (emphasis added). God's way is not always logical to what our way would be. Isaiah 55:8-9 makes it clear that God's ways are not our ways. His ways are higher—better—than our ways. We must choose to operate in God's way.

When you learn how to give sacrificially, you will begin to receive supernaturally!
(Written by Bob Nichols)

APRIL 28
CHOOSING THE RIGHT ROAD
PROVERBS 14:12

Proverbs 14:12 "There is a way that seems right to a man, but its end is the way of death" (New King James).

If ever man had a need, it is for grace from God. From the most talented person to the one who feels least qualified, grace from God is desperately needed. The natural mind, the sense ruled or carnal mind, wants to feel self-sufficient, capable of handling anything.

But the truth is that each of us is inadequate in many areas of life. When Adam and Eve decided to go it alone, to live independently of God and His ways, they were shut out! The way that seemed right ended in death. And down through the ages the road they decided to travel became broad and well traveled, still Jesus said, "leading to destruction."

And in a similar fashion, the way of grace and faith became the straight and narrow. A way that few discover still, a way that leads to eternal life.

The successful businessman may lack the skills to influence his family and develop a healthy home life. A wife may be a good homemaker, yet come short of the spiritual strength needed for a stable household. And good people, faithful to their church, can still fail miserably at living in the power of the Holy Spirit and living obedient to what the Word of God teaches.

God has made Himself available to supply all with the ability to do His will and enjoy His blessings. His grace can enable you to accomplish in life the things that God demands in His Word. He has longed to remove from you the limits of sin and sensuality and open to you the riches of His grace.

He is on your side! *(Written by Marshall Townsley)*

APRIL 29
WAIT A MINUTE. BACK UP!
LUKE 6:38

Luke 6:38 "Give and it shall be given unto you . . . . "

"Why have I given through the years and seen so little in return?" As a pastor I have heard this statement many times. Dedicated tithers and givers have struggled with little or no harvest in their financial lives. "Doesn't the Bible say if we give it will be given back to us?" Yes it does.

But let's back up a bit and get a running start at verse 38. The thought begins in Luke 6:35. This teaching begins with "love your enemies." Love toward friends is often not difficult. But love toward our enemies takes a great deal of faith. This is the true love of Jesus. He loved His enemies so much He died for them.

Second, we are told to "do good." This is the production of good works. Our light is to be seen by the world, not just God Himself.

Third, we are told to "lend, hoping for nothing." How many people out there owe you? You loaned them something and they have never given it back. Forget it. Forgive them. God will take care of you.

Next, we are to "be merciful" and "judge not." Instead of rising up with a critical attitude, be merciful to those who have spitefully used you. This can be tough.

"Condemn not" and "forgive" are the next commandments. Your mouth and your heart are connected in this thought. Let your attitude and words be gracious as you forgive others.

Let's put this all together and find out God's plan for prosperity. *"Love your enemies, do good, lend, be merciful, judge not, condemn not, forgive . . . give and it shall be given unto you, good measure, pressed down, shaken together and running over shall men give into your bosom."* *(Written by Bob Yandian)*

APRIL 30
HOW DO YOU VALUE JESUS?
JOHN 12:1-9

John 12:3 "Then took Mary a pound of ointment of spikenard, very costly, and anointed the feet of Jesus, and wiped his feet with her hair: and the house was filled with the odour of the ointment."
This verse says that the ointment Mary anointed Jesus with was very costly. That is because the spikenard plant that this ointment came from grew in the Himalayan mountains at elevations above 11,000 feet. It had to be transported over 6,000 miles to Palestine and was more expensive than gold. Many scholars believe that it was more than one year's worth of wages. That would be the modern equivalent of more than $30,000.

It greatly offended Judas Iscariot to see Mary bestow such wealth and affection on Jesus. If this same thing was to happen today, many modern day Christians would be offended too. We have to remember what Jesus did for Mary. This was the Mary, who along with her sister, Martha, had known Jesus for a long time. They had entertained Him in their home and Mary hung on His every word (Lk. 10:38-42). Greatest of all, Jesus raised Mary's brother from the dead.

How do you put a price on seeing your dearly loved brother raised from the dead? No amount of wealth is worth a human life. Mary's lavish affection for Jesus was consistent with what Jesus had done for her. The problem was that Judas didn't value Jesus as much as Mary did. In just a few days, Judas accepted 30 pieces of silver to betray Jesus. That was less than half the amount of Mary's ointment.

What value do you place on Jesus and what He has done for you? Your answer will determine whether you become a Mary or a Judas. Make sure you value Jesus more than anything else in your life. *(Written by Andrew Wommack)*

MAY 1
GOD IS GOOD
JAMES 1:16, 17

James 1:16, 17 "Do not be deceived, my beloved brethren. Every good gift and every perfect gift is from above and comes down from the Father of lights, with whom there is no variation or shadow of turning."
God sent Jesus, through whom He would pour out His love on mankind. For God to judge you now and bring hardship into your life would be equal to rejecting the death of His Son. Romans 8:34 poses the question, *"Who is he that condemns? . . . Christ that died . . . ."* If Christ died for you, is He now going to condemn you? No! God did not come to condemn the world, but to save it. You need to know this because of all the judgment preaching that is being given to the Body of Christ.

God is a good God. James 1:16-17 says, *"Do not be deceived, my beloved brethren. Every good gift and every perfect gift is from above and comes down from the Father of lights, with whom there is no variation or shadow of turning."* If this is true, why then is God blamed for every bad thing that happens to mankind? We have let too much religion cloud our thinking. We have to be careful of what we hear.

Remember, God is not a schizophrenic. He changes not. He did not send His Son to set us free from the law of sin and death, only to change His mind and decide to put the curse of the law back on us again. As we know, it is the devil who brings sickness, poverty, and bondage and then tries to get us to blame God for it! Romans 3:24 says that we are justified by grace, apart from works. In the same way we receive healing, miracles, and all the other promises of God by grace, not works. There are no conditions on what we are freely given other than the need for faith.

Let's stop making what we believe so complicated and simply believe what He has said and act on it. Be encouraged and receive what has already been given to you. *(Written by Dave Duell)*

MAY 2
HE WAS MADE YOUR SIN
2 CORINTHIANS 5:21

2 Corinthians 5:21 "For He made Him who knew no sin to be sin for us,
that we might become the righteousness of God in Him."

In Isaiah we read, *"He was wounded for our transgressions, He was bruised for our iniquities . . . "* (53:5). On the cross, Jesus became sin. He bore the weight, the penalty and the pain of our transgressions. He Himself was pure, holy, the unblemished Lamb of God, yet, because of His love for you, He took upon Himself your sin and the penalty of death. Then He conquered death and hell by raising Himself from the dead. Hallelujah!

Not only did He become sin, but He also became a curse. Notice Galatians 3:13: *"Christ has redeemed us from the curse of the law, having become a curse for us; (for it is written, 'Cursed is everyone who hangs on a tree.')"* He has taken your place in judgment. All the forces of darkness overwhelmed Him, so when He raised Himself from the dead, His victory became yours.

The curse of hopelessness under judgment has been done away with. Listen my friend, God is not angry with you today. He is not looking for a reason to bring you harm. God is more concerned about perfecting you than punishing you. His wrath has been resolved through the sacrifice of His Son. His judgment has been satisfied in the life, death and resurrection of His Son. You can rejoice today! You can face any challenge with confidence; if God be for you, who can be against you? *(Written by Mike Fehlauer)*

MAY 3
GOD'S CONCEPT OF GIVING WILL WORK ANYWHERE
ACTS 10:34-35

Acts 10:34-35 "Then Peter opened his mouth, and said, Of a truth I perceive that God
is no respecter of persons: But in every nation he that feareth him,
and worketh righteousness, is accepted with him."

God's Word works; His way works. It will work for preachers, it will work for housewives. It will work for businessmen, teenagers and children. It will work for missionaries. God's concept of giving will work anywhere for anyone.

I've seen it work in Calcutta, India. The most prosperous people I saw in Calcutta were givers. I think one of the greatest lessons I ever learned was in Calcutta with Dr. Mark Buntain and his great mission work. I saw tithes and offerings working in the middle of leprosy and disease. Calcutta has long been known as a decayed civilization. At that time, when the door on the airplane opened, the stench would just knock you back. It was so intense that many ministers would come, stay in the only decent hotel and then take the next plane out. They couldn't handle it. I saw Dr. Buntain teach the people tithing and out of that church came some of the most outstanding, creative people all over the world—educators, neurosurgeons, doctors, even the assistant chief of police of all Los Angeles County.

God's concept of giving will work anywhere when people put feet to their faith. Start with what you have and reach out and stretch a little further in faith. If it will work in a third world nation, it will work for you. *(Written by Bob Nichols)*

MAY 4
CONFIDENCE BEFORE GOD
LUKE 1:74

Luke 1:74 "To grant us that we . . . might serve Him without fear . . . . "
How many Christians do you know who are afraid of God? They have no confidence regarding their relationship with Him and thus live in fear of judgment.

Zacharias, the father of John the Baptist, prophesied about God's direct intervention into the earth by the sending of the Messiah. Jesus would bring redemption to people so they could have a relationship with God that was without fear. The Holy Ghost went on to say through Zacharias that we would be able to live *"In holiness and righteousness before Him all the days of our life"* (Luke 1:75).

What a promise for a prosperous life—that you can confidently relate to Almighty God with no fear or dread of punishment; that God will see you as holy and righteous before Him all the days of your life!

This means that you can stand before God without consciousness of sin. When you have consciousness of sin, you want to hide your face from God. God wants you to have a face-to-face relationship with Him because you are only conscious of your right standing before Him.

This type of relationship is what Jesus came to accomplish. He is the One Who made you holy and righteous by taking the penalty of your sin on Himself. Accept all that He accomplished for you! *(Written by Bonnie Duell)*

MAY 5
WHO MOVED?
1 JOHN 1:7

1 John 1:7 "If we walk in the light, as He is in the light, we have fellowship one with another . . . . "
Do you want to know where Jesus walks? He always walks in the light. This light is God's will. The light is also God's Word. If we want to be successful, we need to walk in God's will and God's Word. This way we will always be walking beside Jesus.

When we walk in God's light we have fellowship with God the Father and Jesus. God's desire is not only to have sons and daughters, but friends. God wants to talk with us and have us talk with Him. The Greek word for fellowship is *"koinonia."* It is more than speaking to one another. It is intimate fellowship—conversation between close friends.

Jesus is always in the light. He never moves. We are the ones who move in and out of the light. Sin removes us from the light of fellowship. Forgiveness of sins brings us back. Verse nine tells us, *"if we confess our sins, He is faithful and just to forgive us our sins and cleanse us from all unrighteousness."* This brings us out of the darkness and back into the light of His presence.

An older couple was driving down the road one day. The wife was next to the door on her side and a great distance was between her and her husband. Who knows how many years ago this began. A young couple drove around them. They were sitting so close together they almost looked like one person. A small tear came down the cheek of the older woman as she remembered the days she and her husband were young and in love. She remarked to her husband, "Do you remember when we used to sit that close to each other?" He replied, "I haven't moved."

Are you wondering why you and the Lord are not as close to each other as you once were? Just remember, He hasn't moved. *(Written by Bob Yandian)*

MAY 6
WHERE'S YOUR HEART?
JOHN 12:1-9

John 12:6 "This he said, not that he cared for the poor; but because he was a thief, and had the bag, and bare what was put therein."

Judas' attitude still lives today in the hearts of many people. It is human nature to put self and personal gain above everything and everyone else. No one wants his greed to be known, but most want what they want when they want it. They just become more skilled in concealing their true motives.

Politicians trumpet their programs as the answers to the problems of society when in truth, many of them only adopt causes because it will get them elected. Many employees only serve their employers because of how it will benefit them personally. Marriages fail every day because of a greater love for self than for one's mate. Many ministers do tremendous damage because they are seeking to build their own kingdoms under the guise of building God's kingdom.

Self love seems all pervasive and inescapable, but there is an antidote. There is a way to live above the grasp of self. You can't just not love self. You have to love someone else more than yourself.

Mary loved Jesus more than her own life. Jesus had done everything for her and her family and she was willing to give liberally of all she had to lavish praise and honor on Him. In contrast, Judas only thought of what he could have done for himself with the money that ointment could have brought. Judas loved self more. Mary loved Jesus more than self.

Which is it with you? You can readily identify where your love lies by where your praise goes. Are you constantly praising Jesus? If not, start today to deny yourself by praising God for all His love and faithfulness. *(Written by Andrew Wommack)*

MAY 7
HANG IN THERE
2 TIMOTHY 3:14

2 Timothy 3:14 "But you must continue in the things which you have learned and been assured of, knowing from whom you have learned them."

We all face the world with its problems and difficulties and we are tempted to quit, but Paul encourages us to continue in the things we have learned. 2 Timothy 3:10-14 says, *"But you have carefully followed my doctrine, manner of life, purpose, faith, long-suffering, love, perseverance, persecutions, afflictions, which happened to me at Antioch, at Iconium, at Lystra—what persecutions I endured. And out of them all the Lord delivered me. Yes, and all who desire to live godly in Christ Jesus will suffer persecution. But evil men and impostors will grow worse and worse, deceiving and being deceived. But you must continue in the things which you have learned and been assured of, knowing from whom you have learned them."*

Paul, one of the chief apostles, speaks of his life and ministry. He endured all kinds of afflictions, persecutions, and perils in his faithful service to the Lord. He wants us to examine his badge of authority for the office of authority.

He is telling us to do two things: look at my life and continue in the things you have learned. He says in Galatians 6:9 not to faint: *"And let us not grow weary while doing good, for in due season we shall reap if we do not lose heart."* Here is the key to his success. Being a man of faith, he simply refused to quit. He believed so much in what he was doing that he continued to do his assignment.

It cost Paul a lot of suffering as we can see. Great success always calls for great sacrifice. I have also found that it will cost you something to follow Jesus and His call on your life. In Paul's writings from jail, he was encouraging us to keep our joy and keep serving Jesus. It's amazing to know that Paul is still reaping from his labors here on earth. It's not how you start, but how you finish. Remember, "It's only forever!" *(Written by Dave Duell)*

MAY 8
HE WAS MADE SICK FOR YOU
ISAIAH 53:5

Isaiah 53:5 "And with His stripes we are healed."
Isaiah 53:4 says that He bore our sickness and disease. All of the sin and disease of the human race was laid upon Jesus at the cross. God not only laid our sickness on Jesus, but He laid us on Him—all of us. The whole man is touched by the power of redemption: Spirit, soul and body. You were nailed to the cross with Him and in Him. Your diseases were part of Him. When we truly believe this, it will end the dominion of sickness over our lives.

If Jesus really was made sick with your sickness, then Satan has no legal right to place sickness on your body. In the name of Jesus you can experience freedom from Satan's power of disease. Just as sin has no dominion over you, neither does disease have the right to have dominion over you. You see, sickness is spiritual. God heals us through the spiritual weapon of the Word. It is the Word that heals your spirit. The Word creates. The Word heals. The Word ignites faith and shows us who we are in Him. Walk in His health today. It is actually your health. It is your right as His child. *(Written by Mike Fehlauer)*

MAY 9
GIVING IS THE MASTER KEY, AND GOD IS THE MASTER GIVER
JOHN 3:16

John 3:16, "For God so loved the world, that he gave his only begotten Son, that whosoever believeth in him should not perish, but have everlasting life."
Giving is the master key that unlocks the door to the blessings and the heart of Almighty God. God is a giver. God gave His best, and gave it with no promise of anything in return. If I really love you, I'm willing to give if I know where and how to give. The biggest giver in the universe is God. He is the one who set the example for us. The Bible shows more examples of this truth: the widow who gave her last bit of meal and oil, the woman who broke the alabaster box and poured the precious ointment on Jesus' head. There are many examples, but God truly is the prime giver.

I've often said that even love is being willing to give your best, asking nothing in return except faith in the seed that you plant. Even giving love to another person is sowing. You sow mercy; you reap mercy. You sow love; you reap love. You sow help; you reap help.

Each day I purpose in my heart to be a giver. It is a response to the goodness of God for all the love and mercy He has poured upon me. Not because of my own goodness, but as it says in 1 John 4:19, *"We love him, because he first loved us."* He is the Master giver. *(Written by Bob Nichols)*

MAY 10
THE THRONE OF GRACE
2 CORINTHIANS 12:10

2 Corinthians 12:10 "When I am weak, then am I strong."

Clearly, one of the most important keys to living the abundant life and the life that's well-pleasing to God is learning how to draw from the wellspring of His grace and live in its provisions.

When Jesus first entered into the garden to pray, He did so with a heaviness that seemed as though it would kill Him. He was facing the darkest moment in His life and prayed that the cup before Him would pass if possible. Three times He prayed. I'm certain that His entire being was resistant to death, as ours would have been. By the time the Roman soldiers came to arrest Him, weakness had given way to God's strength and grace. When He stood identifying Himself as the one they sought, the soldiers fell under the manifest power of God.

This was no longer the burdened Jesus who entered into the garden. There had been a dramatic change between the time He went in to pray and the time He emerged.

What made the difference in the garden? Hebrews 4:16 gives us the answer: *"Let us therefore come boldly unto the throne of grace, that we may obtain mercy, and find grace to help in time of need."*

That's what Jesus did. He made His way to His Father in prayer. He came to the throne of grace and found strength and ability to do what He could not do. He chose to rely upon the heavenly Father, just as you and I must in our times of need. He came into the presence of His Father and found all that He needed.

And now, because of Jesus and His finished work on our behalf, we have open access to the very presence and throne of God. The outgrowth of time in God's presence is the heart set free by His grace. *(Written by Marshall Townsley)*

MAY 11
SOMEBODIES OUT OF NOBODIES
1 KINGS 19:19

1 Kings 19:19 "So he departed . . . and found Elisha . . . plowing with twelve yoke of oxen . . . . "

God delights in turning nobodies into somebodies. People who are important in their own eyes are in for a letdown when they want to be used by God. God uses people who do not think too highly of themselves (Romans 12:3). When God finds a somebody, He sends him to the backside of the wilderness until he is a nobody. Moses in the Old Testament and Paul in the New Testament are examples of those who were used after a stay in the wilderness, away from the view of people.

Elijah had become too important in his own eyes. He told God that he was the only one serving Him. Everyone else had torn down His altars and were serving Baal. Elijah thought God would surely agree with Him. Elijah also thought if God was going to replace him it would be with one of the existing sons of the prophets. They were important young men. They had degrees from the school of the prophets. After all, Elijah had a big mailing list, hundreds of tapes to be duplicate daily and a rigorous schedule to keep. He had spent years perfecting his ministry. It would take someone special to take over such an operation.

God had another idea. He told Elijah he would find his successor plowing a field behind twelve yoke of oxen. *Elijah would be replaced by a farmer.* A nobody would replace Elijah. This was a little hard on Elijah's ego, but he threw his mantle around him anyway. But after all, wasn't that what God did when He found Elijah? Elijah was a nobody God made into a somebody.

God never changes. Why do we think God stopped with us? We look for highly qualified people to fulfill positions of ministry. God first looks for people with good attitudes, not good resumes. *(Written by Bob Yandian)*

MAY 12
LITTLE BY LITTLE
DEUTERONOMY 7:12-26

Deuteronomy 7:22 "And the LORD thy God will put out those nations before thee by little and little: thou mayest not consume them at once, lest the beasts of the field increase upon thee."
The Lord promised His people total and complete victory: not only over people who were their enemies, but also over sickness, barrenness, crop failures and problems with their animals. He made provision for every area of their lives. God is a good God and He receives pleasure from our prosperity (Ps. 35:27). Yet this verse makes a startling statement. The Lord wouldn't grant them these victories all at once.

"Why not?" most of us would ask. If it is God's will for us to succeed in these areas, why doesn't He just do it all at once? The Lord's answer is that we aren't able to handle success all at once. In the case of these Israelites, if the Lord had driven all their enemies out of Palestine all at once, the beasts of the field would have taken over the land before the people could have possessed it. The houses would have fallen into decay. The crops would have been overtaken with weeds. It would have ceased to be a land flowing with milk and honey, and the curse would have dominated it.

Likewise, the Lord will not grant us victories faster than we can possess them. Success without the character to manage it properly would lead to our own destruction. Letting a child drive before he is ready could kill him and someone else. Our heavenly Father loves us much more than to do something like that. God wants us to prosper (3 Jn. 1:2), but our maturity dictates the timing.

Make maturing in the Lord your focus and you will find that your Father will grant you the things you need as soon as you are able to handle them. *(Written by Andrew Wommack)*

MAY 13
GOD WILL NEVER LEAVE YOU IN A NEGATIVE POSITION
I TIMOTHY 6:12

I Timothy 6:12 "Fight the good fight of faith, lay hold on eternal life, to which you were also called and have confessed the good confession in the presence of many witnesses."
Let's look at a few great men and see their "great faith." Moses had a desire to quit. He asked God to kill him. The desire to die is the ultimate quit. We live in a society where it is easy to quit. If it's hard, quit. It's easy to quit a marriage, a pregnancy, to quit working—when the time gets hard. Moses wanted out, but God wouldn't let him.

Elijah, one of the greatest men we read about in the Bible, wanted to quit. He was involved in a tremendous victory when he called fire down from heaven and killed 400 prophets of Baal. One woman said she didn't like him and he wanted to die. Criticism can make a person want to quit, even if he is doing the right thing. God would not let Elijah quit. God is not a quitter.

Job was a great man of his day. In six months of his life he lost everything and he wanted to quit permanently. It was a quick, violent attack of Satan, but God delivered Job. Jonah, a prophet of God, wanted to quit. Things did not go as planned and he wanted out, but God would not let him out.

If you are in any of these situations, you are in good company. But that's not the end of the story. God will never leave you in a negative position. He is with you.

Let's look again at these men. Moses saw God's glory and received the Ten Commandments and God was his pallbearer. He ended up on the Mount of Transfiguration with Elijah and Jesus.

Job stuck it out and was healed and ended up with twice as much as he had in the beginning. He became the New Testament example of patience and the Lord's dealing. Jonah is tied with Jesus for all time. Jesus used him for a sign. The greater the battles, the greater the victories. The greatest victories are the ones you had to fight to gain. Read Hebrews 10:35-11:1 and I Timothy 6:12-14. *(Written by Dave Duell)*

MAY 14
YOU WERE BURIED WITH HIM
ROMANS 6:4

Romans 6:4 "Therefore we were buried with Him through baptism into death . . . . "
We have seen how He became sin with our sin, and how He became our substitute, bearing our diseases. Let's look at how we are buried with Him in death. Remember how the Philistines rejoiced in their victory over Samson after they blinded him and left him helpless? What a day of rejoicing there must have been in hell the day Jesus died. Here is the One who raised Lazarus from the dead, Who ruled the winds and sea, and exercised power over disease and sickness. Now it seemed to Satan that he had conquered Jesus—that is until three days later. Then everything changed for you and me.

The disciples took Jesus' body down from the cross. They laid His body in a borrowed tomb supplied by a man named Joseph. Roman soldiers were ordered to seal the tomb and guard it. No one understood what was happening behind the large stone or in the spirit realm. For three days and three nights Jesus was our substitute in hell. He was there for you. He was there waiting for the claims of justice to be met. When they were, He rose victorious, defeated our enemy, and claimed victory for all who would believe.

Being buried with Him does not mean that we identify with His pain and suffering, but rather His victory. The truth of what He accomplished is greater than the world. It is greater than sickness, depression or any failure. His life carries more authority than life in this world. This is true prosperity. Today as you go through your day, remember this truth—His truth in you. *(Written by Mike Fehlauer)*

MAY 15
IF YOU DON'T LIKE WHAT YOU'RE REAPING, CHECK WHAT YOU'RE SOWING
GENESIS 1:11

Genesis 1:11 "And God said, Let the earth bring forth grass, the herb yielding seed, and the fruit tree yielding fruit after his kind, whose seed is in itself, upon the earth: and it was so."
Sowing and reaping is a foundational biblical principle. God told Noah in Genesis 8:22, *"While the earth remaineth, seedtime and harvest, and cold and heat, and summer and winter, and day and night shall not cease."* We've heard it many times that if you want to grow wheat, you don't plant corn seeds. It's the same with your giving, because *giving is sowing.*

We've sown in helping many ministers get their own cars. Then the Lord gave us a brand new car—totally unexpected. I've sown shoes and received shoes. I've sown suits. Whatsoever a man sows; that shall he also reap. This is a positive for the believer. *If you don't want it coming back, don't sow it.*

We've helped small churches in desperate situations with their payments. We've sown to help other churches, ministers, and people in general. We've sown into helping people with medical bills in a time of need. It's built my faith and my confidence that, really, whatever I need, I know that my God will supply my need. The concept is that we're givers, not takers.

Haggai 1:6-7, *"Ye have sown much, and bring in little; ye eat, but ye have not enough; ye drink, but ye are not filled with drink; ye clothe you, but there is none warm; and he that earneth wages earneth wages to put it into a bag with holes. Thus saith the LORD of hosts; Consider your ways."* The Israelites were setting up nice comfortable homes for themselves while the house of God was lying in waste. The good news is, they repented and God restored them.

If we judge ourselves, we will not be judged. It's good from time to time to give ourselves a spiritual checkup. Remember, if you don't like what you're reaping, check what you're sowing. When we make sure that we put God first, we can be sure that all our own needs will be taken care of in the process. *(Written by Bob Nichols)*

MAY 16
YOU ARE QUALIFIED
COLOSSIANS 1:12

Colossians 1:12 "Giving thanks to the Father who has qualified us . . . . "
For what has the Father qualified you? *"To be partakers of the inheritance of the saints in the light"* (Colossians 1:12). You have already been transferred out of the dark kingdom, out from under Satan's authority, into the kingdom of the Son of His love. You have been redeemed through His blood and have received the forgiveness of sin.

Your sin is no longer held against you. Jesus took your sin upon Himself on the cross and paid the penalty you deserved. Now you can stand tall and say with confidence, "I am purified, I am holy, I am worthy to receive all Jesus bought for me!" Jesus qualified you and made you acceptable and eligible for partaking of His inheritance now.

You have the ability to live victoriously over and above the invisible powers of darkness. You now live in another kingdom, the kingdom where God rules and reigns through you on this earth. And His kingdom is within you and it is *"Righteousness and peace and joy in the Holy Ghost"* (Romans 14:17).

The quality of your life depends on whether or not you believe God and what He has said. Choose a prosperous life. Choose to believe His Word.

Be aggressively thankful that God has qualified you! *(Written by Bonnie Duell)*

MAY 17
NEVER LOSE YOUR CONFIDENCE
2 CORINTHIANS 5:6

2 Corinthians 5:6 "Therefore we are always confident, knowing . . . . "
How would you like to have a confidence which is everlasting? Or, as this verse says, be "always confident." Confidence is not a feeling. It is not an assurance based on circumstances. Because things go your way should not be a reason for confidence. If confidence is based on circumstances, you will be confident at times and not confident at others. How can you be confident always?

This verse goes on to tell us how "knowing" brings confidence. Confidence is based on knowledge. What you know brings you confidence. The Bible does not give you confidence. *Knowing* the Bible gives you confidence. Jesus did not tell us the truth would make us free. He said *knowing* the truth would make us free.

Because you can know at all times, you can be confident at all times. You can be confident when you are hungry or when you have plenty to eat. You can be confident when you have money or when you do not know where your next penny is going to come from. When your confidence is in the Lord and in His Word, you can be confident He will come through. You may not know where the food or money is coming from, but you have confidence it will arrive. Knowing the faithfulness of God is your confidence.

David gave us a look into his own confidence when he said, *"I have been young, and now am old; yet have I not seen the righteous forsaken, nor his seed begging bread"* (Psalm 37:25). When we are cared for by the Lord and taken care of by His faithfulness, we can boldly declare, "I will not be forsaken nor left begging bread." Confidence will remain at all times as an eternal stabilizer in our lives. *(Written by Bob Yandian)*

MAY 18
BLOOM WHERE YOU ARE PLANTED
2 KINGS 5:1-14

2 Kings 5:2 "And the Syrians had gone out by companies, and had brought away captive out of the land of Israel a little maid; and she waited on Naaman's wife."
The healing of Naaman's leprosy is one of the greatest things the Lord did through Elisha. Yet this never would have happened if it hadn't been for a young servant girl who informed Naaman's wife about God's healing power. Without her speaking out, no miracle would have taken place.

This is especially meaningful when you realize that this young girl was an Israelite who had been captured during a Syrian raid and taken back to Syria as a slave. The Hebrew word used for "maid" in this verse means "a young girl from the age of infancy to adolescence." This means she certainly wasn't out on her own yet. She was taken from her parents. It's possible that her parents were killed by the Syrians or made slaves themselves. She could have been bitter and not have told Naaman about God's healing power. Leprosy was considered by many in those days to be God's judgment on sin. She could have thought it served him right. She could have been praying for his death as vengeance.

Instead, she showed concern and compassion for her master. She apparently had forgiven him and gotten over any bitterness. This allowed God to use her as an instrument to touch the highest ranking general in the Syrian army. No doubt many Syrians came to faith in the Lord because she had moved on with her life.

We can't change the past, but we can affect the future for ourselves and others. Regardless of what situation you find yourself in, bloom where you are planted. It's possible that the very ones you have grievances with would respond to the touch of God if you reach out to them. Give someone God's love today. *(Written by Andrew Wommack)*

MAY 19
IN CHRIST
EPHESIANS 1:3

Ephesians 1:3 "Blessed be the God and Father of our Lord Jesus Christ, who has blessed us with every spiritual blessing in the heavenly places in Christ."
Receive these nuggets for yourself.

Ministry is a product of who you are, not what you do. When what you do is the product of who you are, it flows out of your heart effortlessly. Ministry works from what I call the Overflow Principle. Whatever you are full of will flow out of you effortlessly. If you are full of hurt, you will hurt people. If you are full of rejection, you will breed rejection in people. If you are angry, you will make people angry. Face it, sad people do not make others feel happy.

Ephesians 4:23 exhorts, *"and be renewed in the spirit of your mind."* In the original this passage literally reads, *"Renew now after spirit your mind."* Your spirit was renewed at salvation. You became all that Jesus died for to make you become. The Bible teaches that IN CHRIST you are holy, blameless, anointed, called, perfected, righteous, healed, loved, accepted and much, much more.

All of this is the result of being IN CHRIST, not a result of doing something. The problem is that we do not believe our identity. We do not know or do not believe who we are. Remember, grace, which is God's ability, works through faith. The grace to walk in our identity cannot come if you do not *believe* your identity.

Like Jesus when living on planet Earth, we are sons of God. Jesus did not need to become a son of God as we do by receiving Him. He was the Son of God. However, He had to believe it so He could experience the grace to operate in it. *"Beloved, now are we the sons of God, and it doth not yet appear what we shall be: but we know that, when He shall appear, we shall be like Him; for we shall see Him as He is"* (1 John 3:2).

You are a son of God right now. When Jesus was on the cross, it did not look like He was the Son, but He was. When you sin or stumble in life, it does not look like you are a son, BUT YOU ARE! There is nothing you can do to make yourself any more of a son. Unless you believe it, being a son will be of no value. *(Written by Dave Duell)*

MAY 20
HE SUFFERED FOR YOU
ISAIAH 53:3

Isaiah 53:3 "He is despised and rejected by men, A man of sorrows and acquainted with grief . . . ."

Jesus endured all that was possible for humanity to suffer. We are talking about deity suffering for humanity. The righteous suffering for the unrighteous. Religion is a system invented by men in their arrogance whereby they attempt to reach God. The gospel is God reaching down for man. In the darkness of hell, three wonders were displayed by Jesus. First, His power was displayed—His power over death and the grave. Second, His love was displayed—a love that transcended human sympathy, pity or even empathy. It was a love that demanded the Divine give His life for all. Third, His faithfulness was displayed. He is faithful even when we are faithless. Fourth, His righteousness was displayed. Jesus had satisfied the broken law. He had lived a sinless life, then took that pure, holy life and broke it open for you and I to receive. And, we received not only His forgiveness, but also His righteousness.

I know that you believe this, but, here is the challenge. Today, you have the opportunity to display the same wonders to this dark world. You are His expression of power today: power over hate, indifference and fear. Power over poverty and lack. You are His expression of love. Love that drives away fear. Love that goes the extra mile and turns away from a suffered wrong. You are His expression of faithfulness—someone others can count on to keep his word, to follow through and finish what they start. You are His righteousness—an example of grace and truth. *(Written by Mike Fehlauer)*

MAY 21
THE STEWARDSHIP FACTOR
LUKE 12:42-44

Luke 12:42 "And the Lord said, Who then is that faithful and wise steward, whom his lord shall make ruler over his household, to give them their portion of meat in due season?"

Stewardship is an important factor when talking about prosperity. We again come back to our principle of starting where you are, doing what you can do, and keep doing it. If you don't take care of what you have, how can God bless you with something better?

A lot of people are very poor stewards. They don't take care of their home or automobile. I believe if you keep what you have clean, if you're a good steward of what you have, then you're a candidate for God to give you something better. The following is a testimony of a precious family in our church. It is a live stewardship success story.

"We bought a car back in the '80s and kept it because we don't like car payments. Over time, we put 178,000 miles on it. The window fell down into the door when you tried to use it and the air conditioning had died. When I went to the car wash, I had to stuff a rag in the window to keep from getting drenched; but I had to keep it washed because I remembered pastor said that you can't expect God to give you something better if you don't take care of what you have. I really desired a particular kind of station wagon, and I found one that was the exact color that I wanted. The dealership did an evaluation on our car, and the bluebook only went back to 1986 - our car was an '84. Our car was worth $250, but they gave us $500. All this time we had been sowing and trying to work the principles we had been taught at church. We kept giving because it was the right thing to do, and we believed the testimonies that came forth. We also refused discouragement from the enemy. We sowed our car money in a particular Sunday morning offering as the Lord led us. People don't know that. The salesman asked if we could put about $3,000 down on it. After we got back in the car, my husband prayed. He said, 'Lord, you are no respecter of persons. If you want us to have that car, you are going to have to make a way.' The next day after church on Sunday a couple came up to us, and they said they felt impressed to give us a check, and it was for $3,000 which was the amount of the down payment. The salesman was also able to find a company that would finance it for a longer period of time. The payments are what we wanted, and it included life insurance! The car is a 1995 model and has a 12-month, 12,000 mile bumper-to-bumper warranty, which is unheard of for a used car. God is good!"

Yes, God is good. Remember, Luke 12:43-44, *"Blessed is that servant, whom his lord when he cometh shall find so doing (being a good steward). Of a truth I say unto you, that he will make him ruler over all that he hath."* *(Written by Bob Nichols)*

MAY 22
BEYOND OUR ABILITIES
2 PETER 3:18

2 Peter 3:18 "But grow in the grace and knowledge of our Lord and Savior Jesus Christ . . . ." (New King James).

Growing in grace enables us to enter into greater and greater dimensions of power in the inner man. God seldom calls us only to what we are capable of doing. He usually calls us to do what we, in our own strength, cannot do. When God calls us into His plan, it's not according to natural talent or intelligence. He looks for those who are determined to do His will regardless of their abilities, and then equips them to do it successfully.

Whatever you are commissioned to do, whatever your part is in God's plan concerning the Kingdom of God, to fulfill it you will need the grace that comes from time spent with Him in His presence.

Grace is that inner quality that will sustain you as things continue to change around you. Someone once said, "Faith overcomes the problems. Grace keeps the problems from overcoming you."

Let me exhort you to come into His presence and grow in grace. Let His ways become your ways, and His thoughts your thoughts. As you do, His ability will emerge from within, and you will see a new strength in His grace. *(Written by Marshall Townsley)*

MAY 23
THE GOD OF THE FEW
EPHESIANS 1:1, COLOSSIANS 1:1

Ephesians 1:1, Colossians 1:1 "Saints and faithful brethren"

This phrase opens both the book of Ephesians and the book of Colossians. It speaks volumes concerning the strategy of God. God does not look for many, but for few. He looks for quality, not quantity. Just like the Marines, God is looking for *a few good men.*

In the Old Testament, God called the "faithful few," the *remnant.* It was with an army of 300 that God defeated the multitudes of Midianites under Gideon's leadership. Gideon was looking for numbers, God was looking for dedication. God is still looking for *"a man among them"* to pray for the nations (Ezekiel 22:30).

Jesus looked for ways to slim down the multitudes that followed him. He was looking for a few who would follow Him no matter what. He had the 12 disciples out of the 70 who followed Him. Out of the 12 Jesus had the three who were closest to Him. Yet, out of the three, only one—John, stuck with Him when He was crucified.

Many times we look for great numbers in prayer. Because our emotions are moved and we feel a greater anointing with larger numbers. God is still more impressed with a few in faith than a multitude in unbelief.

Just as in New Testament days, churches are filled with saints, but only a few are *faithful brethren.* Although the Great Commission tells us to make disciples of all nations (Matthew 28:19), we are too busy making converts instead. Converts are many, disciples are few. A disciple is one who continues to follow the Lord despite the circumstances. He is faithful no matter who else follows the Lord. Jesus said, *"If you continue in my word, then are you my disciples . . . "* (John 8:31). Continuing in God's Word sets you apart from the multitude of converts. It makes you more than a saint. It makes you a faithful brother in Jesus. *(Written by Bob Yandian)*

GO ALL THE WAY
2 KINGS 5:1-14

2 Kings 5:14 "Then went he down, and dipped himself seven times in Jordan, according to the saying of the man of God: and his flesh came again like unto the flesh of a little child, and he was clean."

Elisha's actions and instructions were strange. What was he trying to accomplish?

For one thing, Naaman hadn't really humbled himself before the Lord, which is a very important part of faith. Jesus said that no one can believe, who is seeking the honor that comes from men more than the honor that comes from God (Jn. 5:44). Naaman was too impressed with himself. That's the reason Elisha didn't even go out to see him.

This incensed Naaman. He headed back to Syria in a rage. Elisha hadn't responded to him as his position deserved. Besides, he thought any Syrian river was better than the Jordan river in Israel. There was definitely a pride issue with Naaman. Yet Naaman's servants prevailed on him to give the instructions of Elisha a try. Need often drives people to do things that they wouldn't otherwise do. Naaman humbled himself and dipped in the Jordan river.

Nothing happened the first or the second time he dipped. His healing didn't come gradually. He was still a leper after dipping six times in the Jordan. By the seventh time, his flesh was completely restored. Naaman nearly missed his miracle because of his pride.

Are there issues of pride in your life that have kept you from doing what God has told you to do? If so, humble yourself and obey. Don't do it halfheartedly. Your deliverance will come when you go all the way. *(Written by Andrew Wommack)*

ACCEPTED IN THE BELOVED
EPHESIANS 1:6

Ephesians 1:6 "To the praise of the glory of his grace, wherein He hath made us accepted in the beloved."

You, like Jesus, have your identity and approval from God apart from your works. Ephesians 1:6 points to the source of your acceptance: *"To the praise of the glory of His grace, wherein He hath made us accepted in the beloved."* There are well over 100 Scriptures in the New Testament that point to your identity IN CHRIST.

We have failed to take our new identity seriously. It seems too good to be true; it is too easy; it is too simple. You became who you are totally apart from any works. You became who you are by adoption, by the new birth. *"Not by works of righteousness which we have done, but according to His mercy He saved us, by the washing of regeneration, and renewing of the Holy Ghost"* (Titus 3:5).

One of the main problems in the Body of Christ is not knowing who we are in Christ. Once you know and believe that you were chosen before the foundation of the world and that you have been adopted as a son by Jesus Christ to Himself, you can live the Christian life like Jesus planned for you to live.

Praise God, the Gospel is Good News and if you believe the words written, you will have the victory in every situation. Jesus meant it when He said in John 10:10, *"The thief does not come except to steal, and to kill, and to destroy. I have come that they may have life, and that they may have it more abundantly."*

I love what the word "abundantly" means. It means superabundance, excessive, overflowing, surplus, over and above, more than enough, profuse, extraordinary, above the ordinary, more than sufficient source. I would call that Blessed.

I believe that Jesus was talking about life after His death, burial, and resurrection. He could see all that would be done by Himself in defeating the devil. All we have to do is believe it and it is all ours. *(Written by Dave Duell)*

MAY 26
YOU ARE ALIVE WITH HIM
COLOSSIANS 2:13

Colossians 2:13 "And you, being dead in your trespasses and the uncircumcision of your flesh, He has made alive together with Him, having forgiven you all trespasses."
Here we witness the miracle of all eternity. It took place in the bowels of hell. I am sure that it shook the foundation of hell itself when they saw Him made alive, break the bonds of spiritual death, and hurl back the forces of death that overwhelmed Him on the cross. God is a faith God. He counted all things that were not as though they were. Down in hell He counted us righteous and counted us alive. He counted us as new creations. The moment we accepted Him as our Savior and Lord, the new birth was made real to us.

His life is flowing through you today. He has infused you with the energy of His life. Light has swallowed up darkness. Life has conquered death. Now is the time to walk and serve in the power of His energy and virtue. Others need to taste of this life today. All they know is artificial life. A substitute. A counterfeit. You carry Eternal Life. It carries with it the power to set the captives free and bring deliverance. Attack your day with His energy.
(Written by Mike Fehlauer)

MAY 27
PAY NOW OR PAY LATER
MALACHI 3:8

Malachi 3:8 "Will a man rob God? Yet ye have robbed me. But ye say, Wherein have we robbed thee? In tithes and offerings."
I remember a couple who made $35 per week. That's all they made, but they were faithful to tithe and give offerings as they could. Their hearts were right and they believed God for more. One day they came to me and told me that their income had increased from $35 to $65. They were excited, but they added that they "couldn't afford to tithe anymore." Let me tell you, you cannot afford not to tithe! They stopped tithing and it wasn't very long after that they lost everything that they had.

I also remember a missionary telling us about a man in Mexico who was in such poverty that all he had was less than a shack of a house. He heard the missionary teach on tithing—that if you have 10 eggs, one belongs to God. If you have 10 coconuts, you give one to God. It was simple. The man started faithfully tithing. The next time the missionary came back to his village, he was amazed to see the nice home and furnishings the man had. The man told the missionary that yes he had really come up in the world. However, the man told the missionary that he didn't know if he could keep tithing. He said, "Really, that's a lot of money to give away," and asked the missionary to pray for him. The missionary looked at him and shrugged, and prayed, "Oh God, take away all these things from this man," but the man jumped in and stopped him, "What are you doing?!" The missionary told him, "If you can't adjust your tithe to match your income, the Lord can certainly adjust your income to match your tithe."

What a hard lesson to learn. It's like Haggai 1:6 says, *"he that earneth wages earneth wages to put it into a bag with holes."* Everything belongs to God anyway. We're just the stewards. You can't ignore God's principles and expect to prosper. The book of Malachi calls it robbing God. I would rather have 90 percent with the blessing of God, than 100 percent that gets put into a bag with holes in it. *(Written by Bob Nichols)*

GOD IS A REWARDER
HEBREWS 11:6

Hebrews 11:6 "He is a rewarder of those who diligently seek Him."
It is important for you to realize the nature of God. God is love. He is good. He is full of grace. He is a rewarder. Unless you believe this in your heart, it will be impossible for you to draw near to Him in faith. Only a revelation of God's grace as demonstrated by the fact that He is a rewarder of those who seek Him can produce faith in your heart.

It pleases God when you have faith to see Him as He really is. If you believe what some preachers say, that God is angry, judgmental and ready to strike you down, you will not even want to seek Him. Many people are in that predicament today because they have listened to the wrong message. Some people even believe God is the cause of their problems.

The faith-producing message that Jesus preached is the revelation of God's grace. God is for you! He is a rewarder! John 1:16 states, "And of His fullness we have all received, and grace for grace." Grace and truth came through Jesus Christ.

The truth is that God loves you unconditionally. He's not mad at you. In fact, He is no longer taking into account your sins and holding them against you (II Corinthians 5:19). He made peace between Himself and all mankind at the cross.

When you get the revelation of God's grace that He is a rewarder, it will produce faith in your heart. *(Written by Bonnie Duell)*

LOOK AND LIVE
NUMBERS 21:8

Numbers 21:8 "And the LORD said unto Moses, Make thee a fiery serpent, and set it upon a pole: and it shall come to pass, that every one that is bitten, when he looketh upon it, shall live."
Why do we want to complicate what God has made simple? We often want to construct seven steps to answered prayer, five steps to healing, six levels of faith or four doors to salvation.

Jesus taught in parables to make difficult teachings simple. He told stories so unlearned multitudes could understand the simplicity of reaching God. Jesus thanked His Father for hiding the profound teachings of scripture from the naturally wise of this world and revealing them to people of childlike faith (Matthew 11:25).

Throughout the Word, faith is compared to simple functions. In Isaiah 55:1 faith for salvation is compared to eating and drinking. Everyone can eat and drink. It requires little human effort. Moral and immoral, fat and skinny, male and female, educated and uneducated, babies and adults, and black and white people can eat and drink. In other words, salvation is for *whosoever will.* It is religion that adds works to the simple plan of God. We want them to believe in Jesus, but we want them to also give money. This limits salvation to those with means. We want people to also be water baptized and join our church. These things are fine, but in no way make us saved. We are simply to *"taste and see that the Lord is good . . . "* (Psalm 34:8).

To demonstrate how simple divine healing is, Moses commanded the people to look at the brass serpent and they would be healed and live. How difficult is it to look? A doctor once told me that the opening of the eyelids requires the least amount of physical effort in the body. What a beautiful picture of faith for healing. Faith is the only thing we can do without doing anything. *(Written by Bob Yandian)*

MAY 30
WHAT DO YOU SEE?
2 KINGS 6:8-23

2 Kings 6:16 "And he answered, Fear not: for they that be with us are more than they that be with them."
The Lord had been giving the king of Syria's battle plans to Elisha who in turn passed them along to the king of Israel. This resulted in Israel escaping Syria's ambushes numerous times. Eventually the Syrian king came to the conclusion that there must be a spy in their ranks, but he discovered that it was Elisha who was the informant. He sent his troops to take Elisha.

Elisha's servant got up early one morning and found the Syrian armies surrounding them. He panicked. He knew why they were there and who they were after. But Elisha was cool. He said there were more with them than with the Syrian army.

How could that be? You could count the enemy by thousands and there were only Elisha and his servant. Two against thousands! Did Elisha lie? No! It could only be considered a lie if all you acknowledge is the physical world with what you can see, taste, hear, smell, and feel. There is a spiritual world that those who are carnal seldom take into account.

In the spiritual world, you have resources that are far greater than your needs. You just can't see them. Does that mean they don't exist? Only to those who are void of faith. *"If thou canst believe, all things are possible to him that believeth"* (Mk. 9:23). You are surrounded by the supernatural ability and protection of God.

Pray that the Lord will open your spiritual eyes today to what you have in Christ and then confess what you really have. *(Written by Andrew Wommack)*

MAY 31
FULFILLING PROPHECY (PART 1)
1 TIMOTHY 1:18

1 Timothy 1:18 "This charge I commit to you, son Timothy, according to the prophecies previously made concerning you, that by them you may wage the good warfare."
I want to share with you the awesome miracle God has done with the Navajo Nation and what we see in the future with these wonderful people. Cindy Jacobs, a prophetess, gave me a prophecy in October of 1994. She said, "You are a part of the healing of this nation with what you are going to do with the Indians. You are going to be financing Indian churches on reservations where they have no place. God is going to use you to get first fruits. The Lord is going to use you to restore their wealth. The Lord will bring to you Indian prophets who will give you the Word of the Lord. There is a real connection that is there in the Spirit. The Lord is going to use you to restore self-esteem and to break the spirit of poverty—tell them poverty is not His plan."

Five years ago, Sammie Begay, a native Navajo-American, was working as a silversmith in Phoenix, Arizona. He always listened to the radio as he worked. One day I was on Andrew Wommack's program talking about the exploits God has done in my life. There was a connection in the Spirit and Sammie ordered my two books, *Faith - Believe or Not* and *Faith - What A Deal.*

Sammie read these books over and over and faith was put into him. He told God that he wanted to meet me sometime. A few years later, Sammie, along with his wonderful wife, Sandy and their two daughters, were asked to be the Pastors in Ganado, Arizona. Day after day, Sammie had me on his mind. Many times he tried to call me but he would put down the phone just before it would ring. This went on for a few years. One morning the Holy Spirit told him to call Dave immediately. I answered the phone and we talked for a while. Sammie asked me to come to Ganado and be the speaker at their camp meeting in July, 1997.

It was exciting to see the fulfillment of the prophecy. Please read on to learn more of the action of the Holy Spirit. Continued. *(Written by Dave Duell)*

JUNE 1
HE IS RIGHTEOUSNESS FOR YOU
ROMANS 3:26

Romans 3:26 "To demonstrate at the present time His righteousness, that He might be just and the justifier of the one who has faith in Jesus" (NKJV).

The moment that you accepted Jesus Christ as your Lord and Savior, He became your righteousness. As God became the righteousness of Jesus, so He becomes the righteousness of the new creation. As He became the life of Jesus, He becomes the life of the new creation. Once we truly accept this truth, it will revolutionize the church. In Ephesians 2:6 we read, *"And raised us up together, and made us sit together in heavenly places, in Christ Jesus."* This could never happen unless you were as righteous as He was.

Surely you can see the courage this can give you in the face of poverty, disease and sickness. It is because of His righteousness that you can have utter boldness to enter His presence. The sense of your oneness with Him should be as real as His sense of oneness with us when He became sin and sickness. Arise and take your place today as a conqueror and victor. Face every situation as an opportunity to live as a king or priest doing the work of Jesus. His plan for you is one of abundance—to live in His fullness and express the reality of His presence. This is your day. *(Written by Mike Fehlauer)*

JUNE 2
WHAT YOU MAKE HAPPEN FOR SOMEONE ELSE'S HOUSE, HE'LL MAKE HAPPEN FOR YOUR HOUSE
PROVERBS 11:24

Proverbs 11:24 "There is that scattereth, and yet increaseth; and there is that withholdeth more than is meet, but it tendeth to poverty."

There is a popular radio minister in our church who was led of the Lord back in 1974 to give $900 to help another minister pay off his ministry tent. At that time money was scarce and that money was originally going to go towards his own house, but in obedience he sowed it. The years that followed brought great challenge and growth through difficult circumstances. They learned some things the hard way and ended up in bankruptcy and had two homes foreclosed.

In 1992 the Lord started speaking to him and his wife to believe for another house. In the natural there was just no way, but they believed God would honor the word He spoke to their hearts. They looked at houses and found a builder who would work with them. He told them, "You give us $2,000 and we'll start the house." Well, at that time they'd never received any more than $20 to $100 in special offerings.

In June of 1993 they experienced revival in what is now their home church. They started to sow into the revival and soon they had $20,000 extra toward their house. By that time, they had been turned down by two or three mortgage companies, but they kept pressing in and giving. They gave into a first fruits offering. You sow where you want to go. It was money that they needed, but God said to help their daughter because she was believing for a house, so they sowed to help her as well.

One night in the fall of 1993 he was in the radio studio and the Lord spoke to him and said, "Do you remember that $900 you gave to me? I am getting ready to give that back to you with interest." He said, "Figure it out with 10 percent a year compounded." It came out to almost $50,000 for 19 years. The minister said, "Oh, my!" Something was about to hit. They found a mortgage company that could help them and they kept giving faithfully.

In April of 1994 the mortgage broker took three contracts to the underwriters; the other two were spotless and the minister's had a bankruptcy and foreclosure on it. The broker said, "You won't believe this," and the minister said, "I might." The broker explained that the other two were turned down, but they accepted his! About a week before closing, all the money was in that they needed. Looking at their bank account, they noticed that the harvest started directly coming in during the revival when they started stepping out and aggressively sowing. That's when it really took off. The whole time they were obedient to tithe, to sow and to believe the Word in faith.

Make a note of this: what you make happen for someone else's house, God will make happen for your house. Do you have a need? Sow some seed. *(Written by Bob Nichols)*

JUNE 3
INTIMACY WITH GOD
2 CORINTHIANS 3:18

2 Corinthians 3:18 "But we all, with unveiled face, beholding as in a mirror the glory of the Lord, are being transformed into the same image from glory to glory, just as by the Spirit of the Lord."

I really enjoy this verse of scripture, first, because it speaks of intimacy with the Lord and second, because it holds one of the most powerful promises in the New Testament.

The phrase, "beholding as in a mirror" speaks of a continuous face-to-face encounter with the Lord. Looking into a mirror is always a face-to-face experience. The Greek word translated "behold" indicates doing it time after time, again and once again, without a break or pause. This word in the Greek language is the antonym, or opposite, of any word meaning occasional or just once in a while.

Paul is drawing from the "face-to-face" experience that Moses enjoyed with God that resulted in, on one visit, the transformation of his countenance by the glory of God. You might remember that Moses insisted on seeing God's glory. Even though God had promised to dwell once again among the children of Israel, Moses hungered for more. He wanted something more intimate and pressed God to grant his desire. He had the abiding presence of God but wanted, and ultimately received, the greater revelation and experience.

This, by the way, is a great picture of what's available to the Christian. But all too often, instead of pressing to know God and to experience His glory in a greater way as Moses insisted on, we stop well short. We are grateful for His abiding, which is glorious, but seldom do we go on to take full advantage of this priceless privilege of knowing Him intimately—of enjoying the deepest fellowship with Him that we can. But that's where most of us stop. And that's why many continue to go unchanged; our lives reflecting more the glory of a weak and sin-stained flesh instead of the glorious spirit of Christ.

Intimacy results, or can result, in genuine transformation. Moses returned from the summit of Mt. Sinai bearing the goodness, grace, and mercy of God on his face because that's what he saw. As we behold Him, we too will be changed just as Paul said, from glory to glory and from grace to grace. What an exciting proposition! *(Written by Marshall Townsley)*

JUNE 4
WHO'S LISTENING?
ROMANS 8:31

Romans 8:31 "What shall we then say to these things? If God be for us, who can be against us."

When Jesus instructed His disciples in faith, he told them to speak to the mountain (Mark 11:23). The occasion for this lesson was a dead fig tree Jesus had just spoken to a day earlier. In another teaching on faith, Jesus told his disciples to speak to a sycamine tree to be plucked up (Luke 17:6). Are you beginning to understand? Faith works as we speak against problems.

When Joshua needed more daylight to finish his battle against five kings, he commanded the sun and moon to stand still (Joshua 10:12).

Paul joins with Joshua, Jesus, and others, when he tells us to speak to the circumstances of life and say, "If God be for me, you cannot be against me." Jesus did not pray to God to heal; He spoke to sickness and demons and told them to go. I cannot find a place where Jesus prayed for sickness. I find over and over again that He spoke to sickness.

If we can speak to mountains, trees, sickness and the circumstances of life, *they must be able to hear.* Jesus said the sycamine tree would obey. If good trees will one day clap their hands at the return of Jesus and oceans will roar at His coming, they must be able to respond to the voice of God's word.

Why not speak to your checkbook as if it can hear? Why not speak to your cancer as if it has ears? Speak to them and say, "Checkbook, I command you to open up the provisions of God. You have been against me too long. Cancer, if God be for me, you cannot be against me. I rebuke you and command you to leave this body in the name of Jesus. Come out by the roots and be cast into the sea." Jesus said they will obey you. *(Written by Bob Yandian)*

JUNE 5
SHUT UP AND GET OUT OF THE WAY
2 KINGS 6:24-7:20

2 Kings 7:2 "Then a lord on whose hand the king leaned answered the man of God, and said, Behold, if the LORD would make windows in heaven, might this thing be? And he said, Behold, thou shalt see it with thine eyes, but shalt not eat thereof."

This famine in Samaria was so severe that people were eating dove's dung and some had even eaten their own children. The king held Elisha responsible because he had captured the Syrian army, but let them go (2 Ki. 6:22-23). The king was intent on killing Elisha. Elisha gave a prophecy that within 24 hours, there would be such an abundance that food would be cheap.

One of the king's servants laughed at Elisha's prophecy and basically said that even God couldn't do a miracle like that. Elisha responded by saying that it would happen and the servant would see it, but he wouldn't partake of the blessing because of his unbelief. It came to pass exactly as Elisha prophesied. The miraculous provision took place, but that servant was trampled to death by the people rushing after the food.

It's easy to say that God can do anything, but when push comes to shove, most people don't really believe it. We all have limits that we put on God. Just like this unbelieving servant, our unbelief keeps us from partaking of the miracle.

Ask the Lord to help you take all limits off of what He can do. As you are in the process of increasing what you can believe God for, at least use enough common sense to not speak forth your unbelief. And certainly don't get in the way of those who do believe. They may trample your unbelief to death. *(Written by Andrew Wommack)*

JUNE 6
FULFILLING PROPHECY (PART 2)
1 THESSALONIANS 5:20

1 Thessalonians 5:20 "Do not despise prophecies."

God did a great work in those few days. I was with Fred White, the director of tourism for the Navajo Nation, in their headquarters. The history of the nation is on murals around the building. I asked Fred how he felt about the white man. I could tell his feelings went very deep. I asked him to forgive us for what we had done. Many tears were shed as we held each other. A great healing took place and history was in motion for the Holy Spirit to do great and mighty things for the Navajo Nation.

That evening in the tent meeting, I had all of the Indian brothers and sisters who had that hatred in their hearts come forward. I chopped all of it off of them. When the power of the Holy Spirit would hit them, they would fly through the air. All were set free. There was dancing like the people had never seen. That was the beginning of relationships that will change the Indian nation.

In five wonderful evenings of meetings, which began around 8:00 p.m. and went until midnight, we saw the Holy Spirit change hundreds of lives, including our own. There was prayer for deliverance, healing of marriages, praying for the elderly women, salvation and the baptism in the Holy Spirit, and healings from all kinds of sicknesses.

The praise and worship went for hours with life-changing demonstrations of the Holy Spirit. Remember, the prophetess said in 1994 that God would send Indian prophets to speak to me. Henry Yazzie, a prophet from Santa Fe, New Mexico, was at the meeting. What a time we had together! The Holy Spirit brought us together in the Spirit and we laughed together, rolled on the floor together, spoke to each other in the Spirit, and demonstrated what the Holy Spirit was saying to us. He gave me an awesome prophecy. The pastors who were present jumped on us. There was a big pile of people on top of us and I didn't feel anything. *(Written by Dave Duell)*

JUNE 7
SATAN HAS BEEN DISARMED
COLOSSIANS 2:15

Colossians 2:15 "Having disarmed principalities and powers, He made a public spectacle of them, triumphing over them in it." Jesus triumphed over Satan. He overthrew the hosts of hell. Here we see that Jesus stripped Satan of the authority and dominion that Satan had taken from man at the fall. You were with Him when that battle took place. Just as you were with Him in His death, burial and resurrection, you are also with Him in His victory over death and the grave. The most amazing part of this whole thing is that the victory is not really His, but yours. He did not need to fight the battle. He did it for you. When Jesus disarmed the powers of Satan, in the mind of the Father it was as though you had done it. You are the devil's master today, just as Jesus was when He rose from the dead. Just like when Jesus conquered the devil when He walked the earth, you too can walk in the same authority.

It is time that we as the church begin to apply the victory over Satan that is ours. Jesus has given us this authority. You are now the righteous victor. You are Satan's master. Satan cannot lord over you any longer. Poverty is under your feet. Disease is under your feet. Sin is under subject to His name from your lips. I challenge you to enjoy His fullness today. *(Written by Mike Fehlauer)*

JUNE 8
THE TITHE IS HOLY
GENESIS 2:15-17

Genesis 2:17 "But of the tree of the knowledge of good and evil, thou shalt not eat of it: for in the day that thou eatest thereof thou shalt surely die.

Tithing is the principle of putting God first. Every believer needs to come to the understanding that the tithe is holy unto God. Leviticus 27:30: *"And all the tithe of the land, whether of the seed of the land, or of the fruit of the tree, is the LORD'S: it is holy unto the LORD."* The opposite of holy is common. The blood of Jesus is holy. The Bible is holy. The name of Jesus is holy. The tithe is holy. Adam was to tend the garden. This was his occupation. The fruit from every tree except one could be used for food. This was a type of tithe. When Adam decided to join with Eve and eat his tithe, he lost his spiritual life. He lost his place to live. The ground became cursed and instead of yielding abundantly as before, it now yielded more weeds than crops. His career became cursed.

Are you seeing the picture here? Although everything belongs to the Lord anyway, He has arranged for us to give Him the first ten percent of everything—the choicest part. Malachi chapter three declares that the Lord will rebuke the devourer for the tither's sake. In Adam's case, the man was the devourer. Tithing is just one point in a life of prosperity, but it is the starting point that must be met to go any farther. Make sure you keep the tithe holy unto the Lord. *(Written by Bob Nichols)*

JUNE 9
PROSPEROUS RELATIONSHIPS
MATTHEW 22:37-39

Matthew 22:37-39 "You shall love the Lord your God with all your heart, with all your soul, and with all your mind . . . And . . . You shall love your neighbor as yourself."

Love God and love people. All the commandments of the law are fulfilled in this. Anything you believe that does not make you fall more in love with God and people is not true.

Love is what makes faith work. You must have a revelation of the love of God for you in order to trust Him. Faith works by believing in the love of God. Faith works because you love people.

"We love Him, because He first loved us" (I John 4:19). You must believe that God loves you first. He accepts you in Jesus apart from your performance. That is unconditional love. When you know and believe you are loved by God, you will be able to make people feel loved too. You can believe that God loves and accepts them first.

You will become like the God you believe in. Your relationships with God and people depend on what you believe about God. If you believe God is judgmental, faultfinding and angry, you will find yourself being that way toward people. If you believe in a loving God, you will become loving toward people.

You will fall in love with God when you realize how much He loves you. When you feel loved by God, you will have the grace to walk in love with people and make them feel loved. *(Written by Bonnie Duell)*

JUNE 10
SOME ADULT CONVERSATION
I CORINTHIANS 14:2

I Corinthians 14:2 "For he that speaketh in an unknown tongue, speaketh not unto men, but unto God . . . ."

When you speak in tongues in prayer or worship, *you speak to God.* That is a powerful statement. What could you possibly say to interest the Creator of the universe? For one thing, your mind could have nothing to do with the conversation. When you pray with tongues, your understanding is unfruitful. In other words, the words come directly from your human spirit to God. Your words are empowered by the Holy Spirit. You are on a conversation level with God Himself.

When I was a child, my mother couldn't wait for me to speak. She wanted to find out what was inside my head. At the proper age, I began to put sentences together and she found out what I was thinking. My vocabulary consisted of cookies, milk, Mickey Mouse and toys. My mother told me she wanted adult conversation so bad she would often go to the neighbor's house just to talk on an adult level. My mother was so happy to see my father come home from work, she would talk and talk to him, seeking adult conversation. She was very glad when I grew up enough and learned how to carry on an adult conversation.

What about God? I am sure He is happy when we approach His throne to ask Him to meet our needs. He is also happy when we come into His presence with praise and worship. But when all of our prayers and praise are in English, He must think they sound a lot like cookies, milk, Mickey Mouse and toys. He must breathe a sigh of relief when we are filled with the Holy Spirit and begin to speak in tongues. Suddenly we speak to God on His level. He must say, "Ahh, some adult conversation." *(Written by Bob Yandian)*

JUNE 11
HOW LONG WILL YOU KEEP DOING THE SAME THING?
2 KINGS 7:3-11

2 Kings 7:3 "There were four leprous men at the entering in of the gate: and they said one to another, Why sit we here until we die?"

These lepers were in a terrible situation. There was a famine in the city of Samaria because of the Syrian blockade. The situation was so bad that people actually cannibalized their own children. These lepers would certainly be the first ones to die. They were outcasts because of their disease. They wouldn't be fed at the expense of others. What were they to do? Something had to change. They decided to go out to the Syrians and ask for mercy. The worst thing that could happen was that they would be killed.

Many people would call that crazy—they were taking too big a risk. *True insanity is to keep doing the same thing and expect different results.* If things continued as they were, death was certain. These lepers made a wise decision that not only resulted in their own salvation, but in the deliverance of the whole city of Samaria.

They had an advantage over other people. They didn't have much of a life. They were cut off from society and were already dead in a sense. They had nothing to lose. They had no fear of loss. Courage flourishes in the absence of fear.

Are you stuck in a rut? Are you continuing to do the same thing that hasn't worked in the past, but you are still expecting different results? Maybe it's time for you to take a radical step and try something different. What have you got to lose? Probably less than you think. You may fail, but failing to try is the worst failure of all. You might just experience a great deliverance as these lepers did.   *(Written by Andrew Wommack)*

JUNE 12
THE POTENTIAL OF ANYTHING IS RELATED TO ITS SOURCE
GALATIANS 4:6

Galatians 4:6 "And because you are sons, God has sent forth the Spirit of His Son into your hearts, crying out, 'Abba, Father!'"

People generally fall into one of three groups—the few who make it happen, the many who watch things happen and the overwhelming majority who have no notion of what happens. The longer I live I can see how we make a difference in this world as we live our lives with a sense of destiny.

Success is not a comparison of what we have done with what others have done. It is simply coming up to the level of our best and making the most of our abilities and possibilities. God has opened up the world to us and I can see so many different ways that we can touch the world with the Good News. We have a man in our church who is awesome with computers in the realm of communication. As he shows me what can be done in this area, it causes me to believe this is one of the largest untapped ways to touch the nations. We are planning to use this tool as much as possible.

I believe we can do more than we are doing right now and that we should not set limits on what we can achieve. You are more than what you have done. We call this potential. Everything in life was created with potential. In every seed there is a tree . . . in every bird a flock . . . in every fish a school . . . in every sheep a flock . . . in every cow a herd . . . in every boy a man . . . in every girl a woman . . . in every nation a generation. Just think—you and I are hooked up with God. THE POTENTIAL OF ANYTHING IS RELATED TO ITS SOURCE.

We are responsible for the potential stored within us. We must learn to understand it and effectively use it. This comes by studying the Bible. We must learn to see ourselves as God sees us.

As believers in these last days, we are part of a special people for whom excellence is the only standard. First Peter 2:9 says, *"You are a chosen generation, a royal priesthood, a holy nation, His own special people, that you may proclaim the praises of Him who called you out of darkness into His marvelous light."*   *(Written by Dave Duell)*

JUNE 13
YOU HAVE BEEN RAISED WITH HIM
EPHESIANS 2:6

Ephesians 2:6 "And raised us up together, and He made us sit together in the heavenly places, in Christ Jesus."
God's ability was unveiled in the resurrection. When He broke through the gates of death, hell was shook to its foundation. Because of the resurrection we are raised together with Christ. We can have victory in every area, over every circumstance. We can go from triumph to triumph. God has lifted you above every rule and authority, power and dominion—not only in this age, but also in the age to come.

He put all things in subjection to you. Because He lives, we have the legal right to use His name. There isn't anything too hard for God. God's ability is the ability that He gives us. Therefore, His resurrection is the proof that we have the right to reign over the works of Satan. Jesus was raised from the dead because He conquered Satan in our place. So today you don't have to live in fear of the unseen forces of darkness. *(Written by Mike Fehlauer)*

JUNE 14
GOD HAS AN ECONOMY AND YOU CAN GET IN ON IT
PSALMS 35:27

Psalms 35:27 "Let them shout for joy, and be glad, that favour my righteous cause: yea, let them say continually, Let the LORD be magnified, which hath pleasure in the prosperity of his servant."
A long time ago, before one of our staff members was on staff at our church, he saw how the gospel of Jesus Christ changes financial disasters. His wife brought him to the church just two days after he received salvation. He was born-agan, but his checkbook wasn't. One of the first things he remembers was hearing me say, "God has an economy and you can get in on it."

He and his wife began to tithe, and they began to give. He said, "How can I tithe? I owe thousands and thousands and thousands of dollars to the IRS. I owe bankers and banks, friends, and family." God told him, "Put Me first." They decided to honor God with their finances. He thought that if God can save and deliver him, He can sure take care of a little money—or a lot of money! He was so under the barrel that anything he got would have to come from God. He figured it up one day and found that he would have to pay $650 per month until he was 70 years old to get out of debt. He was 32 at the time. Finally, God told him that if he would get his eyes off of his lack, and put them on His abundance, He would get them out of that mess. They purposed to get out of debt, and they quit spending money. They tithed for two years and it seemed like nothing was happening. When you can't see something happening in the natural, it's happening in the supernatural. He was in the real estate business. God brought him favor and brought him real estate clients in a time when the market was severely hurting. In less than 20 months, God paid off every bit of that debt!

There are things we can do to get in on God's economy. We tithe, we give, and we always put God first *(Written by Bob Nichols)*.

JUNE 15
RECEIVING BY FAITH
PHILIPPIANS 4:13

Philippians 4:13 "I can do all things through Christ who strengthens me"
(New King James).

Paul experienced the grace of God in his weakest moments and so can you and I. Grace will come from God to you by faith and you will be transformed. It does not matter what you're up against. Nothing shall be impossible to those who believe. Believe what? Believe by faith that God has grace to meet every need.

The Bible speaks of a woman who had an issue of blood for 12 years and had suffered many things at the hands of many physicians. She had spent all that she had and was still not cured. She had exhausted not only all her money, but her property as well, and she continued to get worse.

The scripture continues to say that when she heard of Jesus she pressed in from behind and touched the hem of His garment. She knew that if she could just get her hands on some part of Him that she would be made whole. Her situation was completely hopeless—no one could help her and she could not help herself. When she made contact with Him she was immediately healed of her condition.

What was it that caused her to put her life on the line, fight her way through the crowd and literally crawl on the ground, in the dust, to get to Jesus? Jesus said it was her faith. Jesus said to her, *"Daughter, thy faith hath made thee whole; go in peace, and be whole of thy plague" (Mark 5:34 King James).*

Grace provided for her healing but it was faith that received it. *(Written by Marshall Townsley)*

JUNE 16
WHAT DO YOU HAVE IN YOUR HAND?
EXODUS 12:11

Exodus 12:11 "And thus shall ye eat it; with your loins girded, your shoes on your feet, and your staff in your hand . . . . "

When something is repeated many times in the Bible, it is for a good reason. The principle of looking to what we have and not to what we don't have is taught over and over again, Old Testament and New. The reason is we repeat the same mistake many times.

It is almost human nature to look at how far we still have to go instead of how far we have come. When I speak to couples with marriage problems, I know the first few months will be the most difficult. Discouragement comes easily when you think of two or three years of work. You won't get out of this situation overnight, but you can come out of it faster than you got into it. There must be an attitude of thankfulness each day for every inch of progress. Every journey begins with the first step. God can multiply one seed into a crop.

When Jesus asked the disciples how much food they had to feed the multitude, they responded with a description of the five loaves and two fishes. But they then said, *"What are they among so many?"* (John 6:9). Jesus then took the loaves and fishes, blessed them and multiplied them.

We need to learn from Jesus to bless what we have even if it looks small. Only by blessing what we have can it ever be multiplied. Instead of blessing the few who come, many ministers complain about the many who did not come. If you keep cursing the empty seats, the full ones will one day be empty too. People do not want to come to a church where they are rebuked week after week for those who did not attend.

Your small amount of talent, teaching ability or money can be much when you bless it and give it to the Lord. With one stick, Moses delivered an entire generation. What can you do in your generation? *(Written by Bob Yandian)*

JUNE 17
HAVE YOU TOLD SOMEONE?
2 KINGS 7:3-11

2 Kings 7:9 "Then they said one to another, We do not well: this day is a day of good tidings, and we hold our peace: if we tarry till the morning light, some mischief will come upon us: now therefore come, that we may go and tell the king's household."

There are many parallels between this situation and ours today. Just like the people in Samaria, people today are starving to death spiritually. Our own sins have surrounded us and are choking the life out of us. This desperate situation causes many to do things that they would never do otherwise, just as these Samaritans were eating dung and even their own children to stay alive.

Certainly every one of them prayed to God for deliverance; however, when God answered their prayers, they didn't know it immediately. They continued in their hunger and despair for a time when there was an abundance of food just outside the gates.

These four lepers were the ones who discovered their redemption. They rejoiced at their own deliverance, but in a short time they remembered the others who were still starving and their responsibility to share their discovery. They brought the good news back to the city.

These lepers could have kept the news to themselves. Remember, the people in the city had rejected them. This would have been a great opportunity for them to get even, but they knew that was the wrong thing to do. People's lives were hanging in the balance.

If you know Jesus and the forgiveness of sins that He brings, then you have been delivered from a fate worse than starvation. Others need to know who and what you know. Don't keep the Good News to yourself. *(Written by Andrew Wommack)*

JUNE 18
RELEASING YOUR POTENTIAL
ROMANS 8:11

Romans 8:11 "But if the Spirit of Him who raised Jesus from the dead dwells in you, He who raised Christ from the dead will also give life to your mortal bodies through His Spirit who dwells in you."

The new birth created a new nation of people born into the same anointing of Jesus. It has placed within ordinary people extraordinary qualities and power. The will to succeed is useless unless you are willing to prepare to succeed. You must go to the Word of God and see how to put yourself in the position of walking in His goodness and blessing.

You must prepare yourself to prosper, receive His healing and health and to know His peace in the face of any opposition. Do not let what you cannot do interfere with what you can do. What you see is not all there is. Potential is dormant ability, reserved power, untapped strength, unused success, hidden talent, capped capability. It is all you can be, but have not yet become; all you can do but have not yet done; how far you can reach, but have not reached; what you can accomplish but have not yet accomplished.

Nothing in life is instant, as you well know. The dreams and visions and prophesies that God has given to you are all out in front of you ready to come into fulfillment as you press on in this war that I call "believing": the battle of the mind. No man can climb beyond the limitations of his own belief. That is what we have been working on all of our lives.

We are what we speak. Our task is not to get Christ into us, but out of us. When man puts a limit on what he can be, he has put a limit on what he will be. Jesus came, not to convince God of anything, but to convince us about who we really are. Just think that you have in you the same Holy Spirit that raised Christ from the dead. To me that shows that "all things are possible to him who believes" (Mk. 9:23). GOD DESIGNED AND PREDETERMINED YOU TO BE A SUCCESS STORY! *(Written by Dave Duell)*

JUNE 19
JESUS IS YOUR HIGH PRIEST
HEBREWS 9:11-12

Hebrews 9:11-12 "But Christ, came as High Priest of the
good things to come . . . . "
I really like the idea that Christ is our high priest of *the good things to come.*
Do you believe that? Is that what you expect—good things from God? Jesus died a
lamb without blemish or sin, but rose the Lord and High Priest. As a high priest,
Jesus took His own blood and He carried it up to the Holy of Holies. It is the red seal
of His precious and pure blood that is the seal of your redemption today. His blood
witnesses the fact that the price has been paid. The law has been satisfied. He
finished the work of redemption. Satan's dominion over us has been broken. Satan's
right to rule us with fear, despair, sickness and ungodly passion is over! Your High
Priest has settled the issue of sin and death.

Don't allow Satan to intimidate you out of walking in Christ's liberating presence
today. Whatever you might be facing, remember your right to His name. His blood has
cleansed you; your High Priest has washed and delivered you. Good things are in
your future. Jesus as your High Priest stands on your behalf constantly bringing His
highest good at all times to you. Celebrate His goodness. You will not have to face
today's challenges or temptations alone. Greater is He that is in you than all the
doubts and fears that have ruled you in the past. *(Written by Mike Fehlauer)*

JUNE 20
NONE WALKS THIS WAY ALONE
1 JOHN 3:16-17

1 John 3:17 "But whoso hath this world's good, and seeth his brother have need,
and shutteth up his bowels of compassion from him, how dwelleth
the love of God in him?"
I don't know who said it first:
"There is a law that makes us brothers. None walks this way alone.
All that we send into the lives of others comes back into our own."
Our whole lifestyle is giving—our time, our talent, our words, our thoughts, even
kind deeds. I'd rather err on the side of generosity than being stingy. If you think the only
time to give is at offering time in church, you've missed it. Look around, there is always
somebody who is worse off than you are. Rather than looking at what we think we lack,
why not look at how we can bless someone else? If you can't sow money right now, sow
time. Find some things in your house and give them to someone who would be blessed
by them: clothes, pictures from your wall. Why not have them over for dinner? Lunch?
Sow into someone's marriage. Why not baby-sit a couple's children so they can spend
time together. What you have or what you can do will bless somebody.

We need each other. I've said it before, and I'll say it again and again. Partners catch
more fish. On any given Sunday, there is enough money to meet every need. Calvin
Coolidge said it well when he said, "No person was ever honored for what he received.
Honor has been the reward for what he gave." *(Written by Bob Nichols)*

JUNE 21
THE PERFECT WILL OF GOD
GALATIANS 5:14

Galatians 5:14 "For all the law is fulfilled in one word, even in this: 'You shall love your neighbor as yourself.'"

Your life will be prosperous in all areas as you walk in the perfect will of God for you. Many Christians today are so concerned about finding the will of God. Some become immobilized by fear thinking they might miss the will of God. Don't try to complicate the matter. The will of God is to walk in love.

First, experience the amazing love God has for you by getting to know Him through His Word and His Spirit. And then give that love to others. God's love has been given to you to share with the world. God's will is not found in rules, laws and regulations. It is not your faultless life that keeps you in the will of God. You walk in the will of God by walking in love.

"Love does no harm to a neighbor; therefore love is the fulfillment of the law" (Romans 13:10). Love never violates another person. It never does anyone wrong. Christians loving each other is what Jesus said the world needs to see to persuade them that we have the truth.

Renew your mind to this truth and you will prove by practice in everyday life that *"good and acceptable and perfect will of God"* (Romans 12:2). You can't miss it.
(Written by Bonnie Duell)

JUNE 22
ARE YOU A PLODDER?
COLOSSIANS 1:7

Colossians 1:7 "Epaphras . . . who is for you a faithful minister of Christ . . . . "

Have you ever heard of Epaphras? He was the pastor of the church at Colosse. Let me tell you what is missing in this verse. We are not told the size of his congregation, or the number in his youth group. We do not know if he had a cell group program or a traditional Sunday School. This is what churches are known for in our day. We are only told one thing—he was faithful. His name was not known well in the ancient world. If Paul would not have mentioned him, we probably would never have heard of him. It didn't seem to matter to Epaphras, he remained faithful.

A faithful person is a plodder. Without a lot of outside inspiration, a plodder keeps moving each day, driven by the Word of God in his heart. We are told we will reap in due season if we faint not. A plodder is one who will not faint. He never seems to give up. Unlike many others, he does not gain great amounts of ground at one time. Yet, when others have given up, thrown in the towel, the plodder is still going.

Many begin a race; beginning is easy. Finishing is difficult. Many who begin with a flash will never make it. They bask in the limelight of popularity, but when the popularity diminishes, so does their stamina. The plodder draws from the wells of inspiration he has in his own heart. He has developed a personal relationship with God and will continue whether anyone stands with him or not. He knows that God will never leave or forsake him.

The important thing is not who starts, but who finishes. Finishing is much more difficult. That is why many are at the starting line, but only a few cross the finish line. God is not so interested in how many begin with Him. He is more interested in how many finish. This is reserved for the plodder. Remember, the one who won the race was the tortoise, not the hare. *(Written by Bob Yandian)*

JUNE 23
GOD HAS NEVER HAD ANYONE QUALIFIED WORKING FOR HIM YET
1 KINGS 19:1-21

1 Kings 19:12 "And after the earthquake a fire; but the LORD was not in the fire: and after the fire a still small voice."

Many times we think we have to do everything just right to have God bless us, but the scriptures certainly don't present that. David sinned greatly, yet he was the man after God's own heart. Moses failed, as did Abram, and just about every other mighty man of God. *The truth is that God hasn't had any one who was qualified working for Him yet.* It's always by God's grace that He uses any of us.

Take Elijah for example. Here he was in such despair that he asked God to kill him. He thought he was the only one left serving God when the truth was that there were thousands who were faithful to the Lord. He had led a revival just days earlier where the whole nation turned to God. Elijah was into self-pity. He was ready to quit.

The Lord spoke to Elijah in a still small voice and told him to do three things. One of those things was to anoint Elisha to take his place as prophet. That was the last thing the Lord told Elijah to do, but it was the first thing he did. As it turns out, it was the only thing he did. He never did anoint Hazel to be king over Syria or Jehu to be king over Israel. He just ignored two-thirds of the things God told him to do in an audible voice.

Was that the end of Elijah? No. I think we can safely say that was a turning point and he never did fulfill God's true potential for his life, but God still used him. Elijah is one of only two people in the Bible who never died. He was actually caught up into heaven in a whirlwind (2 Ki. 2).

Do you think that God is through with you because you've failed Him? Take courage from Elijah. Regardless of your failures, you can still walk with God in a powerful way. *(Written by Andrew Wommack)*

JUNE 24
THE RUSSIAN CONNECTION!
MARK 16:15

Mark 16:15 "And He said to them, 'Go into all the world and preach the gospel to every creature.'"

It was in 1989 that I first entered the former USSR, at a time when foreigners were not welcome in many places. On the streets of Riga, Latvia, my two companions and I were praising God as we walked along. A Latvian man, who could speak no English, heard us say, "Hallelujah!" He shouted back, "Hallelujah!"

That "chance" meeting eventually opened doors into the vast land of the former USSR which spans 13 time zones. A Bible school was started that sent students out to plant over 1,000 churches. Large meetings were held throughout the land where tens of thousands received Jesus Christ.

Rick Renner and I traveled to the former USSR in 1991, and Rick knew immediately that God was calling him to move there. In 1993 Rick and Denise Renner and their three sons, Paul, Philip and Joel, moved from Tulsa, Oklahoma to Riga, Latvia in order to reach millions through weekly TV teaching programs, literature, planting a church, and starting an association for pastors and leaders. The TV program is now being broadcast throughout Europe and the U.S.

I was reminded that when I went to Latvia for the first time, I visited the TV station in Riga and boldly proclaimed that the Gospel would be preached from that station. Now it is happening.

A report has already come back of a prayer cloth taken to a young girl who had twisted feet with extra bones. A creative miracle took place instantly! Her twisted feet became normal and X-rays showed NO extra bones! Thank you, Jesus!

One woman, now on Rick's administrative staff, recalls being at the 1991 meeting at the Jelgava Palace where Rick and I ministered. "My grandmother, 74, could not walk. She was driven 200 kilometers to the meeting. We had to carry her into the room. Dave chopped her. She got up and danced all over the stage. She is 82 today and is still dancing!" *(Written by Dave Duell)*

JUNE 25
RELEASING HIS ABILITY TO YOUR PROSPERITY
2 CORINTHIANS 5:17

2 Corinthians 5:17 "Therefore, if anyone is in Christ, he is a new creation; old things have passed away; behold all things have become new."
The more I meditate on this truth, the more excited I become. Just think of it—we have God's life in us. Notice the scriptures say that we are new creations. We are created in Christ. We are the workmanship of God. In 1 John 5:13 we read, *"These things I have written unto you . . . that you may know that you have eternal life, and that you may continue to believe in the name of the Son of God."* We have His life, His nature and His love within us. You may not feel that today. You may be feeling anger, frustration, fear or despair. These feelings don't change the eternal truth of what God has done in us. We have become partakers of His divine nature. The object of His coming is that we might have life, and have it more abundantly.
As you go through the affairs of your day, trust in His life and His nature within you. This means that no matter what questions you might have, He is your wisdom. No matter what weaknesses you might experience, He is your strength. His ability is in you. You are a carrier of His glory and life. Draw on Him today and give His love to others. *(Written by Mike Fehlauer)*

JUNE 26
YOU CAN'T CLAIM PROMISES WHILE VIOLATING PRINCIPLES
ACTS 5:1-11

Acts 5:4 "Whiles it remained, was it not thine own? and after it was sold, was it not in thine own power? why hast thou conceived this thing in thine heart? thou hast not lied unto men, but unto God."
Integrity is the key word here. In this real life account in Acts 5, of *"a certain man named Ananias, with Sapphira his wife . . . "* we see how deception and greed wrought the demise of a couple in the early church. Today, there are still people who think that they can live however they please and still be blessed. Not so. Maybe not today, maybe not tomorrow, but payday cometh. Galatians 6:7 says, *"whatsoever a man soweth, that shall he also reap."*
In our church there is a family who had just one vehicle—an old, worn-out pickup truck. They were a family of six trying to get around by fitting as many as they could in the cab, and piling some in the back. One day the husband found out that a relative had *once again* given a car to his brother, who was not even serving the Lord. I said, *once again.* Now this family was in dire need of a vehicle and could have gotten very jealous and upset about this. Instead, they decided that it was none of their business and that their own heart attitude was what was important. They chose to have a good attitude. They kept giving and believing God. Two weeks later, a man in the church called and told the man that they had been trying to get a hold of him. They had something for him. They connected and the gift they received was astounding. They were now the proud owners of a family van—clear title and all.
Learn this: you cannot operate in strife or violate any other principle of God and expect to claim His promises of blessing. I believe that if they had chosen to get offended at their relative, or their brother, that they may not have been on the receiving end of that van. Let's choose peace, to walk in love and to stay grounded in the principles of God's Word. Then nothing can stop the blessing of God from flowing in our lives. *(Written by Bob Nichols)*

JUNE 27
RESTING IN GOD
HEBREWS 4:1-3

Hebrews 4:1-3 "Let us therefore fear, lest, a promise being left us of entering into his rest, any of you should seem to come short of it. For unto us was the gospel preached, as well as unto them: but the word preached did not profit them, not being mixed with faith in them that heard it. For we which have believed do enter into rest . . . ."

Here, the writer of the book of Hebrews makes a distinction between those who did rest in God and those who did not. The people were the same and the message was the same, but one group mixed faith with what they heard while the other group did not. To our knowledge, that was the only difference between one group entering into God's rest and the other not getting to go. In a similar way, God's grace has appeared unto all men unto salvation. But only those who receive it through personal faith in God will benefit from it.

The New Testament is filled with one account after another concerning this simple principle. God may see fit at times to overrule our faithlessness or our unbelief and grant us His help. But from the information that we have available to us through the Scriptures, this action would be more the exception than the rule.

Faith is an inner assurance that the things we hope for actually exist, and the conviction that they are already ours even though we cannot see them. It's not the greatness of my faith that moves mountains, but my faith in the greatness of God. Oral Roberts once said, "The important thing is not the size of your faith—it is the One behind your faith—God Himself." *(Written by Marshall Townsley)*

JUNE 28
ARE YOU WORRIED?
MATTHEW 6:25-28

Matthew 6:25-28 "Take no thought (don't worry) for your life, what ye shall eat, or what ye shall drink, nor yet for the body what ye shall put on . . . Behold the fouls of the air . . . Consider the lilies of the field . . . ."

When Jesus told us not to worry about the necessities of life, He gave us two examples. Jesus was sitting on a mountain with His disciples and said, "behold . . . consider." He said this because birds were overhead and lilies surrounded them. Their object lesson was in front of their eyes.

Do birds worry? How about flowers, do they worry? For both the answer is NO. The birds do not read the paper, watch the news, or look for stock market results. The needs of the birds are always met. Do you ever hear birds flying through the air saying, "I wonder if I will have enough to eat today?" The birds never knew we had a Great Depression. Only people jump out of windows in fear and panic of what is coming.

Flowers are always dressed nice. They do not wait for the new styles, or become concerned they are wearing last season's clothes. God provides for them and they do not even have a job. Neither birds or flowers live in our daily world. Well, as Christians, we are in the world but not of it. We do not live in this world either.

To worry about your food is to put yourself below the level of a bird. To worry about clothing is to put yourself below the level of a flower. People are created superior to the animals and plants. Jesus watches over nature, but Jesus did not die for birds or flowers. He went to the cross for people. He loves nature, but He loves us more.

God will supply for us according to His riches in glory. God's supply for us is not according to Wall Street or the First National Bank. The stock averages can go up and down. But the economy of heaven will never fail. *(Written by Bob Yandian)*

JUNE 29
DON'T LOOK BACK PART 1
HEBREWS 11:1-15

Hebrews 11:15 "And truly, if they had been mindful of that country from whence they came out, they might have had opportunity to have returned."
This verse is saying if Abraham and Sarah had been mindful of the country they left, they would have been tempted to return. However, since they weren't mindful of that country, they weren't even tempted to return. What a revelation! Their temptation was linked to their thoughts. You can't be tempted with something you don't think about; therefore, control your thinking and you can control temptation. Any of us could be powerful men or women of God if we could stop being tempted. We can do just that by controlling our thinking.

Many people have missed this simple truth. They try and control their actions but they don't realize that actions are a direct result of the way they think. They allow themselves the luxury of thinking things they shouldn't, and then when temptation comes they struggle to remain faithful to God. Often they wonder why they are so tempted. It's because of their thoughts.

God has called all of us to leave things behind. It may not be a country. It might be a lifestyle or friends. Maybe there are habits or hobbies the Lord has asked you to lay down. The secret to walking away from them, is not dwelling on what you've left behind. Thinking "what if . . . " is a faith killer. We don't need to be looking back; we need to look forward at the things God has promised us.

Don't be mindful of what you've left behind. Take a look ahead through faith at what God is calling you to. You'll find that your positive thoughts will bring you hope instead of temptation. *(Written by Andrew Wommack)*

JUNE 30
YOU HAVE TO REPLACE THOUGHTS PART 2
HEBREWS 11:1-16

Hebrews 11:16 "But now they desire a better country . . . . "
Did you know that you can't get rid of negative thoughts by rebuking them? You have to replace unwanted thoughts with new thoughts.

Think of an apple. Now quit thinking of an apple. I rebuke thoughts of an apple. Do not think of an apple in Jesus' name. Refuse to think about apples. Are you still thinking about apples? Of course you are. In that method of trying to control your thoughts, you are mentioning and continuing to focus on apples. That's not the way to get rid of thoughts.

Instead, think about strawberries. See a beautiful plump red strawberry. Think how sweet it would taste. Imagine a whole strawberry patch with all the delicious berries just begging to be picked. Or think about bananas. See a whole bunch of them and imagine going to some tropical island and picking them yourself. Wouldn't that be great?

If you continue that line of thought, in just a short time, you will have lost the thoughts about apples. You can only get rid of thoughts by replacing them with other thoughts.

Sometimes our efforts to resist negative or sinful thoughts actually strengthen their hold on us. The better way is to replace them with God thoughts. God thoughts come from His Word. As we read God's Word, His thoughts begin to control our thinking and soon the negative thoughts are gone.

Abraham found something better to think about than what he left behind. Don't you have something better to think about today? *(Written by Andrew Wommack)*

JULY 1
GOD WITH US
MATTHEW 1:23

Matthew 1:23 "'Behold, the virgin shall be with child, and bear a Son, and they shall call His name Immanuel,' which is translated, 'God with us.'"

Isaiah and Matthew both echo the greeting, "Behold a virgin shall be with child and shall bring forth a Son, and they shall call His name Immanuel . . . which being interpreted is "God with us."

What does it mean? Not since the Garden of Eden had God been with man like He wanted. The birth and ministry of Christ began a new relationship between God and man. Once again shall the God of all the earth be with His man and He also shall be in Him.

Jesus' birth signified a new beginning for God's man. A new creation was to enter the earth, all God and all man. God put on skin, an earth suit. Jesus' birth was the prototype, the example, the foreshadowing of what was to come—a new species of being that never before existed.

The birth of Christ is a facsimile of the new birth. The new birth is unspoiled and virgin in nature. The new birth is only by the Holy Spirit. And the new birth produces a new creature. God with us and in us. Paul said that he had Christ in him and the life He now lived, he lived by the faith of the Son of God, not faith in the Son of God. Of course we also have faith in the Son of God.

We see a man with God in him. A man who had faith on the inside of him. A man who had new insight into his divine inheritance. One who was born of faith and righteousness and could stand before God as though sin never touched him, without sin, guilt, or inferiority.

Two children were busy at the kitchen sink talking. Their mother had gone away for a few days and had left them with their father. The little girl asked her not-so-much older brother, "What if Mom never comes back?" "Elizabeth!" answered her brother, "I know she's coming back; she left some of her most valuable stuff here—US!"

We know Jesus is coming back for us—His most valuable possession. *(Written by Dave Duell)*

JULY 2
HIS NAME BRINGS ABUNDANCE
JOHN 14:13-14

John 14:13-14 "Whatever you ask in my name, that I will do, that the Father may be glorified in the Son. If you ask anything in my name, I will do it: "

I am sure that you know these scriptures. I am sure that you have quoted them more than once. This is not prayer. It is not a petition or request. It is commanding the forces of darkness to recognize the authority already established by Jesus through His name. It is the way Peter used His name when he approached the lame man at the gate Beautiful. That beautiful, wonderful name is yours. You may not have taken advantage of it. You may have been timid in using it, but Jesus has given you the power of attorney to use His name against the works of Satan. Matthew 28:18-19 says, *"All authority has been given to me in heaven and on earth. Go therefore and make disciples of all nations. . . ."*

This belongs to you today. Not only do you have authority over the powers of darkness, but you also have His authority to bring others into His kingdom. You can release this authority today through His name. When sickness attacks your home, His name drives out sickness and disease. When poverty threatens your household, His name drives out the spirit of poverty. Fear has no place, no authority over His name. Cancer must bow to His name. Depression must surrender to His name. *(Written by Mike Fehlauer)*

JULY 3
NO FARMER EVER HARVESTED WHAT HE INTENDED TO SOW
ECCLESIASTES 11:4

Ecclesiastes 11:4 "He that observeth the wind shall not sow; and he that regardeth the clouds shall not reap."

Excuses. It is often said that the road to hell is paved with good intentions. But good intentions never paid a bill, and they certainly never blessed anyone. No farmer has ever reaped a harvest on seed that he intended to sow. Can you imagine a farmer saying, "Nope, I don't believe I'll go out and plant this corn today. It looks like it might rain a bit and I sure don't want to get my new John Deere wet." So he tosses the seed in a barn someplace. Come harvest time, what do you think that farmer will find in his fields? Nothing. If you don't plant seed, you cannot expect a harvest.

Ecclesiastes 11:6 says, *"In the morning sow thy seed, and in the evening withhold not thine hand: for thou knowest not whether shall prosper, either this or that, or whether they both shall be alike good."* It is our job to sow seed. Whenever you have the opportunity, whenever you can, put some seed in good ground. If you want to prosper, don't just scatter your seed to the wind, and don't hoard it. Sow it in faith believing. If you sit on your sack of seed the only thing you will get is a seed sack sofa! *(Written by Bob Nichols)*

JULY 4
STRONGHOLDS IN THE SOUL (MIND)
2 CORINTHIANS 10:4-5

2 Corinthians 10:4-5 "For the weapons of our warfare are not carnal but mighty in God for pulling down strongholds."

Your soul will never prosper if it is filled with strongholds. Strongholds are any thoughts that oppose God's will and Word. Strongholds in your mind will cause oppression, mental confusion and a sense of unworthiness. Strongholds are wrong thought patterns that allow the enemy access to you.

Your mind will lie to you. It will speak false allegations to you in the first person and say, "I am a failure." Or, "I am afraid of failure." Notice your mind does not say, "You are . . . . " It wants you to believe that these wrong thoughts are true. Did you know that fear of failure is the number one immobilizer of people?

These faulty imaginations and arguments in your mind can destroy you. They are "high things" that exalt themselves against the knowledge of God. That is called pride. When you give into thoughts that put you down and are the opposite of what the Word says, you are in pride. You may think it is being humble, but it is actually being stupid.

To be humble is to believe what God says about you. It is humility to accept His assessment even when it doesn't line up with your thoughts. That is why it says in verse five to bring *"every thought into captivity to the obedience of Christ."* Cast down those arguments in your mind. Forcefully tell your mind what to think. Pull down those strongholds—overthrow, demolish, destroy and put them to an end.

Live in the freedom you rightfully possess in Jesus. *(Written by Bonnie Duell)*

JULY 5
ANSWERS AND PROBLEMS
1 CORINTHIANS 10:13

1 Corinthians 10:13 "God is faithful, who will not allow you to be tempted above what you are able; but with the temptation will also make the way to escape . . . ."

Ask yourself a question: Who was here first, God or Satan? The answer is God. Ask yourself another question: Is God your problem or is He your answer? God is your answer. Satan is your problem. If God is your answer and He was here before Satan, then your answers were here before your problems existed.

There is not a problem you can experience that can take God by surprise. In fact, God planned each answer, knowing ahead of time what the problem would be. Problems may take *us* by surprise, but never God. God was not taken by surprise when Lucifer tried to overtake heaven's throne. God had an answer prepared. When Adam and Eve sinned, do you think God looked at Jesus or the Holy Spirit and asked, "What do we do now?" Do you think either One looked back at the Father and said, "We don't know. We did not know this was going to happen"? No! God's Word tells us that Jesus was the Lamb slain before the foundation of the world. God had an answer prepared for every problem creation could face before creation existed.

This verse tells us God has made a way of escape. You can enter each problem in thanksgiving and praise, knowing the way of escape was created before the problem existed. It is next to blasphemy to think you can face a problem that God has not planned for and cannot deliver you from. If God planned for, and created an answer for the biggest problem in your life—your salvation, then how could He possibly fail now in the smaller areas of your life such as your health, finances, family or your happiness? *(Written by Bob Yandian)*

JULY 6
HOW DETERMINED ARE YOU? PART 1
MARK 5:25-34

Mark 5:27 "When she had heard of Jesus, came in the press behind, and touched his garment."

One of the ingredients of faith is determination which is defined as "the power to make choices, set goals, and to act upon them firmly in spite of opposition or difficulties." This woman was determined. She had already spent years and all her money on doctors. Yet nothing had helped. She was actually worse. Most people would have just given up by then, but this was one determined lady. She heard of Jesus and knew that she would get her healing through Him. She found Him but there was another obstacle: A multitude thronged Him.

The Greek word for "throng" that was used in verse 31 means "to compress, i.e. crowd on all sides." How would this frail sickly woman ever make it through the crowd? On top of all this, the woman's issue of blood made her unclean. She was not supposed to be in public because she would defile them. If someone recognized her and revealed her uncleanliness, Jewish law allowed the crowd to stone her to death. She would not be deterred.

She crawled her way through the crowd and touched the hem of Jesus' garment. That's the only way she could have done it. You can't just bend over and touch the hem of a garment in a throng of people. She was on her hands and knees. This woman would have done anything to get her healing.

Most people would not do what this lady did. They wouldn't go to all that trouble. They wouldn't put their lives in jeopardy by being in a crowd that might stone them. They wouldn't get on their hands and knees and crawl through a throng of people. And they probably wouldn't get healed either. Most people lack her type of determination.

What stands between you and what you need from the Lord? Make sure that it is not your lack of determination. *(Written by Andrew Wommack)*

JULY 7
THE LAWS OF FAITH PART 2
MARK 5:25-34

Mark 5:30 "And Jesus, immediately knowing in himself that virtue had gone out of him, turned him about in the press, and said, Who touched my clothes?"

Was it possible that Jesus really didn't know who touched Him? Certainly it was. Jesus was God manifest in the flesh but His physical mind had to grow in wisdom (Lk. 2:52). That means that Jesus had limitations to His physical mind just as we do. It was through His Spirit that He was able to draw on the mind of God just as we are. When the woman didn't come forward on her own, Jesus perceived who she was (Lk. 8:47), but this happened after she was healed.

The significance of this is that Jesus didn't size this woman up before virtue went out of Him to heal her. That's the way most people feel God does things. They bring their requests before the Lord and He evaluates them on whether they have enough faith or holiness and so forth. If they pass the test, God heals them. If they don't, their requests get denied. That's not accurate.

God's power is governed by laws. He doesn't make a case by case determination of who receives what. He has provided all that we need and if we put His laws into motion, then His power flows. That's what this woman did.

This woman was determined (Lk. 11:5-13; 18:1-8). She also spoke her faith by saying, "*If I may but touch his clothes, I shall be whole*" (Mk. 11:23-24). She acted on her faith and the power of God flowed (Jas. 2:17).

If you grab a live electrical wire, the electric company doesn't send a special jolt of electricity out to shock you. No! There are laws that make that electricity flow. It's not personal. Likewise, there are laws that govern the flow of God's power. Learn what they are and start receiving from God today. *(Written by Andrew Wommack)*

JULY 8
CHILDREN OF THE RESURRECTION PART 1
PHILIPPIANS 3:10

Philippians 3:10 "That I may know Him and the power of His resurrection, and the fellowship of His sufferings, being conformed to His death."

We understand that the resurrection is the very heartbeat of Christianity, the central theme of the new covenant. The resurrection of Jesus Christ is what takes Christianity out of the realm of religion and philosophy and makes it a living reality in our lives.

The birth of a new race of people took place on that day. A New Covenant came forth. Fellowship with the heavenly Father came into being just like Adam had before he sinned. God received His family back. Jesus dealt with sin and the law. It was one of the greatest days on earth.

Crucifixion is an act, but resurrection is a way of life. Jesus' resurrection was for our benefit. It was not just a one-time historical act, but a daily life-changing reality. Paul was saying that he wanted to be more than just a Christian. He wanted to walk in the power and reality of the resurrected Christ. I do too!

Resurrection life is in progress at this very moment in the lives of millions of believers around the world. We have nothing to fear. We are stronger than anything hell can manufacture. Faith in the Word and faith in the Spirit will always put us over the top and raise us up in power and authority.

Faith is voice activated. Even though we are sometimes overwhelmed, we still have the victory. Faith never recognizes defeat. Faith keeps us spiritually alive. Faith is resurrection life in action. Faith can definitely change the unchangeable. We are children of the Resurrection! *(Written by Dave Duell)*

JULY 9
CHILDREN OF THE RESURRECTION PART 2
JOHN 11:25

John 11:25 "I am the resurrection and the life, he that believeth in me though he were dead, yet shall he live."

The Captain of our salvation has already declared, *"I am the resurrection and the life, he that believeth in me though he were dead, yet shall he live"* (John 11:25). I am ruled by the abundance of God. We do not know how to stay down, for we have not inherited a quitting spirit. We know that without Jesus, life is a hopeless end, but *with* Jesus' life, is endless hope. We abide in His life-giving presence. Because He lives, we live.

It is certain that when Adam lost, we lost, and it is just as certain that when Jesus won, we won. When He arose out of the grave, we arose triumphantly with Him and in Him. When He ascended upon high, far above principalities and powers, we ascended with Him and in Him (Ephesians 2:6).

We share His position of rest, victory and authority—right now! We are free from condemnation—right now. We are in Him . . . and in Him is life, renewing life, restoring life. So through the precious Blood of Jesus, we have a new beginning every day.

Jesus left this spiritual position of authority in this world, ascended to heaven, and told us to occupy until He comes. We have been commanded by God to assume the reins, to take over where Jesus left off and to do it all for His glory. We are so blessed to be linked to the source of all life and all love. We are actually a part of Him. We are in Christ and He is in us.

God has now given us everything we need in life. The way was made for us to receive the mighty Holy Spirit. We are blessed above all creatures. We are children of the Resurrection! *(Written by Dave Duell)*

JULY 10
HIS LIVING WORD ABIDES IN YOU
COLOSSIANS 3:16

Colossians 3:16 "Let the word of Christ dwell in you richly . . . . "

What does God's Word accomplish in us? What is it working? It is admonishing us. It is training and teaching us. At times it corrects as it builds faith and love in our spirits. In Acts 20:32 the Apostle Paul says, *"Now brethren, I commend you to God, and to the word of His grace, which is able to build you up, and give you an inheritance among those who are sanctified."*

The Word of God makes you and me know of our inheritance. It is His Word that builds us up in Him. Through the Word, the relationship of abundance and prosperity is unveiled to our souls. The Word of Christ healed the servant. Jesus said that His words are spirit and they are life. They carry His life to every area of our lives. It was the Word of God that framed the worlds and sustains the laws of the universe. It is His Word that stands forever.

This same powerful "Word" is living in you. We have the privilege of speaking His Word. His Word on your lips creates miracles and defeats demons. You will have the opportunity to speak the words of defeat today or His Word of life and victory. Make up your mind now, that no matter what happens, you will speak His life-giving, creative and sustaining Word. *(Written by Mike Fehlauer)*

JULY 11
TITHING IS A PRINCIPLE OF PUTTING GOD FIRST
DEUTERONOMY 14:22

Deuteronomy 14:22 "Thou shalt truly tithe all the increase of thy seed, that the field bringeth forth year by year."
Many people read about tithing and use the excuse, "Yeah, but that was Old Testament stuff." Jesus said Himself in Luke 11:42, *"But woe unto you, Pharisees! for ye tithe mint and rue and all manner of herbs, and pass over judgment and the love of God: these ought ye to have done, and not to leave the other undone."* He wasn't saying that the New Testament was coming and that nobody should tithe anymore. Nothing could be further from the truth. It is a spiritual principle. He specifically said, *"these ought ye to have done."* When we put God first, all of our needs will be met. Matthew 6:33, *"But seek ye first the kingdom of God, and his righteousness; and all these things shall be added unto you."* I heard someone say, "No man is really consecrated until his money is dedicated."

The tithe was not founded so that God could get our money or as a payoff to get something out of God that He didn't want to give us. It was designed as a vehicle to get the blessings of God to us so that we could be blessed. When we tithe, we are showing the world, the devil, God, and even ourselves, that God is first in our lives—in every aspect. When you are faithful in tithing, it shows that you have victory over greed. It shows that you have understanding of spiritual things.

The tithe is God's. It is holy to Him, and it belongs to Him. It is only a starting point. When we can, we should be faithful to give above and beyond that in offerings, but the tithe is the start. If you want your business to be successful, make faithful tithing your business! *(Written by Bob Nichols)*

JULY 12
OUR GOD IS MORE THAN ENOUGH
ROMANS 5:20

Romans 5:20 "Where sin abounded, grace did much more abound."
This word "abound" means not only to exist in abundance, but carries with it the idea that this abundance is more than enough. That grace exists in superfluity; that it is over and above. So the literal translation of this verse would read, "Where sin existed in abundance, grace was in superabundance, and then some more added on top of that."

The Amplified Bible reads this way, *"But where sin increased and abounded, grace (God's unmerited favor) has surpassed it and increased the more and superabounded."*

There is enough, no, more than enough grace in God's heart of love to save and keep saved for time and eternity, every sinner who has ever lived or ever will live, and then enough left over to save a million more universes, were there such, and then some more.

There is enough grace available to give every saint constant victory over sin, and then some more. There is enough grace to meet and overcome all the sorrows, heartaches, difficulties, temptations, testings, and the trials of human existence—and more added to that. God's salvation is an oversized salvation. It is shockproof, strain proof, unbreakable and all-sufficient. His grace is equal to every emergency and 911 call. Grace will be on the scene long before the ambulance ever gets to your home and will be more than enough to meet the need.

What the doctor can't do, grace can. What the lawyer can't figure out, grace can. When your money doesn't go far enough—thank God grace never runs out! What your husband or wife can't provide for you—grace can. Grace will never disappoint. *(Written by Marshall Townsley)*

JULY 13
ARE YOU GOING TO GET OUT AND PUSH?
2 THESSALONIANS 1:7

2 Thessalonians 1:7 "And to you who are troubled, rest with us . . . . "

According to this verse, rest is not something that drops on you from heaven. It does not come by a sovereign decision of the Holy Spirit. It is something you decide to do in times of trouble. Rest is a choice.

Think about this: What good does it do to worry? Jesus told us that worrying about the problems of life will not add one cubit to our stature (Mt. 6:27). You do not increase yourself, you actually chip away at your life and cut it short. Peter told us to cast the whole of our care (worry) on the Lord (1 Pet. 5:7). Many years ago, I was flying to Michigan for a church meeting. My flight went through Dallas/Fort Worth and our plane was sitting on the taxi way preparing to take off for Detroit when the pilot announced we were sitting next to a new Concorde supersonic jet. Everyone looked out the window because this was the newest, state of the art aircraft. Our pilot told us that in the same amount of time it would take us to fly to Detroit, the Concorde could fly from Dallas to Paris.

While flying to Detroit, I could not get the Concorde off my mind. I was not happy; I was angry. Why wouldn't our government allow our aircraft companies to make a supersonic aircraft? After all, we *invented* the airplane. While we were flying at 35,000 feet, the Concorde was flying at 61,000 feet. Why couldn't the plane we were in fly faster? What was wrong with our country for letting the Europeans create this aircraft?

Then the Lord said to me, "What are you going to do, get out and push?" I had to laugh at myself. How useless it is to worry about something I can do nothing about. I might as well sit back and enjoy the ride.

You cannot hurry the plan of God by worrying about anything. Why not sit back, enjoy the ride and rest in the promises of God? *(Written by Bob Yandian)*

JULY 14
FINANCIAL PROSPERITY IS PART OF CHRIST'S ATONEMENT
2 CORINTHIANS 8:1-15

2 Corinthians 8:9 "For ye know the grace of our Lord Jesus Christ, that, though he was rich, yet for your sakes he became poor, that ye through his poverty might be rich."

This verse couldn't be any clearer. It is a part of Christ's atonement for us to be financially rich. Yet many Christians persist in their belief that God delights in poverty for His children. That is not true.

The way many people have gotten around the obvious truth of this verse is to say that Jesus came to make us rich spiritually, not financially. But the whole context of this verse deals with money. Jesus died to produce financial prosperity for us. He would no more make us poor than He would make us sin. He died to free us from both sin and poverty. We need to get the same attitude towards poverty that we have towards sin.

There is no doubt that many people have learned lessons as the result of their sins. People have been broken and come to the end of themselves because of their own disobedience. But does that mean God led them into sin? Did God want them to commit adultery so they could learn the value of the mate God had given them? Certainly not.

Likewise, people can learn things through poverty. They can learn the value of things that money can't buy. But poverty itself is a killer. We should seek to overcome poverty the same way we seek to overcome sin. God put poverty in the same category as sin and redeemed us from it. We should do the same. Those who don't take advantage of the prosperity God has provided are not taking advantage of the atonement of Christ in its entirety. *(Written by Andrew Wommack)*

JULY 15
PRESS ON
PHILIPPIANS 3:12

Philippians 3:12 "I press on, that I may lay hold of that for which Christ Jesus has also laid hold of me."

Every moment you spend thinking about the past is a moment lost to your future. We can't do one thing about the past, but we must pursue what God has for us to do.

Paul said, *"I press on, that I may lay hold of that for which Christ Jesus has also laid hold of me"* (Philippians 3:12). Paul knew that he had a destiny.

His destiny was described for him by Jesus in Acts 26:16 where Jesus said to him, *"I have appeared to you for this purpose, to make you a minister and a witness both of the things which you have seen and of the things which I will yet reveal to you."*

Did Paul fulfill his destiny? Absolutely. Are you fulfilling your destiny? Are you pressing on, ministering and witnessing all that Jesus has shown you? Your calling and destiny is similar to Paul's, to open people's eyes, *"in order to turn them from darkness to light, and from the power of Satan to God . . . . "* (Acts 26:18).

We are determined to press on. I was in a meeting when the Holy Spirit called out to me in a loud voice, "Don't you dare give up, if you don't pursue it the people won't get it." I believe that our decisions affect the lives of thousands of people. As for me, my decisions will affect the lives of millions of people.

Whatever desires God has placed in your heart are His specific destiny and calling on your life. Continue to say "yes" to Him, be totally committed to your call to spread the gospel, and expect Him to bring it to pass. *"I press toward the mark for the prize of the high calling of God in Christ Jesus"* (Philippians 3:14).

God usually calls us to do what we think we cannot do, so He receives the glory. You will never feel equipped with what He has called you to do. We have to depend on His anointing to complete the task every time. We have a God of faith. Just think, He called you and me and we have to have faith in His faith. *(Written by Dave Duell)*

JULY 16
ABUNDANCE COMES FROM WITHIN
COLOSSIANS 1:27

Colossians 1:27 "To them God willed to make known what are the riches of the glory of this mystery among the Gentiles: which is Christ in you, the hope of glory."

You have everything you need to live in God's victory and abundance. It is in you. *He* abides in you. Some of you may be carrying inside of you a great author. An anointed singer. A successful businessman. Each one has gifts and callings from God. These are to further His kingdom and bring His prosperity to our lives. Yet, for many, these gifts go undeveloped. Hidden treasures of personal accomplishments and wealth. I want to encourage you to first believe that you have a purpose—a reason for being here. A calling. Then I want to challenge you to find out what your purpose is. Discover the untouched treasures that have been stored away inside you. It is going to require drive. Personal discipline. It will mean sacrifice. Nothing worthwhile comes easy.

You have within you, given to you by God, that blueprint for success. Only you can take those blueprints and build them into the buildings of God's purposes for your life. Put yourself on a mental diet—not one of idle dreams and fantasies. I am talking about real mental work. Renew your mind to His Word. Attack thoughts of defeat and resignation, of mediocrity. Expect the best. Think big, plan big, believe big and pray big. It is in you, but only you can bring it out. *(Written by Mike Fehlauer)*

JULY 17
EVERY NEED IS MET IN THE PRESENCE OF GOD
PHILIPPIANS 4:19

Philippians 4:19 "But my God shall supply all your need according to his riches in glory by Christ Jesus."

No matter what need a person has, no matter what emergency occurs, no matter what the problem, God is the answer. I cannot tell you how many times I was faced with seemingly impossible situations and I would get out my prayer towel and get down on my face before the Lord. I would cry out to God, sometimes all night, but when I got up, I knew in my spirit that I had my answer. Listen, God doesn't just make a way where there *seems* to be no way; God makes a way where there *is* no way. Nothing is impossible with God.

The Bible tells us in Ephesians 1:18, *"The eyes of your understanding being enlightened; that ye may know what is the hope of his calling, and what the riches of the glory of his inheritance in the saints."* Also, Ephesians 3:16 says, *"That he would grant you, according to the riches of his glory, to be strengthened with might by his Spirit in the inner man."* Colossians 1:27, *"To whom God would make known what is the riches of the glory of this mystery among the Gentiles; which is Christ in you, the hope of glory" (emphasis added).* The glory is the manifest presence of God. He wants us to know that when we enter into His glory, all the riches of heaven are there to meet our needs.

I have seen people who have struggled and struggled with something with seemingly no results. I've seen those same people come, sit in the glory of God, and in five minutes God took care of what was impossible for years! Oh, child of God, if you have a need, get into His presence. Look up! Keep your eyes focused on Jesus. Worship Him and you will see that every need is met in the presence of God. *(Written by Bob Nichols)*

JULY 18
FEAR HAS TORMENT
I JOHN 4:18

I John 4:18 "There is no fear in love; but perfect love casts out fear, because fear involves torment . . . . "

God desires that you live in peace in your relationship with Him which will cause your soul to prosper. When you experience any fear in your relationship with Him, realize that it is not God condemning you. Fear denotes that which causes flight; hence, fear, terror, dread. Our English word "phobia" is a transliteration of the Greek word for fear, "phobos."

I have lived much of my life with torment inside because of fear. This came from wrong teaching about God. I was always feeling condemned, thinking that God was displeased with me, thinking that I wasn't doing enough for Him. How wonderful to be able to renew my mind to the truth that God loves me and accepts me. The torment has gone and peaceful rest has come.

Another fear many people have is the fear of speaking publicly. Many will say, "I am too shy." No, you are selfish. God has given you things to say to bless others in the Body. We taught our children from an early age that they would have the privilege of giving to others that which God had given to them. They may not have appreciated this at the time, but today all four of our daughters can speak before any size audience. Remember this, shyness is not a fruit of the Spirit. It should have no place in you.

Dwell on God's perfect love for you and watch fear and its torment flee! *(Written by Bonnie Duell)*

JULY 19
PRESSURE EXPOSED THE CRACK
ROMANS 5:3

Romans 5:3 "We glory in tribulations . . . knowing that tribulation works patience."

The Greek word for "works" in this verse means, something on the inside working itself to the outside. When we trust God, tribulation causes patience, which is already inside us, to be worked to the outside. Tribulation works out patience. This is why we can glory, or rejoice, in tribulations. We know that more than receiving an answer to a problem, we are developing our godly character. Long before patience is brought forth in us, the pressure of circumstances brings much more to the surface. A friend of mine told me a story about a summer job he had between years in college. He worked on the off-shore oil rigs in Louisiana. Being a newcomer and a temporary employee, he had the jobs not too many others would take. One of them was testing oil pipe before it was put in use. The oil company did not fully trust the manufacturer and would test each piece of pipe before putting it below the water in the gulf to handle great amounts of oil flow. To test whether the pipe would handle the oil pressure, my friend would pump in water under great pressure to see if any hidden flaws or cracks were overlooked in production.

Often, when the pressure would reach a few hundred pounds per square inch, a small stream of water would shoot from a section of the pipe. My friend would turn down the pressure, weld the crack and file it smooth. One day, when a stream of water shot from a small crack in a pipe, the Lord spoke to my friend and said, "The pressure did not create the crack, it revealed it."

We often blame Satan for our anger, bitterness or temper flare ups. The pressure did not create the character flaw, it revealed what was already in us. We need to fix the crack, repent, receive forgiveness, and then patience will develop. *(Written by Bob Yandian)*

JULY 20
HOW DO YOU FEEL ABOUT MONEY?
1 TIMOTHY 6:1-11

1 Timothy 6:10 "For the love of money is the root of all evil: which while some coveted after, they have erred from the faith, and pierced themselves through with many sorrows."

Money is not the root of all evil. It's the love of money that is the root of all evil. Many people who have very little money have a greater love and lust for money than people who have lots of it. The amount of money one has is not the issue. It's the attitude one has towards money that Paul is warning against.

If money itself was evil, then we would all be in trouble because we all have to have money to exist. And having just enough evil to survive wouldn't be any better than having a lot of evil. Money is not evil and those who have less money aren't any more holy than those who are rich. Money is amoral. That is, it is neither good nor bad. It's the person's attitude who has the money that determines how the power of money is used—for either good or bad. A $20 bill can be a blessing or a bribe. The money can't determine that. It's the holder of the money that directs its power.

Money is like food. We have to eat to exist. But an abnormal desire to eat will kill us. So will an abnormal love for money and what it can produce. But on the other extreme, a hatred for food will also lead to death. It takes a certain amount of food to keep us healthy and alive. It also takes a certain amount of money to keep us going and it takes even more money to allow us to be the blessings God wants us to be. There is a right amount of food for each of us and there is a right amount of money also.

Do you have enough money to do all the Lord wants you to do? If not, increase your hope today and get ready to prosper. *(Written by Andrew Wommack)*

JULY 21
MIND YOUR HEAD
PHILIPPIANS 2:5

Philippians 2:5 "Let this mind (attitude) be in you which was also in Christ Jesus."
I was in a building in England and as I was walking downstairs I saw the sign "Mind your Head." I thought this would be a title for a sermon. We are what we think and believe. We can be born again and have a messed up mind. Our hearts are perfect, but we can have a head problem. Our theology, what we believe will determine everything we will receive in life.

We are either the masters or victims of our attitudes. It is a matter of personal choice. Who we are today is the result of choices made yesterday. Tomorrow we will become what we choose today.

There is a power that is in negative thinking. Why is it so hard for us to take the Bible at face value in the areas of healing, prosperity and deliverance? Why do we have so much trouble accepting that His promises written in the Bible are for us!

The answer is negativism. It is all around us and affects our faith. We are programmed from childhood to think negatively, to expect bad instead of good. As a result, we limit ourselves to what we can accomplish in life. How easy it is to fall into the trap of confessing the Word with our mouths but wavering in our hearts. Negativism attacks and ultimately destroys our faith and hope until our dreams are abandoned in an atmosphere of frustration and despair.

I grew up with negative thinking in my family. Even at a early age I knew it was wrong and I was not going to speak like that, so I became one of the most positive people that I know. Words have so much power in them for good and evil. It was the Holy Spirit that came up with the confession message. We just have to understand what He meant. I believe the correct way to confess the Word is this way. I don't confess the Word to get something from God, I confess the Word because I already have it. Second Peter 1:3 says, *"as His divine power has given us all things that pertain to life and godliness, through the knowledge of Him who called us by glory and virtue."* (Written by Dave Duell)

JULY 22
BELIEVE IN WHAT HE HAS PUT IN YOU
COLOSSIANS 1:27

Colossians 1:27 *"To them God willed to make known what are the riches of the glory of this mystery among the Gentiles: which is Christ in you, the hope of glory."*
Everyone has a gold mine of untapped potential in him. Everyone has God's kind of success hidden away in his soul. No man is a failure. You have heard of the old saying, "God doesn't make junk," well, He doesn't make failures either. The difference between those who struggle through life, and those who conquer life is very small. The difference is that the successful ones discover the key that unlocks their God-given potential. They dared to believe. They accepted their value. They had a sense of destiny—of purpose.

I read a story about a father who was dying. He had two sons. The two boys had always felt that the father had gold hidden away somewhere on their farm land. The father had always been sickly, so he had never developed his farm land. In the back of the house there were ten acres of stump land. This is where the boys suspected the father had hidden the gold. As the father was dying, he said over and over again, "The stump lot, the stump lot." These were his last words.

After the funeral, the boys began to tear up the stump lot. They removed every stump and turned over every piece of dirt in those ten acres. They never found the gold. But after they had finished, they saw that the land was in such good condition, they decided to plant corn. Come harvest time, they had the richest crop of corn they had ever seen. You have a stump lot in you. Only you can farm the land that can bring God's harvest in your life. (Written by Mike Fehlauer)

JULY 23
JESUS HAS GIVEN US A BLANK CHECK
JOHN 16:23-24

John 16:23-24 "And in that day ye shall ask me nothing. Verily, verily, I say unto you, Whatsoever ye shall ask the Father in my name, he will give it you. Hitherto have ye asked nothing in my name: ask, and ye shall receive, that your joy may be full."

Many believers have a poverty mentality. The Bible says in 2 Corinthians 8:9, *"For ye know the grace of our Lord Jesus Christ, that, though he was rich, yet for your sakes he became poor, that ye through his poverty might be rich."* Some would say, "Well, I don't think Jesus would wear fancy clothes like that." No? Even Jesus wore clothes that were so nice that the guards wanted them. His coat was the best available at the time because, *"the coat was without seam, woven from the top throughout. They said therefore among themselves, Let us not rend it, but cast lots for it, whose it shall be . . . . "* (John 19:23-24)

Jesus told us to ask. Now, if what you want is not in line with God's Word, you have no business asking for it. God will not give you something out of selfish motivation or greed. He will not answer a prayer that involves manipulating the will of someone else—that is witchcraft. But, 1 John 5:14-15 says, *"And this is the confidence that we have in him, that, if we ask any thing according to his will, he heareth us: And if we know that he hear us, whatsoever we ask, we know that we have the petitions that we desired of him."* Hallelujah!

Jesus has given us a blank check. All we have do is to sign it. I don't have to live on "Poverty Lane" or "Barely Get By Street." When I want something in line with God's Word, I'll sign my blank check on "Abundant Blessing Boulevard" by asking the Father in Jesus' name, in faith believing, and I know that I will have the petition that I desire of Him! *(Written by Bob Nichols)*

JULY 24
CHEERFUL ENDURANCE
HEBREWS 10:36

Hebrews 10:36 "For ye have need of patience, that, after ye have done the will of God, ye might receive the promise."

Answered prayer often requires waiting, while trusting God often means dealing with unanswered questions. Patience is developed as we cling to God with our faith while meeting with resistance. Now, the source of patience is not tribulation, but God Himself and the grace He gives. I was taught growing up that if you asked God for patience that He would give you tribulation. But the Bible doesn't teach that. It's just another religious idea that we need to forget. When we hold true to our faith under difficult or opposing conditions, then our patience is developed, but tribulation cannot give birth to patience.

One of the greatest mistakes any of us can make as believers is to take something that God has promised and try to rush ahead of Him by attempting to bring it to pass in our own ability. The end result will almost always be wasted time and effort, at a minimum, or missing God's will altogether.

This is none more obvious than when Sarai came up with the idea to give her handmaiden, Hagar, to Abram to make a baby with. Abram consented to Sarai's wishes and Hagar bore them a child by the name of Ishmael. But Ishmael was not to be the heir of promise. He represented Abram and Sarai's best efforts but was not accepted by God. He grew up to be a man whose life was filled with and followed by strife, contention, and war.

Our best efforts and intentions seldom contribute to what God really wants done. They can complicate things seriously. Long-term consequences can be devastating. We need grace to overcome the weakness of our flesh. *(Written by Marshall Townsley)*

JULY 25
AN ATTITUDE OF WILLINGNESS
EXODUS 35:29

Exodus 35:29 "The children of Israel brought a willing offering unto the LORD, every man and woman, whose heart made them willing to bring for all manner of work, which the LORD had commanded to be made by the hand of Moses."

Above the amount a person gives in an offering, the Lord is looking for the right attitude behind the giving. Willingness is the heart condition God wants. Moses requested that no one bring an offering unless he or she was willing to do so (Ex. 35:4,5). The offerings were so great for the building of the tabernacle, Moses had to tell the people to stop giving.

God's desire for willingness has not changed in the New Testament. Paul told of the willingness of the Macedonian believers to give to the need of the saints at Jerusalem (2 Cor. 8:3). Paul told of the same dilemma that Moses faced. So much money came in to Paul for the saints' needs that Paul had to constrain the Macedonians not to give (2 Cor. 8:4). Imagine a church service today in which the offering is so large the pastor asks the people to stop giving. More than enough is received, yet the congregation compels the pastor to continue receiving their gifts. This is the power of willingness.

It is not only obedient giving that brings financial prosperity, but the attitude of willingness that backs the giving. *"If ye be willing and obedient, ye shall eat the good of the land"* (Isa. 1:19).

Your heart can be made willing through studying the promises of God, prayer and an openness to the Holy Spirit. Openness means looking for opportunities to sow. Before you go to a church service, a seminar or evangelistic meeting, take your checkbook with you. During the meeting, be open to the Holy Spirit as to what to give. If the Holy Spirit does not speak to you, purpose in your own heart what you will give and the Holy Spirit will bless and multiply it (2 Cor. 9:7). *(Written by Bob Yandian)*

JULY 26
TRUE PROSPERITY ISN'T SELFISH
2 CORINTHIANS 9:1-15

2 Corinthians 9:8 "And God is able to make all grace abound toward you; that ye, always having all sufficiency in all things, may abound to every good work:"

Most Christians who oppose financial prosperity do so because they equate it with greed. There is no doubt that many Christians err in this regard. The love of money is the root of all evil (1 Tim. 6:10), but true prosperity as the Bible teaches it, isn't selfish. As this verse says, the Lord prospers us so that we can have enough to give to every good work. Those who are unable to give to everything they would like to have not yet reached the level of prosperity that God has provided for them.

Another verse that makes this point is Ephesians 4:28 which says, *"Let him that stole steal no more: but rather let him labour, working with his hands the thing which is good, that he may have to give to him that needeth.* God prospers us so that we can bless others. Therefore, the individual with the biblical concept of prosperity isn't selfish at all. He wants to prosper so he can be a blessing to others. And, as the money flows through there's always plenty for you.

The person who says, "I have enough. I would never ask God for any more," shows that he thinks prosperity is for himself. With that attitude, it would be selfish to believe for more money. But once you see that prosperity isn't only for yourself, but so you can be a channel of God's supply to others, then this, "I have enough" attitude becomes selfish.

What's your reason for wanting to prosper? Is it all for selfish reasons or do you want to be a blessing to others? If God can get it through you, He will get it to you. *(Written by Andrew Wommack)*

HOPE , AN ESSENTIAL ELEMENT OF FAITH
HEBREWS 11:1

Hebrews 11:1 "Now faith is the substance of things hoped for, the evidence of things not seen.
Hope is an essential element of faith. I do not mean the kind of hope that says, "Someday God might do something for me." The word translated hope in the New Testament means "confident expectation of good." Biblical hope is the breeding ground of faith. Without a confident expectation of good, we will never be able to operate in real faith.

Once hope, the confident expectation for good, is destroyed, fear takes over. Fear is the opposite of Biblical hope, it confidently expects the worst. Fear is the breeding ground for unbelief which always leads to disobedience. This process of fear and unbelief starts in childhood and often lasts a lifetime.

Jesus told us that we must become as little children in Matthew 18:3. Young children possess a quality that is essential to achieving their dreams. They know no limits. They do not know what they can't do, so they dream big dreams. They are limited only by their imagination. Research shows that few adults can be classified as highly creative, whereas 95 percent of all four-year-olds studied, were considered creative. Only four percent of all seven-year-olds studied retain their creativity. What happened to these children? The answer is obvious. They started school and began to learn what they couldn't do.

The only limitations that God has are those in your mind. When we get saved we have to renew our minds so that we may know what is that good and acceptable and perfect will of God. (Romans 12:1,2)

When you received Jesus, you became a new creation. All the old has gone, and the new has come. To live this new life to the fullest of your potential, you must change your thinking. Otherwise, you will always limit what God can do in your life by negative thinking. As for me, I cannot meditate on one negative thought. If I did, I would wind up in a white jacket. That's how powerful it is to me. Philippians 4:8 is our verse to meditate on and live by. *"Whatever things are true . . . noble . . . just . . . pure . . . lovely, and . . . of good report . . . virtuous and . . . praiseworthy, meditate on these things."* (Written by Dave Duell)

DISCIPLINE YOURSELF
2 PETER 1:3

2 Peter 1:3 "As His divine power has given to us all things that pertain to life and godliness, through the knowledge of Him who called us by glory and virtue."
I heard a preacher say once, "What you do for yourself counts far more than all that others have done or can do for you." Growth and maturity does not necessarily come with age. It does come though with the acceptance of responsibilites. It is up to us to develop God's potential within us and see His prosperity in our lives. No one else is gong to do it. They do not have the interest or time. And, it isn't their job—it's yours. There are three areas where we must have mastery: Our tongues, our appetites and our tempers. These three have destroyed kingdoms. These three undisciplined, have brought men of great giftings down to a place of medocrity or failure.

Temper: The man who cannot rule his temper will be ruled by the situations of life. He will become a slave to circumstance. He will destroy the very building he erects. Proverbs tells us not to make friends with an angry man. Anger is so compelling to the carnal nature. It is an expression of fear and mistrust. Anger comes because we are afraid that God didn't mean what He said. That His Word cannot be trusted.

The tongue: All injury and damage that is done to character, homes, businesses and relationships is done with the tongue. The book of James tells us that it is an unruly member. Yet, it has the power to bless, heal and inspire. It also has the power to curse, destroy, hurt and damage. That is why the scriptures tell us that if we can rule our tongues, we can govern our entire lives.

Appetite: I am speaking about more than food. I am talking about the passions that we allow to govern our lives. The emotional realm of our souls. (Written by Mike Fehlauer)

JULY 29
YOUR "LITTLE BIT" CAN FEED A MULTITUDE
MARK 6:41-44

Mark 6:42 "And they did all eat, and were filled."
Most people are familiar with this account in the life of Jesus. In John 6:9 we found out that it was a little boy's sack lunch that fed the multitudes: *"There is a lad here, which hath five barley loaves, and two small fishes: but what are they among so many?"* Jesus was out teaching a multitude of people—five thousand men, not including women and children (Matthew 14:21). It had been a long time since anyone had eaten. The disciples wanted Jesus to send the people away so they could go try to find some food. But that wasn't what Jesus had in mind. He had compassion on the multitude. Matthew 14:16: *"But Jesus said unto them, They need not depart; give ye them to eat."* He took what the little boy offered out of love and multiplied it to feed a huge crowd. Mark 6:43: *"And they took up twelve baskets full of the fragments, and of the fishes."* They had enough to go around, and more to spare. Our God is able to do exceeding abundantly above all that we ask or think, according to His power that works in us according to Ephesians 3:20. Don't look at your insufficiency—look to God's all-sufficiency!

This isn't the only time we see Jesus feeding a multitude in Scripture. Again in Matthew 15, a multitude of people crowded around Jesus to hear the Word of the Lord. Those people were so hungry for God that in three days time they didn't budge, not even to eat. (Many Sunday morning churchgoers could take a lesson from that too.) Again, the disciples looked at their lack and wanted to send the people on their way to fend for themselves. And, once again, Jesus having compassion on these people said, *"they continue with me now three days, and have nothing to eat: and I will not send them away fasting, lest they faint in the way"* (Matthew 15:32). He took the little bit that they had and multiplied it so that all four thousand men (plus women and children) were completely satisfied and they even had seven baskets extra. God is the God of more than enough!

We can learn a powerful lesson in giving if we'll just keep our hearts like the heart of that little boy with the little lunch. I have purposed in my own heart that I will give my "little bit" to Jesus so that He can multiply it to abundantly meet needs. *(Written by Bob Nichols)*

JULY 30
GOD WANTS A FAMILY
I JOHN 3:1

I John 3:1 "Behold what manner of love the Father has bestowed on us, that we should be called children of God . . . . "
Prosperity is being a part of the greatest family on earth. We have been adopted as sons by Father God. (You could say children, but if God wants to call me His son, I don't mind. In Old Testament society, only sons could inherit from the father. So now male and female are called sons because we all receive the inheritance. Hallelujah!) It is astonishing that God's ultimate goal in creating us was to have a family of love children who would be just like Jesus. We are capable of receiving and participating in His love.

God is Father and we are His family. He didn't call you into an army (although there are aspects of your Christian life which require battle). He called you into relationship and fellowship. God does not love you for your performance. He loves you unconditionally as His son.

When you feel this love God has for you, you feel prosperous inside. You are able to give love to the people around you. You are able to help them see that God loves them and believes in them. You do not have to try to get them right. You can help them to become a part of His family.

Do you have an awareness of God's love? Do you make people around you feel loved? *(Written by Bonnie Duell)*

JULY 31
PROFILE OF AN AMBASSADOR
2 CORINTHIANS 5:20

2 Corinthians 5:20 "Now then, we are ambassadors for Christ . . . . "
First, an ambassador is a high ranking minister of state, often chosen from a royal family, sent to another country to represent his own nation.

We are all members of the royal family of God. There is no higher family in the universe and no greater royalty than God's family. We are chosen from the best family to represent the Lord Jesus on earth.

Second, an ambassador does not become a citizen of the country in which he is living, but remains a citizen of the country he came from. Philippians 3:20 says, *"Our citizenship is in heaven. "* The moment we were born again, our citizenship was changed from this world to heaven. We are truly in this world, but not of it. When Satan tries to put the sickness, disease and poverty of this world on us, we can claim diplomatic immunity.

Third, an ambassador's needs are not met by the economy of the country he is in, but by the country he is from. An ambassador does not care if the economy of the country he is in collapses; his needs are supplied from his home country. Our needs are not supplied by Wall Street, or the First National Bank, but by God's riches in glory. Just like God supplies for the birds (Mt. 6:25,26), He supplies for us. Birds are not concerned about the stock averages. They did not even know the Depression occurred. They ate just as well. So can we.

Fourth, ambassadors do not live under the laws of the country they are in, but live by the laws of the country they are from. Our laws are written in the Word of God. The only way we can be put under the laws of the world is to be ignorant of God's promises. Satan can only deceive us when we are ignorant of who we are in Christ and what our privileges are. *(Written by Bob Yandian)*

AUGUST 1
PUT GOD'S NEEDS FIRST
MATTHEW 6:24-34

Matthew 6:33 "But seek ye first the kingdom of God, and his righteousness; and all these things shall be added unto you."
The main principle that is expounded here is that we can not do two things effectively at the same time (vv. 24-25). Our true strength lies in being single-minded. But how can we keep from being focused on providing the basics of life, for ourselves and for our families? Jesus gave us the promise that if we put His kingdom first, then God the Father will provide for our needs. It's that simple.

Because it is so easy to get caught up in a lust for money and what it can provide, the Lord gave us a better system. We should use our jobs and other revenue producing abilities to first and foremost advance the kingdom of God. If we do that, then the Lord will make sure that our needs are met. We can literally live to give instead of living to get and just give occasionally. Giving can be our focus.

How do you know if you are seeking first the kingdom of God with your money? One sure way to tell is in your giving. Do you give a tithe and offerings first, before paying bills and fulfilling personal wants, or do you first take care of your needs and give what's left over? That's not putting first the kingdom of God.

Someone may say, "I don't have any extra." But you do have God's promise. He promises that if you put His kingdom first, He will provide these other things. You may not be able to see this, but that's why we call it faith. If you honor the Lord first with your money from a true heart, God will make miracles and blessings come your way. You will not be without. That's His promise. *(Written by Andrew Wommack)*

AUGUST 2
WISDOM PART 1
PROVERBS 2:1-2

Proverbs 2:1-2 "My son, if you receive my words, And treasure my commands within you, So that you incline your ear to wisdom, And apply your heart to understanding;"

Here are some nuggets on wisdom. In Proverbs 2:1 it says, *"My son"* which refers to relationship. "If" means decision. Everything that is happening in your life is with your permission. *"If you receive my words."* When God wanted something, He spoke. When He wanted something to begin, He spoke. Words change your life—Words that you are listening to, and saying. Words contain your future.

Verse four states, *"If you seek her as silver."* You will never possess what you are not willing to pursue. If you don't pursue it, you won't get it. You have to pursue what you believe God wants you to have.

Verse six, *"The LORD gives wisdom."* The only problem on earth is a wisdom problem. There is no such thing as a financial problem. Increase wisdom and increase wealth. The only difference between people is between their ears. Hosea 4:6 says, *"My people are destroyed for lack of knowledge . . . ."* Proverbs 11:9 states, *"through knowledge shall the just be delivered."* Proverbs 1:5 says, *"A wise man will hear and increase in learning . . . ."*

The difference between today and tomorrow is wisdom. If you enter tomorrow with the same information that you entered with this morning, tomorrow will be just like today. No future, but just a longer day.

Life is based on choices. Everything happens because of your choices. Many people use God as their excuse for something they did not want to do. *(Written by Dave Duell)*

AUGUST 3
WISDOM PART 2
PROVERBS 2:6

Proverbs 2:6 "For the Lord gives wisdom; From His mouth come knowledge and understanding;"

What you respect, you will attract. What you respect will come toward you, what you don't will move away from you. You can't make fun of a man who is used of God for healing and expect to get healed. You can't belittle a man who preaches prosperity and expect to prosper or wonder why money is uncomfortable in your hands. Those who do not respect your assignment disqualify themselves for a relationship.

In my life very close friends have come against the vision that God gave me and the relationship was severed. It is not an easy issue in life to deal with, but God's will comes first and we must continue with what He has given us to do.

What you are willing to walk away from, God will use as seed to multiply back to you. God told me this when we left Greeley to move to Denver to begin this work. As the years have gone by since the move I can see the hand of God in this move. We could not have accomplished what God had assigned us to by staying in our hometown.

If your desire is harvest, God will position you for harvest. And in our obedience, God will open the doors.

If what is in your hand is not big enough to be your harvest, it must be your seed. Whatever God tells you to do is not impossible. It is always bigger than ourselves—God never gives a small vision or assignment. If your visions and dreams don't wake you up at night, you are dreaming too small. I found out that God will terrify you before he will edify you. *(Written by Dave Duell)*

AUGUST 4
THOSE WHO PROSPER ARE THOSE WHO KEEP ON KEEPING ON
HEBREWS 6:12

Hebrews 6:12 "That you do not become sluggish, but imitate those who through faith and patience inherit the promises."
There are few in life who have reached the top, who did not have to climb up through adversity. Obstacles always wait for those who dare to climb. I read a statement once that said, "The inward drive to plod on when one is tired is the thing that makes one a strong, self-reliant conqueror." The conqueror sees hardship as a part of winning, and serving God. It is just a fact of life to him. Adversity is just an opportunity for a greater victory in the mind of a soldier for God. No one is a failure until he is laid under the sod of the earth. As long as there is breath in your lungs, there is the opportunity to overcome. Paul said in Romans 5:3-4 that we can glory in tribulation. Why? Because we know that tribulation is an opportunity to demonstrate patience and endurance which are true God-like characteristics.

Failure is not final—nor is it fatal. Cultivate the will to win. Allow the Holy Spirit to put in you a constitution of fighting. You may face tribulation today. Adversity may show up at your home or office. You may experience what seems to be a setback. Do not fear. Face it with courage knowing that if God be for you, then no one can successfully be against you! *(Written by Mike Fehlauer)*

AUGUST 5
GOD IS NOT A CHEAPSKATE
1 KINGS 5, 6
1 Kings 6:14 "So Solomon built the house, and finished it."
God is not a cheapskate or stingy God. He is not a mediocre God, and is certainly not a poverty-minded God. When God does something, He does it with excellence. He expects His children to do the same. That means to use what we can to obtain the best resources available in whatever we do. Now don't get me wrong, more expensive is not always better, but the key is *excellence.*

The Illinois Society of Architects did a study in 1925 to determine the cost value of Solomon's temple. Those figures were adjusted into 1997 inflation dollars. Vallapardus states that the talents of gold, silver and brass used for construction, were valued at well over 315 billion dollars ($315,439,838,700), with the jewels close to the same figure! WOW!

When looking at the records of ancient historian Flavius Josephus, the vessels of gold were valued at what today would be 17 billion dollars ($17,207,335,492.55) and the vessels of silver, almost 30 billion dollars ($29,772,422,400). If you want to nit pick about the type of suits that ministers are wearing, look at the priests' vestment and the singers' robes—they were 92 million dollars ($92,158,500)! Those would be some choir robes, wouldn't they? The trumpets alone would have been nine million dollars ($9,170,000) by today's currency rates.

Now, add into the mix the expense of the building materials, labor, and so forth. It took 10,000 men hewing cedars; 70,000 bearers of burden; 80,000 hewers of stone; 3,850 over-seers (managers/supervisors); all of which were employed for seven years. Besides wages, Solomon gave them $308,752,845.45 in bonuses! That comes to $1,884.36 per person for their bonus alone!

Solomon took care of his workers. The cost for daily food for the workers for the seven years and six months it took to complete the temple has been estimated at $3,158,014,484.80. Materials other than gold, silver, jewels, and so forth, cost $116,703,701.45.

If you add all of the estimates of everything pertaining to Solomon's temple, the temple would have cost close to 800 billion dollars ($797,790,000,000)! Astounding! No wonder the Temple was the wonder of olden times!

God wants His people to prosper and to be blessed so that they can be a blessing. There is no lack in heaven and there should be no lack in the life of a believer. The key is to know your source. God is our source. Meditate on 2 Corinthians 9:8, *"And God is able to make all grace abound toward you; that ye, always having all sufficiency in all things, may abound to every good work."* *(Written by Bob Nichols)*

AUGUST 6
GRACIOUS JOANN
EPHESIANS 2:7

Ephesians 2:7 "That in the ages to come He might show the exceeding riches of His grace in His kindness toward us in Christ Jesus" (New King James).
There was a special woman by the name of Joann Harbert who lived next door to my wife and I while we were living and ministering in west Texas some years ago. I guess it must have been back in the mid 70s. Cindi and I were both very young and very green in the ministry; like most, mature in some ways and very immature in others. We were very much in love with God and felt at the time that we were right where God wanted us.

But it was also the first time in our lives together that we were really away from all the people and surroundings that we were most accustomed to and comfortable with. It was for us and at that time, a huge step of faith. We experienced, along with many others in that area, some of the greatest miracles no doubt that we will ever see. But alongside some of the greatest highs that we experienced were also some difficult and lonely times. We had periods of deep poverty where we couldn't find work and didn't eat.

Anyway, back to Joann. During our stay in west Texas, it seemed that Joann took a special interest in us. And looking back, we know now that she probably felt some special unction from God to look after us. She would come by when we were away from the house and put food in our refrigerator when it was empty and we would often find money tucked away in some of the strangest places. We had some exciting treasure hunts in our little home from time to time.

Hebrew scholars tell us that the word *grace*, as it is used in the Old Testament, denotes a free and spontaneous willingness to bestow good on him that is destitute of it either in a way of kindness or compassion. This word, they say, excludes all idea of merit in the object of free favor. In other words, grace is not a reciprocal response toward someone who might be deserving. It is an act of favor, mercy, compassion or pity initiated by the one who is gracious within and of himself. It is unmerited favor—*not a favor returned.* *(Written by Marshall Townsley)*

AUGUST 7
AUTHORITY OVER SATAN'S POWER
LUKE 10:19

Luke 10:19 "Behold, I give unto you power (authority) to tread on serpents and scorpions, and over all the power of the enemy: and nothing shall by any means hurt you."
Jesus did not give us power over Satan, but authority over his power. To be truthful, authority is greater than power. That is a radical statement today. With all of the fitness magazines and karate movies, we are led to believe that we will have confidence in life when we have large muscles and great physical strength. This whole idea puts the emphasis in the wrong place.

Satan may be more powerful than us, but we have control over him. One demon was stronger than the seven sons of Sceva. Before the seven could reach the front door of the house, one demon possessed man overcame them, wounded them and tore off all their clothes (Acts 19:16). Jesus has given us authority through His name over all the strength of Satan and his kingdom.

A police officer standing in an intersection simply raises his hand and traffic comes to a halt. He does not have to be a big, muscular man. The cars, busses and trucks are more powerful than the police officer and could easily run over him. Yet, the drivers of these powerful vehicles recognize the officer's authority. They stop at a simple hand signal and go when he allows them to go. They know if they resist his authority, they will face the power. The police officer simply calls the station and the police department will bring more officers, guns, and dogs if necessary, to stop the lawbreaker. Power backs authority.

When we as believers use the name of Jesus, all hell comes to a halt. We may not be big or physically strong, but Satan has to stop. He knows if he runs over us, He will have to face the power, AGAIN. He faced it once, at the cross, and lost. Jesus has given us authority over all the power of Satan. *(Written by Bob Yandian)*

AUGUST 8
YOUR GIVING DETERMINES YOUR HARVEST
2 CORINTHIANS 9:1-15

2 Corinthians 9:6 "But this I say, He which soweth sparingly shall reap also sparingly; and he which soweth bountifully shall reap also bountifully."
This verse is saying that there is a direct relationship between the seed we sow and the harvest we reap. Another way of saying this is, you can determine your harvest by the amount of seed you sow.

In the natural realm this is an indisputable fact. No one would argue that a farmer harvests proportional to his sowing. We would consider a farmer crazy if he sowed very little seed but expected a big harvest. Yet in the spiritual realm, people do this all the time. Many people give very little money, if any at all, to the Lord and then wonder why the Lord doesn't supply their needs. That's crazy! Big harvests demand big sowings.

A farmer doesn't just plant seed from what he has available. He predicts what his needs will be and then sows enough seed to meet those needs. He borrows money if he has to, but he sows enough seed to meet his projected needs.

What are your needs? Is the money you are giving to the Lord's work enough to reap the harvest you want? If it isn't, then you need to increase the money you are sowing into God's kingdom.

Try this: Instead of just giving a tithe on what you have, move up to the next level. What income do you need? Start tithing on that figure and watch the money come in. Your giving determines your harvest. *(Written by Andrew Wommack)*

AUGUST 9
GOOD NEWS
ROMANS 10:15

Romans 10:15 "And how shall they preach unless they are sent? as it is written, "How beautiful are the feet of them that preach the gospel of peace, who bring glad tidings of good things!"
A little boy in a Christmas program had one sentence to say, "Behold, I bring you good tidings." After rehearsal he asked his mother what "tidings" meant. She told him tidings meant "news." The program began and he was so afraid before the large congregation that he forgot his line. Finally the idea came back to him and he blurted out, "Hey, I have news for you!"

I looked up the words "glad tidings." They come from the Greek word "evangelizo" which means good news, glad tidings, God, Jesus Christ, salvation, grace of God, peace, the promises, the truth, faith, hope, and immortality—the general blessings of the New Covenant called the gospel. The gospel of the kingdom is not only the coming kingdom, but it is salvation and all the benefits of the Good News of Jesus Christ.

Romans 10:15 says *"How beautiful are the feet of them that preach the gospel of peace, who bring glad tidings of good things!"* Not every preacher has beautiful feet. Not every preacher walks in the pathway of peace. It says those who preach THE GOSPEL OF PEACE, THOSE WHO BRING GLAD TIDINGS OF GOOD THINGS, those are the ones who are sent.

Hearing the gospel of peace will build faith and trust. Hearing bad news about works, law and performance will destroy confidence, trust and faith. The message of peace makes one run to God: the message of judgment makes one run away from God.

Expectation of good things should be the general view of all Christians. In every situation we should be expecting good things from God. This will never be if we are hearing teaching that label God as the source of all our hurts, trials, problems and tribulations. That kind of teaching promotes the expectation of bad things from God.

Either hope or fear will rule our lives in every situation. When one is not confidently expecting good, he is in fear or worry. *(Written by Dave Duell)*

AUGUST 10
NO LONGER A VICTIM
JOHN 5:1-8

John 5:6 "When Jesus saw him lie, and knew that he had been now a long time in that case, he saith unto him, Wilt thou be made whole?"

In this scripture we have a story of Jesus healing a crippled man at the pool of Bethesda. There are several interesting facts within this story that shed light on the enemy of faith which is "the victim mentality."

As Jesus approached the pool of Bethesda, He asked the lame man the question, "Do you want to be made well?" Jesus wanted to know where his faith was—what the lame man's desire was. Had this lame man resigned himself to his infirmity? Did he really want to be made well? Or, did he enjoy the freedom from responsibility that his sickness afforded him? Notice the crippled man never directly answered Jesus' question. When asked if he wanted healing, the lame man began to complain that he had not received the breaks in life that others had experienced. It was someone else's fault that he was still sick.

This mentality is the very reason why we are not able to rise above the circumstances of life. The truth of the matter is that the moment we received Jesus as Lord, we were redeemed from the authority of darkness. You now have His nature. Contained within you is the seed of greatness. the greater One lives on the inside of you! In Romans 5:17 we read that we can reign as kings in this life through Jesus Christ. The question is, "Who are you going to identify with? If we identify with the past, the symptoms, the lack and the fear, we will imprison ourselves with our own infirmities. We will be impotent in life, always seeing ourselves as the ones in need instead as the ones who help meet the needs of others. As we choose to identify with the Greater One, powerful things happen. Courage replaces timidity. Confidence replaces shame. Faith replaces fear, and love conquers bitterness. Choose to identify with Him today. *(Written by Mike Fehlauer)*

AUGUST 11
THE POWER OF PARTNERSHIP – (PARTNERSHIP, PART 1)
LUKE 5:1-7

Luke 5:7 "And they beckoned unto their partners, which were in the other ship, that they should come and help them. And they came, and filled both the ships, so that they began to sink."

Partnership is powerful. A partner is someone who helps you to do what God has called you to do. It is people coming together, working together, believing together, giving together and pooling resources together. Alone, I cannot accomplish what I would be able to do with partners linked together with me in faith. When you sow into the finances of your church, you are partnering with them. You become a partner with Jesus. You become a part of everything that the church does and you reap the reward for every life it touches.

Jesus needed to get the Word of God out, and He needed someone to help Him do it. There were no radios, televisions, videos or cassette tapes to do it. He needed partners to help Him reach out, and so do we. The disciples needed help too. They were fishermen who fished all night and caught nothing. They had bills to pay. The sailors wanted their paychecks. The insurance companies didn't understand that they didn't catch any fish the previous night. They still wanted their premiums. The payment on their boats was coming due. The disciples needed some fish. They needed some money. Jesus and the disciples came together in partnership. It was a divine connection, a divine appointment. Together they would prosper more than they would individually. We need faith partners in our lives. If you do not have faith in an area, find someone who does and partner with him.

Matthew 18:19 says, *"if two of you shall agree on earth as touching any thing that they shall ask, it shall be done for them of my Father which is in heaven."* Ask God to send you Holy Ghost faith partners and see the power that is released into your life to prosper. *(Written by Bob Nichols)*

AUGUST 12
CAN JESUS BORROW YOUR BOAT? (PARTNERSHIP, PART 2)
LUKE 5:1-7

Luke 5:3 "And he entered into one of the ships, which was Simon's, and prayed him that he would thrust out a little from the land. And he sat down, and taught the people out of the ship."

Today, Jesus is still looking for partners and saying, "Can I borrow your boat? I want to partner with you." What if Jesus walked up to you and said, "I'd like to go out to lunch with you. Would you buy my lunch?" Why, you'd beg, borrow, or do anything you had to do to get enough money to take Jesus out to lunch. And, you wouldn't take Him to some low-budget, fast food place. You'd take Him to some place a little bit nicer than that, wouldn't you? But please realize that today Jesus is saying, "I want to partner with you. I want to partner with your bank account. I want to partner with your time. I want to partner with your business, your family, your talent."

Some people see Malachi, chapter three as negative. Friend, that is not negative, because the same Lord who said to bring all the tithe into the storehouse, also said that He would rebuke the Devourer. He said, "Bring all your tithe and I will help you. I will take care of the insects, and I will take care of anything negative. You do your part, and watch Me go to work on your behalf. Watch Me multiply your little loaves and fishes. Watch Me help you do what you're not able to do on your own." When you are obedient to bring your tithes and offerings, or anything else the Lord asks of you, you are not throwing it away. You're sowing it. It is not waste, it is not throw-away. Some people look at big beautiful churches and say, "This is a big church. They don't need my money." They miss the whole point. Tithing is God's way to get it back to you, multiplied. Tithing is not a get-rich scheme.

Jesus is appealing for partners today. I want to be the partner of the Lord Jesus Christ. Let us pray, "Lord, I will be your partner today. You can use my boat. You can use my talent. You can use whatever you want to use. Sign me up." God blesses people who enter into faith covenant partnership for the kingdom of God.
(Written by Bob Nichols)

AUGUST 13
PARTNERS CATCH MORE FISH (PARTNERSHIP, PART 3)
LUKE 5:1-7

Luke 5:7 "And they beckoned unto their partners, which were in the other ship, that they should come and help them. And they came, and filled both the ships, so that they began to sink."

Idle nets produce nothing. Only the net that is cast into the water catches fish. The more nets, the more fish. Why partner? So we do not lose the harvest that God has given us. When Peter obeyed the Lord in casting his net once again, he did not realize the blessing that was going to come. It was a net breaking, boat sinking load! There were so many fish that he had to call out to his partners to help bring in the haul. Partners catch more fish. If it were only Peter in his boat, they would have lost all those other fish. How many fish would they have caught if they had more partners?

It's like the lady that is retired and at home. Physically she may not be able to go out on the street. Physically she may not be able to go out to the prisons or do some of the things you are able to do because of certain limitations that she may have. When she sends her tithe in to her local church she instantly becomes a partner with the Lord Jesus Christ. She makes it possible to bring in a bigger haul of fish. She can't go, but she is sending someone who can. She is partnering with Jesus.

There is no shortage on fish, because there is no shortage on sinners. If you reach one pastor, you are reaching hundreds or thousands of lives. Peter allowed Jesus to use his boat so that He could get the Word to the people. God always pays for His order. Fishing was Peter's livelihood. Jesus more than paid for the use of that boat by the haul of fish Peter and his partners brought in. By partnering with the Lord to get the gospel out to people, you will prosper. Remember, partners catch more fish. *(Written by Bob Nichols)*

AUGUST 14
GOD WANTS YOU TO DO WHAT YOU CAN'T DO (PARTNERSHIP, PART 4)
LUKE 5:1-7

Luke 5:7 "And they beckoned unto their partners, which were in the other ship, that they should come and help them. And they came, and filled both the ships, so that they began to sink."

The just really shall live by faith. If the devil can get you away from faith in God, you will go down. I often say that I'm out there so far now, I cannot make it without faith. You cannot play conservative, run of the mill church games, walking in fear, and have God's best. There comes a time you have to cut the cord and go for it. There just comes a time when you have to launch out into the deep.

I heard a minister bring out an observation from Luke, chapter five that was life changing for me. The minister said that while he was visiting the Holy Land, Israel, he asked some fisherman about their nets. They explained that there were different kinds of nets. They were using shallow water nets—the kind they do not use out in the deep. The Galilee is deep, and when Jesus said, "Launch out your nets into the deep," He was saying, "Do what you can't do." Those nets were not made to catch all kinds of fish, but He said, "Do what you can't do." You will never know faith until you do what you cannot do. You will never really know the wonderful blessing of faith until you do what you can't do.

As long as I do what I have the ability to do, it is just me—my strength. I do not need God so much in the things He has naturally gifted me to do. But when I get out there, when it is beyond me, that is when it becomes supernatural. That's when God can get tremendous glory.

When the disciples did what Jesus told them to do, they caught a whole bunch of fish. In fact, they caught so many they had to call for partners. That is why we need partners nowadays. We are out there in the deep water catching some big fish. You can stay in the shallow water the rest of your life and catch minnows, or you can get out there where the big fish are. The choice is yours. Do what you can't do. *(Written by Bob Nichols)*

AUGUST 15
GOD WILL NEVER GO BANKRUPT (PARTNERSHIP, PART 5)
2 CORINTHIANS 1:20

2 Corinthians 1:20 "For all the promises of God in him are yea, and in him Amen, unto the glory of God by us."

Godly partnership is an investment that, when we enter into it in faith, is a sure investment. Have you ever heard one of those "great opportunities" on the radio? They pull the same thing they do when they tell you about super car deals. After the wonderful ad, the next little voice that comes in rapidly mumbles a bunch of things and you have to say, "What did he say?" It is a disclaimer because nobody can promise, and guarantee without failure, a return on your money. They may look good and have a good track record—there are certain signposts you can look for, but there is no one on the face of this earth that has a guaranteed return except for God Almighty.

Partnership cannot be guaranteed on this earth, but when you give to the kingdom of God, it is. Partnership with Jesus always pays because He is a debtor to no man. Anything Jesus wants, let Him have it. Give Him your time, your talents, your ability, your finances. Then you will experience the joy of reaping the harvest together. Doing things God's way, partnering with Him, will guarantee a return in your life and the lives of those around you. He's kept every promise He's ever made. Everything God ever said, He's either done it, in the process of doing it, or—rest assured—He will do it. It shall come to pass. Jesus Christ is the same yesterday, today and forever. God has never gone bankrupt and He never will go bankrupt. Invest in His kingdom to have capital gain here on earth and a crown of glory in the world to come. *(Written by Bob Nichols)*

AUGUST 16
PEACE WITH GOD
LUKE 2:14

Luke 2:14 "Glory to God in the highest, and on earth peace, good will toward men!"

A multitude of angels appeared to shepherds in the middle of the night to praise God for the birth of the Baby Jesus. They had already been told by the angel of the Lord, *"Do not be afraid, for behold, I bring you good tidings of great joy which will be to all people"* (Luke 2:10).

The angels were proclaiming that this Baby Jesus would be the One who would bring peace between God and mankind. Jesus would provide the way whereby mankind could have a relationship with God. To have an intimate, face-to-face relationship with God makes you the most prosperous, successful person possible.

Peace denotes a state of rest, quietness; calmness; an absence of strife; tranquility; a perfect well-being. It is talking about harmonious relationships between God and men, men and men, nations and families.

Jesus is the Prince of Peace and He accomplished the ability for you to have peace in your relationships through His death, burial and resurrection. When you accept what He accomplished, you experience peace in your relationship with God. You have no fear or dread of punishment. You experience rest and tranquility because you live in total acceptance before God.

Peace in your heart then allows you to live in peace with others. People will open their lives to you because you will be able to encourage and strengthen them rather than criticize and find fault.

Glory to God in the highest! *(Written by Bonnie Duell)*

AUGUST 17
WHAT IS AN EXCUSE?
LUKE 14:18

Luke 14:18 "And they all with one consent began to make excuse . . . ."

In this parable, those who were bidden to come to the supper are compared with those invited to come to a church service. Church services are each designed not only to bring a person to Jesus, but to cause him to grow up into a disciple filled with God's Word. Just as today, many people in Jesus' day began to make excuses why they couldn't come.

Just what is an excuse? An excuse is a facade to cover your own weakness. An excuse is not the real issue, but a diversion. An excuse puts the blame or responsibility on someone else or something else. An excuse does not accept responsibility. Therefore, an excuse is a lie. Listen to the first excuse in this parable: "I have bought a piece of ground, and I must needs go and see it." What kind of person would buy a piece of property and THEN go look at it? You look at property before you buy it. Where did the man gain the money to buy the land? He must have been faithful to the house of God, listened to the word and grew in wisdom and prosperity (3 Jn. 2). When his financial need was gone, and extra money was in hand, the house of God was less important. The love of God was replaced by the love of money.

A reason, on the other hand, is honorable. A reason accepts responsibility, knowing circumstances or emergencies arise from time to time. A reason is the truth. You may have a reason for missing a church service, but you have no excuse. A person with a reason will be back next week. Excuses lead to more excuses and rarely will you see that person again.

God has asked us to study His word daily. He has asked us to praise His name from the rising of the sun to sunset. He also wants to fellowship with us daily through prayer and meditation on His promises. What is your excuse? *(Written by Bob Yandian)*

AUGUST 18
WHY DOES GOD WANT YOUR MONEY?
PSALM 50

Psalm 50:12 "If I were hungry, I would not tell thee: for the world is mine, and the fulness thereof."

Have you ever wondered why the Lord told us to give to Him? It's not because He needs it. This is what He says in Psalm 50: He tells the people that he isn't going to eat their sacrifices. He owns all the cattle on a thousand hills. What did He need their sacrifices for? If God was hungry, would He look to us to satisfy Him? Certainly not! Then why did He ask for the sacrifices? Why does He ask us to give if He's not in need?

God doesn't want Sunday only Christians who give Him only an hour or two per week. He loves us and wants to be involved in every part of our lives. We spend a majority of our time earning a living. How does He get involved in that part of our lives? He asks us to give Him ten percent.

If there was no God, and if what we give is not multiplied back to us, then giving away ten percent of what we have is foolish. It's moving away from our goal instead of towards it. That's just the point. It takes faith in God and in His Word to give away a portion of what we have. That's the reason He asks us to do it. It's so we can move into faith in the financial part of our lives.

Therefore, the person who wants to give and plans on giving when he has some extra cash, is missing the main purpose of giving. It is to thrust us into a realm of faith. If you wait to give until it takes no faith to trust that God will multiply it back to you, then you've missed the point.

Give in faith to the Lord today. It's your faith that the Lord really wants. *(Written by Andrew Wommack)*

AUGUST 19
FAITHFULNESS
LUKE 16:10

Luke 16:10 "He that is faithful in that which is least is faithful also in much: and he that is unjust in the least is unjust also in much."

Faithful men (meaning, mankind) are the bedrock of the church, the nation, and the world. God commits the leadership of His church to faithful men.

Faithfulness means to be firm in adherence to promises or in observance of duty. It also means, true to the facts, to the standard, or to an original. Faithfulness is synonymous with words such as loyal, constant, staunch, steadfast, and resolute. It implies unswerving adherence, firm resistance to the temptation to betray; firmness of emotional attachment; fortitude and resolution; steady unwavering in love, allegiance or convictions.

Faithfulness is a mark of maturity. God requires men to be faithful. So if men are required to be faithful, what about God?

God is faithful. All the qualities of faithfulness are found in His very being. God doesn't act or feel faithful, He simply is faithful. I Corinthians 1:9 says, *"God is faithful, by whom you were called into the fellowship of his Son, Jesus Christ our Lord."*

God has given us many prophesies over the past years and now they are all coming to pass. God told me in the beginning of my life that patience will pay. I can truly say in my life that God is faithful, no matter how much time goes by. He told me that in the realm of faith, the time element is not involved.

Decisions determine destiny. My decision to be effective will affect the destinies of millions of people's lives. Success always erases failure. God is moving in our lives—our greatest hour is now! *(Written by Dave Duell)*

AUGUST 20
TURNING YESTERDAY'S SORROWS INTO TODAY'S TRIUMPHS
PHILIPPIANS 3:13

Philippians 3:13 "Brethren, I count not myself to have apprehended: but this one thing I do, forgetting those things which are behind, and reaching forth unto those things which are before."

One of the greatest temptations of Satan is to steal our hope by convincing us to live in the past. The past for you may represent those things that happened before you were born again. Or, it may be something that happened yesterday. Whatever the case may be, Paul was clear that we must forget those things that are behind. The principle is that you can only conquer your past by focusing on your future. How can we conquer our past?

First, we must learn to stop defining who we are by what we have done. It is only when we understand about the righteousness of God that we can successfully do this. Our righteousness is not based on what we do, but on what Jesus did 2000 years ago. In 2 Corinthians, chapter five, we read, *"For He made Him who knew no sin to be sin for us, that we might become the righteousness of God in Him"* (v.21). We must come to the place where we accept our lives and ourselves as God's Word declares us to be. It is as you begin to accept God's divine opinion of you that you will no longer be plagued by your past and will begin to have great hope for the future.

Through the shed blood of Jesus you have been redeemed from shame, guilt and fear. God's love has set you free. You have been delivered from the power of darkness and jammed into the kingdom of love in His Son. Don't allow yesterday to steal today's victory. *(Written by Mike Fehlauer)*

AUGUST 21
IN YOUR FACE GRACE
LUKE 6:35

Luke 6:35 "But love your enemies, do good, and lend, hoping for nothing in return; and your reward will be great, and you will be sons of the Most High. For He is kind to the unthankful and evil" (New King James).

Let's say that someone came to your door, out of work, hungry, and he offered to do some odd jobs around the house for you in exchange for some groceries or just a little money to buy some. You say no to his kind offer but invite him to come in and make himself comfortable in your living room while you go to the kitchen to get a couple of sacks and fill them with things from the pantry.

Because you did not require that person to work for wages or earn their right to your food, your act of kindness would be considered by biblical standards an act of grace. You showed grace and he received grace.

Let's add a new twist to our illustration. Let's say that while you're in the kitchen loading up a couple of grocery sacks, the guy in the living room notices your wallet on the small table in your entry hall. As you return to the living room to deliver the groceries, you find him with *your* money in hand and an embarrassed look on his face as he reaches for the front door. As he begins to apologize and make his way out the door, you stop him, turn him around, put the groceries in his arms and send him on his way.

Now that's a depth of grace that leaves someone speechless; there's absolutely nothing left to say except "thank you" and be on your way. It is a "turn the other cheek" or a "go the extra mile" kind of grace.

The work of Jesus on our behalf was more than just an act of kindness toward an otherwise deserving mankind. The wages of sin is death and all have sinned. But in the face of a criminal, sinful, nature toward God, Jesus commended His love toward us and poured out His life for us. God's love is an "in your face" act of grace. *(Written by Marshall Townsley)*

AUGUST 22
THE MIGHTY PALM TREE
PSALM 92:12

Psalm 92:12 "The righteous shall flourish like the palm tree, He shall grow like a cedar in Lebanon."

This is a strange thought. Why would God compare the righteous believer to a palm tree? How can you put a cedar and a palm in the same verse? What is majestic or beautiful about a palm tree? Very few palms are good for fruit and they give little shade.

You have to look at the context of this verse. David was watching the seeming prosperity of his enemies. David felt small among the mighty nations on the earth in his day, yet he knew they would eventually fall and Israel would endure forever. He also knew those kings who rose up against him would come to destruction, yet his kingdom would never end (vv. 9,10). David had God's word on it. David's attitude was that he would not only survive, but FLOURISH.

Can you name a tree that not only exists in harsh conditions, but flourishes? The palm tree. Palm trees grow in deserts. Where there seems to be little or no water you will find palm trees. Where the heat is unbearable for humans, let alone for vegetation, you will find palm trees. They not only survive, they grow and grow tall. You can see them from some distance away.

The secret of the palm tree is its system of nourishment. A palm tree is different than any other type of tree. All other trees receive water and minerals through the bark. If you cut the bark completely around the tree (ring it) you will kill the tree. Yet with the palm tree, you can not only cut the bark, but weave it or even remove it and the tree lives. Why? A palm tree pulls it's life through the inside of the trunk, not through the bark.

A strong believer will not only survive in terrible circumstances and in the midst of his enemies, but like the palm, will flourish. This follower of God does not live by his flesh, his outward man, but draws his strength from his spirit, his inward man, which is filled with the Holy Spirit and God's promises. *(Written by Bob Yandian)*

AUGUST 23
BEGGAR OR BELIEVER? PART 1
MARK 10:46-52

Mark 10:46 "And they came to Jericho: and as he went out of Jericho with his disciples and a great number of people, blind Bartimaeus, the son of Timaeus, sat by the highway side begging."

Prior to this time, Bartimaeus had no option but to be a beggar. Man had no cure for his blindness. But that day, there was one passing by that wasn't only a man. Others had told Bartimaeus about how Jesus healed blindness. His plea to the Son of David showed that Bartimaeus recognized Jesus as his Messiah. This was his day. God was passing by. Nothing else mattered.

Bartimaeus could have made a different choice. A multitude was passing by. He could have made more money begging that day than he would have received in months. This was the break of a lifetime. Beggars think that way.

But that day, Bartimaeus became a believer. He wasn't thinking about an opportunity to continue his beggarly existence for another month or two. He was thinking of a brand-new life. A life free from begging. A life of independence where he could make it on his own. A life where he could help someone else.

What choices are you making? Are you so occupied with continuing the status quo that you are missing your opportunity to change your life? Are you so busy making a living that you don't take time to study or pray? Are you unable to go to church because of the demands of your business? That would be like Bartimaeus not calling out for his healing because of his great opportunity to beg.

Today, don't let the demands of everyday life cause you to miss Jesus as He passes by. Don't be a beggar, be a believer. *(Written by Andrew Wommack)*

AUGUST 24
HOW DESPERATE ARE YOU? PART 2
MARK 10:46-52

Mark 10:48 "And many charged him that he should hold his peace: but he cried the more a great deal, Thou son of David, have mercy on me."

It is amazing how much influence other people have on us. There is an intense desire for each of us to conform to those around us. We want to be part of the group. We don't like to stand out from the crowd. We want to be accepted. But the crowd is never going to go all the way with God. Those who receive God's best always have to buck the crowd. Therefore, a herd mentality is a tremendous detriment to serving God.

Bartimaeus was compelled to conform to what others expected of him. Others could choose where they wanted to live or what they wanted to do for a living. A blind man had no choice but to beg. I'm sure Bartimaeus hated the way his life was headed. But what choice did he have? Man had no cure for his problem.

However, Bartimaeus had heard about someone who was more than just a man. He had made other blind men see, maybe he could do the same for Bartimaeus. Inside that blind beggar's body was the heart of a believer. Bartimaeus was longing for the day when Jesus would pass his way.

When that day came, he wasn't going to let anyone stop him from receiving his miracle. Others were embarrassed at his outburst, but he had spent a life in embarrassment and shame, and was not going to continue in it. If he didn't do something differently, things would never change. It was now or never.

There is something powerful about desperation. Are you desperate enough to do whatever it takes to change? Don't let others stop you from receiving God's best. *(Written by Andrew Wommack)*

AUGUST 25
GOD RESPONDS TO FAITH PART 3
MARK 10:46-52

Mark 10:49 "And Jesus stood still, and commanded him to be called. And they call the blind man, saying unto him, Be of good comfort, rise; he calleth thee."

Certainly, there were many people in this crowd who needed a touch from God. That's why they were following Jesus. Many needed healings, deliverances, prosperity or other miracles. But there is no scriptural account of any one else receiving his miracle except blind Bartimaeus.

When Jesus heard Bartimaeus calling out to Him for mercy He stood still. What could possibly stop Jesus in His tracks? It was faith. Jesus told Bartimaeus that his faith had made him whole (v. 52). Others called for help but Bartimaeus called out in faith. Faith makes the difference. Faith gets the ear of God.

The scripture doesn't say that prayer will save the sick. James 5:15 says, *"And the prayer of faith will save the sick . . . ."* A multitude of people touched Jesus as He passed through Galilee, but only the woman who touched the hem of His garment in faith was made whole (Mk. 5:29).

Many people look to God for help, but not all of them receive what they need. It's not because God doesn't want to give it, but it takes faith to receive the blessings of God. In Jesus' hometown, He couldn't do many mighty works because of the people's unbelief (Mk. 6:5-6).

Don't just call out to God in fear or desperation. Move beyond those things into faith and God will stop and command your miracle too, just like He did for Bartimaeus. Your miracle is just a call of faith away. *(Written by Andrew Wommack)*

AUGUST 26
PREPARE FOR SUCCESS PART 4
MARK 10:46-52

Mark 10:50 "And he, casting away his garment, rose, and came to Jesus."

In Bartimaeus' day, beggars wore clothing that distinguished them as beggars. Therefore, for Bartimaeus to cast away his garment was significant. He wasn't planning on going back to begging. He was believing God for a miracle and he acted accordingly.

Bartimaeus was blind, so of course, he couldn't see the clothing he wore. But others could see it, and he was obligated by the society he lived in to wear the clothes appropriate to his place in life. Beggars weren't like every one else. They weren't productive members of society. They might be tolerated or pitied, but they weren't admired and they weren't allowed the same privileges as those who were normal. Bartimaeus must have hated the differences that his blindness imposed on him.

No doubt, he dreamed about what it would be like to have his sight. And since he had heard of Jesus healing the blind, he probably became very specific in what he would do if Jesus ever passed his way. One thing he knew for sure: If Jesus came by his place, he would let no one or nothing stop him from receiving his healing. He would never go back to begging. He knew he would be healed and wouldn't need his beggar's clothes ever again.

How convinced are you that God is going to answer your prayer? Have you held on to your "old clothes" just in case nothing happens so you can go back to your old beggarly existence? That's not faith. Meditate on God's promises until you see yourself receiving whatever you need and then make no plans to go back to where you were before.

(Written by Andrew Wommack)

AUGUST 27
THIS IS THE YEAR FOR GOD TO ACT
LUKE 4:19

Luke 4:19 "To preach the acceptable year of the Lord."

In Luke 4:16, Jesus speaks in the synagogue and reads from Isaiah 61 quoting Himself. In verse 19 it says, *"To proclaim the acceptable year of the Lord."* In *The Message*, a contemporary English translation of the New Testament, it says *"This is the year for God to act."* The Holy Spirit told me that He is acting upon the words of prophesy that He has given to us over the last years.

This passage also means in Greek, "That in which He is pleased to show mankind extraordinary favors." Jesus was also referring to what God had spoken to Moses in Leviticus 25 about the year of Jubilee, or the year of freedom, or the great year of the Lord. The year of Jubilee was like none other. The people went free—free of debt, free of bondage. No one could remain a slave. It was a great year of freedom.

Jesus stood in the midst of the congregation at Nazareth and boldly declared, *"This day this scripture is fulfilled in your ears"* (vs. 21). In other words, He was saying, "Your Jubilee has come and I am He! I am sent to preach the Gospel to the poor, heal the brokenhearted, and preach deliverance to the captives. Your Jubilee has come and I am here."

The moment He said those words, the Jubilee was no longer a year in time, but it became a person. Jesus is the great Jubilee of God, the Anointed One who has come to set man free.

Your Jubilee has come. He came on the day of Pentecost. He is dwelling in us today, anointing and honoring us with His power—the same message that was preached by Jesus 2000 years ago. We need to sound our trumpets of freedom. We are free from the authority of darkness and translated into the kingdom of God's dear Son. We are free from sickness and disease in our bodies. We are free from fear, and debt and all the rest that goes along with the old man or old life. *(Written by Dave Duell)*

AUGUST 28
TURNING YESTERDAY'S SORROWS INTO TODAY'S TRIUMPH'S   Part 2
PHILIPPIANS 3:13

Philippians 3:13 "Brethren, I count not myself to have apprehended: but this one thing I do, forgetting those things which are behind, and reaching forth unto those things which are before,"
We previously looked at what is necessary for us to walk away from the shame of the past. We looked at how important it is to accept a righteousness that is not ours, but is through the finished work of Christ. Another principle that is necessary for us to understand how to get past the past, is choosing to find our identity in Jesus.

The Apostle Paul wrote in 1 Corinthians 6:17, *"he that is joined unto the Lord is one spirit with Him."* As far as Satan is concerned there is no difference between us and God. As far as the pressures of the world are concerned, when they attack you, they attack our Lord. Through the death and resurrection of Jesus, we have the opportunity to identify with Jesus' death and His life. Everything that Jesus has is ours. You have exchanged your old life for His new life of power and love. Ephesians 2:5-6 says, *"Even when we were dead in trespasses, made us alive together with Christ (for by grace you have been saved) and raised us up together, and made us sit together in the heavenly places in Christ Jesus."* His victory has become your victory. His life has become your life. Greater is He that is in you, than all the fears and shame that have ruled you in the past.   *(Written by Mike Fehlauer)*

AUGUST 29
YOU'RE NEVER ON YOUR OWN
EPHESIANS 6:10

Ephesians 6:10 "Be strong in the Lord and the power of His might" (New King James - emphasis added).
One of the things I actually looked forward to, growing up as a young boy, believe it or not, was the opportunity to mow our lawn. I had watched my father and my older brother do it time and time again from our front porch. There came a time where I literally could not wait to prove that, I too, could mow a lawn! One hot and humid afternoon, while watching television in a nice air conditioned room with my brothers, one older and one younger, my Dad stepped into the room and announced that the lawn needed mowing before it rained. My older brother reluctantly got to his feet and started out the door when my father stopped him and looked my way. After a brief pause he said, "Marshall, do you want to give it a try?" Boy, I jumped to my feet, stuck my chest out, gave my brother a "watch this" look as I passed by him and said, "Sure, Dad. I thought you would never ask."

I got the mower started, which was no small task, and began pushing it through the thick, tall grass little by little, row by row. I just knew the whole neighborhood was watching. What an achievement. But you know, the mower was heavy, the handle was as tall as I was and that grass was a lot thicker than what I remembered. Before getting even half done I ran out of steam. I was exhausted, embarrassed and just hung my head in disgust, my sweat mixed with tears.

Suddenly, the mower seemed to move forward on its own. For the first few minutes I honestly did not know what was happening. When my eyes cleared I saw my father's hands on the handle of that mower next to mine and when I looked up (my father was very tall) I saw him smile. He didn't say anything until we finished our work together and sat down on the porch side by side. That's when he said, "Son, I never intended for you to do this all by yourself, this is something I looked forward to doing with you."

The heavenly Father never intended for you to go it alone. Life is too vast to take the challenge alone. When God speaks to you to do something, He also gives you the grace to perform it. Don't try to live without Him. You, too, will end up drowning in your own sweat and tears unable to press on. There is a line from a wonderful Christian song that says, "The grace of God won't lead you where the grace of God can't keep you." Enjoy the journey.   *(Written by Marshall Townsley)*

AUGUST 30
A SERVANT CALLED MONEY
MATTHEW 6:24

Matthew 6:24 "No man can serve two masters: for either he will hate the one, and love the other; or else he will hold to the one, and despise the other. Ye cannot serve God and mammon (money)."

We do not really own the money in our pockets. We do not really own our homes, cars, clothes or jewelry. Who owned them before you were here and who will own them when you are gone? *"For we brought nothing into this world, and it is certain we can carry nothing out . . ."* (1Tim. 6:7).

God does not call us owners of this world's goods, but stewards. He is the real owner of everything (Ps. 50:10, Hag. 2:8). A steward is hired by the owner to distribute the goods as the owner sees fit. A steward is responsible for the goods and servants of his master. God is the master, money is the servant and we stand in between. We are a servant of God and money is our servant. Money is a terrible master, but a good servant. God is the true and wonderful master.

Money is a great servant. A servant takes orders and accepts no credit. The servant gives all credit to the one who sent him. A servant is like another set of hands and feet for his master. He can go where the master cannot go and do what the master cannot do. Yet the master receives the credit.

The great commission tells us to go into all the world. We know there are those who are called to go into other countries, but some must stay "by the stuff," or work at jobs to support those who go. When we send our finances into the uttermost parts of the earth to support a prophet, evangelist or teacher, our money allows more people to receive Jesus, be filled with the Holy Spirit, be discipled and healed. It is as if we went ourselves. We are rewarded equally with those who went to battle. The money does not receive the credit for all the changed lives. We receive the credit and God receives the glory. *(Written by Bob Yandian)*

AUGUST 31
DIVINE HUNGER
MATTHEW 5:6

Matthew 5:6 "Blessed are they which hunger and thirst after righteouseness, for they will be filled."

Jesus said that it was those who hunger that are filled. It is a law of the depths of the Spirit. God doesn't respond to needs. There are many who have desperate needs. Most of those never see the hand of God move in their lives. God responds to hunger mixed with faith in Him. Every great move of God's Spirit in the earth was in response to a cry of hunger from a heart of faith.

You see, God by His Spirit plants the seeds of what He desires in our hearts. When we are in tune with His heart, we in turn redirect God's will back to Him in the form of hunger and faith. God then responds to our heart cry. He desires for us to be co-labourers with Him. That way we learn of Him. We discover a greater place of intimacy. It all starts with hunger. Hunger for rightness. Rightness in our families, our finances, our bodies and our minds. What have you been hungry for? Healing in your body? To see others come into the kingdom? Restoration of your marriage? Don't grow weary in well doing. The promise is, *"Blessed are they which do hunger and thirst after righteousness: for they shalll be filled"* (Mt. 5:6). You will see God Himself fill the empty, dry or desolate areas of your life. He loves you and is with you right now—today! *((Written by Mike Fehlauer)*

SEPTEMBER 1
EVERYTHING AFTER ITS OWN KIND
JOHN 3:6

John 3:6 "That which is born of flesh is flesh, and that which is born of Spirit is spirit"

There is a spiritual law found from the very beginning of the Bible: everything produces after its own kind (Genesis 1:12). This is true with plants, animals, fish, birds and man. It is true in the spiritual kingdom as well as in the natural. It's also true with God.

Love produces love and hate produces hate. Green beans produce green beans, turnips produce turnips, cats produce cats, dogs produce dogs and people produce people. God produces spirits.

Every living thing passes on attributes. Turnips smell, taste and look like turnips. Cats have whiskers, dogs have tails and people have hands and feet. I received all of man's attributes when I was born. I have the same feet and hands I was born with. I did not go to the doctor when I was two years old and have my original hands removed and two year old hands attached. My original hands have the ability to grow to their present size. I simply learned to use what was given to me at birth. These hands which at one time could not hold a bottle can now drive a car.

When you were born of God you received all of His attributes. You have the same love, joy and patience you were given when you received Jesus as your savior. You also have the same measure of faith. You do not have to trade your faith in for more. One of the most unscriptural prayers you can pray is, "God give me more faith." That is like saying, "God give me more hands." Just like the hands on your natural body, you need to learn to use the faith you were given at the new birth. Your faith which at one time could not trust God for a pair of socks can today believe Him for the house payment, divine healing and souls to be won. Like developing a natural muscle, your faith needs to be fed and used. It will grow. *(Written by Bob Yandian)*

SEPTEMBER 2
ESTABLISHING THE PATH OF SUCCESS
1 JOHN 4:17

1 John 4:17 "Because as He is, so we are in this world."

I know that I have said this before, but I want to repeat it: EVERYTHING you need to prosper and succeed in this life is IN YOU! God has provided within us, all we need to live and reign as kings in this world. Please believe this. No man has the power to determine your destiny. It is impossible for anyone to control your future— unless you let him.

We have the ability to control and determine our future as well as our present. You have the ability to create an environment of success or failure. Before you go to the office, the store, or home, create around you an atmosphere of victory. How? By spending some time meditating on His greatness and ability. Meditate on the truth that He lives within you. Guard your environment from defeat, weakness and unbelief. Associate with people who have won; they will help you go to the top. Associate with those who love people and fear God. Avoid those who gossip about others or are critical of others. Don't hang around the water cooler wasting time through loose talking. Pray in the Spirit. Sing loud. Give thanks fervently. You can go out today with a consciousness of the Greater One within you. You are going out to work today as a victor. *(Written by Mike Fehlauer)*

SEPTEMBER 3
THE RICHES OF HIS GRACE
EPHESIANS 1:7-9

Ephesians 1:7-9 "According to the riches of His grace which He made to abound toward us in all wisdom and understanding . . . . "

God is a generous Father. He made His grace, His favor and ability, to abound toward us. Abound means to have in excess, greatly surpass, excel. God lavished, or wastefully poured, His grace upon us.

To fall from grace has nothing to do with losing your salvation. Falling from grace is when you fall from the realm where grace works. It leaves you to work in your own ability, to try to be justified and made righteous by works of the law. Paul told the Galatians that they had fallen from grace. In Galatians 5:4 he states, *"You have become estranged from Christ, you who attempt to be justified by law; you have fallen from grace."*

Wouldn't you rather live in the lavishness of God's grace? It is His ability at work in you. It is grace that gets you saved, that gives you power over sin. It is by grace that you fulfill your call.

Thank you, Father, for being so generous with us, your children. Thank you for giving us, by the riches of your grace, all things that pertain to life and godliness through the knowledge of You (2 Peter 1:3). *(Written by Bonnie Duell)*

SEPTEMBER 4
FIRST GIVE YOURSELF
2 CORINTHIANS 8:5

2 Corinthians 8:5 "And this they did, not as we hoped, but first gave their own selves to the Lord, and unto us by the will of God."

How many times during a church offering have you thought, *This church just wants my money?* Even worse, have you ever thought that is all God wants from you? With all the teaching in the Old and New Testament on giving, you might just think that.

God has chosen the giving of money throughout history to fund the preaching of the Gospel. God could send angels to do this work, but He would rather use redeemed people. He could raise up many rich people, give them gold and silver mines and relieve us of the responsibility of giving tithes and offerings.

Why offerings and why everyone? Every time we give an offering into the spreading of the Gospel, it is a test of our love for God. Far beyond the giving of money, is the attitude behind the giving. Finances are a very important part of your life, one of your highest priorities. Jesus told us, *"Where your treasure is, there will your heart be also"* (Mt. 6:21). If you want to find a person's love, their highest priority, find out where they spend their money.

GOD DOES NOT WANT OUR MONEY FIRST—HE WANTS US. If God has us, and our hearts, He has our money. He has everything we own. This is why God wants willing givers. He wants us to present our *"bodies a living sacrifice"* unto Him (Rom. 12:1).

Many Christians give to get God off their backs. They will give money to relieve themselves of the guilt of not serving God. In other words, they buy God off or bribe Him. God cannot be bought. He does not want money without our hearts. He would rather we not give if our hearts are not right with Him (Mt. 5:23,24). *"Every man according as he purposeth in his heart, so let him give; not grudgingly, or of necessity: for God loveth a cheerful giver"* (2 Cor. 9:7). *(Written by Bob Yandian)*

SEPTEMBER 5
ATTITUDE CREATES ATMOSPHERE
EPHESIANS 4:23

Ephesians 4:23 "And be renewed in the attitude of your minds."
JOY . . . PEACE . . . LOVE . . . FAITH . . . HOPE.

These are all attitudes. These are heart expressions in response to the challenges of life. These attitudes were experienced by the early Christians during times of intense persecution. Webster defines an attitude as, "A state of feeling of mind about a person or situation." Our attitude is a reflection of what we have chosen to think about and value. If we have chosen to think about the cruel words of others, and have valued those words over God's, then our attitude will be one of bitterness and depression. If on the other hand, we dwell on God's faithfulness in the midst of criticism, then our attitude will be one of joy and faith.

The same applies in the realm of financial prosperity. If we constantly dwell on the bills we have, or the lack we are experiencing, then our attitude will be one of fear and frustration. Faith is a powerful force. It not only repels the darkness of Satan's kingdom, but it also is a magnet that attracts the blessings of God. The atmosphere of faith creates an attitude of expectancy. Expectancy causes us to look at problems as opportunities. Expectancy causes us to prepare and make room for blessings, just as an expectant mother prepares a room and bed for her unborn child. There is a supernatural dynamic that is in an attitude of expectancy. Blessings just seem to come to one who lives with an expectant heart.

Today, expect God to bless and prosper you. Allow holy anticipation to be a part of your day. Resist the temptation to allow your present circumstances to dictate your attitude. He is for you. Today, not tomorrow, God is looking for an opportunity to bless you.
(Written by Mike Fehlauer)

SEPTEMBER 6
UNIQUELY GIFTED
EPHESIANS 1:3-4

Ephesians 1:3-4 "Blessed be the God and Father of our Lord Jesus Christ, who hath blessed us with all spiritual blessing in heavenly places in Christ: according as he hath chosen us in Him before the foundation of the world, that we should be holy and without blame before Him in love" (King James).

Everything in the Christian life is grace. Like Paul (and I don't say this presumptuously) you and I were also chosen before the foundation of the world to be that unique expression of Christ that no one else can possibly be and to fulfill that particular ministry to which we have been called.

Many Christians think they have no special place in God or in His work because they aren't involved in what they might consider full-time ministry. Like the Apostle Paul, you have been separated and called by God's grace to those to whom He will lead you. If you're a believer, you are just as much a minister of the Good News as anyone who stands behind a pulpit week to week ministering to a congregation of people, or anyone else, for that matter, who might be recognized as in the ministry. Because of the grace on your life, you can reach some that others cannot. Every member of the Body of Christ is in full-time Christian service whether he knows it or not—whether he fulfills it or not.

You're unique and hold a special place in God's eyes, not because of anything you've accomplished but because of His resident grace in your heart. *(Written by Marshall Townsley)*

SEPTEMBER 7
STEWARDS MUST BE FAITHFUL
1 CORINTHIANS 4:2

1 Corinthians 4:2 "Moreover it is required in stewards, that a man be found faithful."
When I was a new pastor, I desired to open a bookstore in our church, that would enable us to place Bibles, good teaching tapes and books in the hands of our congregation. I tried to think of every qualified person among our people to open and maintain a book shop. I talked with many who had handled money or worked in retail shops, but no one wanted the position.

A young girl worked in our audio department as a faithful and dedicated volunteer. On a few occasions I thought of her to take the position in our bookstore. She was faithful, but was not qualified, so I forgot her.

One Saturday I was walking through our empty auditorium praying for the Sunday service, and I caught her out of the corner of my eye. She was faithfully volunteering on Saturday to set up the microphones, audio tape and speaker levels for the Sunday service. When I looked at her, this scripture came out of my heart, *"Moreover it is required in stewards, that a man (person) be found faithful."* The Amplified Bible says "essentially required." Faithfulness is not requested, but required. God told me in that moment, "You have been looking for qualifications, I look for faithfulness. You can teach a person qualifications, but you cannot teach them faithfulness." Let faithfulness be our highest priority in ourselves and others.

Paul told Timothy to take the word and, *"the same commit thou to faithful men, who shall be able to teach others also" (2 Tim. 2:2).* When Timothy found them, they were only faithful. One day they would learn (be able) to teach.

Although Paul was a qualified man when God saved him and called him, God placed him in the ministry for his faithfulness: *"He counted me faithful, putting me into the ministry"* (1 Tim. 1:12).

When we stand before the Lord, He will not say to us, "Well done thou good and qualified servant." God will reward us for our faithfulness (Mt. 25:21). *(Written by Bob Yandian)*

SEPTEMBER 8
OUR LIGHT AFFLICTION
2 CORINTHIANS 4:17

2 Corinthians 4:17 "For our light affliction, which is but for a moment, is working for us a far more exceeding and eternal weight of glory."
Do you realize that most dreams are destroyed because we believe other people's discouraging words. There was a quote in the Wall Street Journal, *"When you make your mark in the world, look out for people with erasers."* Abraham Lincoln, at his peak of popularity, once said: "If I tried to read, much less answer, all the criticisms made of me, and all the attacks leveled against me, this office would have to be closed for all other business."

The Bible is full of stories of people just like you and me who overcame these same types of circumstances. These were people who led lives of victory, power and effectiveness because they learned to put God's Word into action and eliminate the destructive influences others exerted over their lives. They came to a place where they saw beyond the vicious spirits that were trying to dominate them. They moved into a realm where there are limitless possibilities because of God and His grace.

"Yesterday people" will rarely enjoy your future. It is normal to want to bring everyone close to you into the chapters of your future success, but few will qualify.

Move away from yesterday. You exhausted its benefits. Refuse to waste your energy on repairing it. Rather, rebuild by focusing on your future. Certainly, yesterday can be a reservoir of wisdom and information. You are not forgetting the precious lives whom God used mightily for your continual survival and success, but you are refusing to abort your future joys and victories through replaying the memories of yesterday's painful experiences.

Paul refused to wallow in the tears of his past. Few made greater mistakes than he. Yet he refused to forfeit his future by focusing on his past. His mistakes were over. His sins were behind him, and even his name was changed.

Let your conversation be more creative, and start using your imagination instead of your memories. Life is a journey and not a destination. Let's make this life the most creative and exciting we can imagine. *(Written by Dave Duell)*

SEPTEMBER 9
HE IS A GOD OF HOPE
ROMANS 15:13

Romans 15:13 "Now may the God of hope fill you with all joy and peace in believing, that you may abound in hope by the power of the Holy Spirit."

Everyone of us goes through times when life seems hopeless. The dreams we have had, seemed to have been crushed by the blow of adversity. Or, the exciting plans for the future have been poisoned by deceit or betrayal. Maybe it is a marriage that has failed, or a child who has turned his back on God.

It makes no difference what you are going through, what your circumstances may be, or how tempted you are; God has not disowned you. Nor has He turned His back on you. The Apostle Paul says, *"If we are faithless, He remains faithful, for He cannot deny Himself"* (2 Tim. 2:13 Amp).

In your moment of need, take God at His Word. In Romans 8:35 and 37 we read, "Who shall separate us from the love of Christ?" and "We are more than conquerors through Him that loved us."

It is the knowledge of God's love that gives us hope. A hope that offers within it, no disappointment. A knowledge of His love gives us the confidence to face any circumstance or situation. Herman Melville said, "Hope is the struggle of the soul, breaking loose from what is perishable, and attesting her eternity."

In your moment of weakness, take God at His Word. Throw yourself, your life, and your situation into the tabernacle of God's love. *(Written by Mike Fehlauer)*

SEPTEMBER 10
GRACE FOR EVERY WEAKNESS
HEBREWS 4:16

Hebrews 4:16 "Let us therefore come boldly unto the throne of grace, that we may obtain mercy and find grace to help in time of need" (King James).

That verse always ministers to me. I guess because I have already resolved for myself that I will always stand in need of His mercy and that I must have His grace to live. There are another couple of verses in Hebrews chapter 12 that say, *"Wherefore we receiving a kingdom which cannot be moved, let us have grace, whereby we may serve God acceptably with reverence and Godly fear: For our God is a consuming fire"* (vv.28-29).

Here, we see that we can't begin to stand before God's magnificent presence or serve Him acceptably, as this scripture says, without grace. And that, again, is why the first verse I mentioned to you is so important. There is mercy and grace for us in our times of need. God is aware of our weaknesses, easily touched with the feelings of our infirmities and offers us strength for them. There is special grace for every weakness. Our fears of failure are silenced; that overwhelming sense of inadequacy that plagues so many is cast out. The spirits of accusation and condemnation are made to hold their tongues in the face of His grace. Even pride is confronted because our merits cease to be the central issue. All of our human inabilities are addressed as we turn to walk toward the throne of His grace and humbly take our place before Him asking for His help. *(Written by Marshall Townsley)*

SEPTEMBER 11
A GOOD RULE FOR REAPING
PROVERBS 6:6-8

Proverbs 6:6-8 "Go to the ant, thou sluggard; consider her ways, and be wise: Which having no guide, overseer, or ruler, Provideth her meat in the summer, and gathereth her food in the harvest."

The ant is a great example to us of God's plan to prosper His children. Ants are diligent workers. You have never seen a lazy ant, have you? God does not prosper believers who will not work.

God told Adam to be fruitful, multiply and replenish the earth. But before he gave Adam a wife and family, He gave him a job. Adam had to tend and guard the Garden of Eden. Having a job is not part of the curse. Even in Paradise, man had to work. Adam was to provide an income and a home before he met Eve.

I heard a testimony of a man who prayed for prosperity and all he received were job offers. Prosperity begins with a job, faith and love: *"Let him labour, working with his hands the thing which is good, that he may have to give to him that needeth"* (Ephesians 4:28). We should look to our job to give us seed to begin giving to others.

But how should we work? The lesson of the ant is: if you can work without supervision, you will have more than enough. Paul warned the Ephesians not to work *"with eyeservice, as menpleasers"* (Ephesians 6:6). This means to work when the boss is looking and quit working when the boss is gone. We are to work as unto the Lord because Jesus is with us at all times. We should work because Jesus is watching over us, not because the supervisor is present.

Christians should be the best workers at the factory or office. As God's representatives, we should be at the office early and leave late. Christians should not spend longer on lunch than needed and should put forth maximum effort at everything they do. We should set the standard for excellence. *(Written by Bob Yandian)*

SEPTEMBER 12
GOD ALWAYS HAS A PLAN
1 SAMUEL 3:1-10

1 Samuel 3:3 "And ere the lamp of God went out in the temple of the LORD, where the ark of God was, and Samuel was laid down to sleep;"

Eli was the high priest of the nation of Israel for 40 years (1 Sam. 4:18). He feared God and served Him faithfully, but his sons did not. They were carrying out the duties of the priesthood but they were wicked. They took more than the portion God had allowed them (1 Sam. 2:14) and they committed fornication with the women who came to the temple of the Lord (1 Sam. 2:22).

Eli was now an old man in his late 90s. He would soon be gone and his sons certainly weren't able to lead the nation in a godly direction. Samuel was chosen by God to fill the void of spiritual leadership. This phrase, *"ere the lamp of God went out in the temple"* was talking about more than just the extinguishing of the physical lamp. It was speaking of the spiritual leadership God had invested in Eli.

Before Eli died, the Lord raised up Samuel as a prophet in the land. There have been times that true godly leaders have been in short supply, but they are always there. Anytime we get to feeling that all the godly people are gone, that's the Elijah syndrome (1 Ki. 19:10), and it is always wrong (1 Ki. 19:18). Samuel was brought to Eli as a young boy of two or three and he was probably a teenager at this time. The Lord had been working on Eli's replacement for quite some time. God always has our provision before we even have the need.

At times it may look like things are out of control and there is little hope. But God always has His man or woman. The world is in desperate need of godly leaders today. Be still, listen for God's call, and then respond as Samuel did by saying, "Speak Lord for your servant is listening." *(Written by Andrew Wommack)*

SEPTEMBER 13
IDENTITY TEMPTATION
MATTHEW 4:1

Matthew 4:1 "Then Jesus was led up by the Spirit into the wilderness to tempted by the devil."

Jesus continues to show us who we are in Him and who He is in us. The more we find out who Jesus is the more we find out who we are. It's not the truth that sets you free, but the truth you know and believe that sets you free.

Let's talk about temptation. Look at Matthew 3:15. Jesus was being baptized and He said that He would fulfill all righteousness. Why would He say these words?

Let's go back to Adam and see what happened in that first temptation. Adam was created in God's image. He was perfect and he did not know anything about sin. The first temptation was misguided information to Adam. "If you eat of this fruit you will be like God." And the truth was that he was already was like God. He was tempted to become something He already was!

Paul tells us what Adam's sin was—UNBELIEF! When Adam sinned, he plunged mankind into extreme darkness of knowledge, knowing that there was something wrong between him and God and a totally wrong perception of what the problem was. Because man's perception was so wrong as to what the problem was, what did God have to do? He gave us the LAW! For what purpose? To declare everybody guilty.

If the first Adam sinned and threw us all into unbelief, what would be the second Adam's goal? To restore us to faith! When Jesus came up out of the water at His baptism and was filled with the Holy Spirit, the heavens opened and God spoke and said, "This is my beloved Son, in Whom I am well pleased." Then the Spirit took Him into the desert to be tempted. The time had come to reverse all things. To restore all things unto God.

But the temptation had to be endured. What temptation? The very temptation that Adam fell in to. Now we have a man on earth who is the first one to know since Adam, that He is the Son of God and He is pleasing to the Father. Jesus had not done one miracle. He was being challenged in His identity to have that identity moved from what God said about Him to His performance. Satan wants you to believe that your performance with God determines your relationship with God. That is demonic, religious and of the kingdom of this world. *(Written by Dave Duell)*

SEPTEMBER 14
BULLDOG OF FAITH
2 KINGS 4:30

2 Kings 4:30 "And the mother of the child said, 'As the Lord liveth, and as thy soul liveth, I will not leave thee.' And he arose, and followed her."

The Shunammite knew in her heart that it was only Elisha that God would use to bring her son back from the dead. She would not settle for anything less. She had left her gift from God, now void of life, to go to Mount Carmel with hope in her heart. "It is well," she said as she departed. She knew her God and she knew how to access His power.

Many times, we are surprised and even shocked when adverse circumstances threaten to steal God's blessings in our lives. We get comfortable and take our ease spiritually with the status quo. We must realize that as long as we live on planet Earth, the battle will not cease. When a skirmish erupts, it's not the time to make a feeble effort and then resign ourselves to the first answer we get. With determination in our hearts and a history with the Creator of the universe, we can hang on until heaven touches earth. *(Written by Mike Fehlauer)*

SEPTEMBER 15
STEAK OR SPAM
MALACHI 3:10

Malachi 3:10 "Bring ye all the tithes into the storehouse, that there may be meat in mine house, and prove me now herewith, saith the LORD of hosts, if I will not open you the windows of heaven, and pour you out a blessing, that there shall not be room enough to receive it."

We are to give God our best. In Proverbs 3:9 it says to, *"Honour the LORD with thy substance, and with the firstfruits of all thine increase."* First fruits are the first, beginning, best, chief or choice part of everything we get. Some people would go out and spend fifty or a hundred dollars or more for a nice night out, but never give more than a dollar or maybe ten dollars to the house of God. God told us to bring Him our best. Don't get me wrong. If that's truly the most you can do, then keep doing it and God will bring increase. He told us to bring all our tithes into the storehouse (the house of God) that there may be meat in His house.

Here are some questions we should all ask ourselves as members of the body of Christ. What kind of meat am I providing for my local church? Am I providing steak, or Spam? Am I giving my best, or am I being stingy in the giving department? These are tough questions that warrant an honest answer from the heart of every believer.

What kind food do you suppose we will be eating at the marriage supper of the Lamb? Cold cuts, Twinkies and peanut butter? I don't think so. If everyone gave like you give, what financial shape would the church be in? *(Written by Bob Nichols)*

SEPTEMBER 16
GOD, THE BIGGEST GIVER
JOHN 3:16

John 3:16 "For God so loved the world that He gave . . . . "

God gave us His very best, His only begotten Son. He gave for a reason— because He loved us. His motivation for giving was love.

As His child, you've inherited His giving nature. Love should be your motivation for giving too. He wants to meet your needs (financial, spiritual, and so forth) and increase your resources to meet the needs of others. He desires that you have an abundance for every good work (II Corinthians 9:8).

When God gave His Son, He expected to receive back many sons. We can also expect to receive when we give. When we give our finances to God, we can believe for a return in people being saved and added to His family.

God is our example. He gave His best so that mankind would be able to have eternal life and so that heaven could be populated. Eternal life is knowing God and Jesus Christ (John 17:3).

Notice that *"God so loved the world"* (Jn. 3:16). God poured out His wrath on Jesus so that the entire world could have a chance to experience God's love. God wants everyone to be saved. He is not excluding those who are homosexuals or abortionists, as some would have you believe. He is offering to all His marvelous salvation.

We are living in the age of grace when God is calling mankind to come to Him. His love reaches out to the world. Can we do any less? *(Written by Bonnie Duell)*

SEPTEMBER 17
JESUS WATCHES YOUR ATTITUDE IN GIVING
MARK 12:41

Mark 12:41 "And Jesus sat over against the treasury, and beheld how the people cast money into the treasury . . . ."

This verse introduces the story of Jesus and the disciples observing the Pharisees who gave large sums of money and the widow who gave her mite. The issue of this story is not how much each gave, but the attitude behind their giving. Notice, Jesus watched how the people gave. Jesus was more interested in the heart behind the giving than the amount. The woman's amount of money was smaller, but her gift was larger. Jesus said she outgave them all.

The quality of giving is weighed more than the quantity. *"For the love of money is the root of all evil: which while some coveted after, they have erred from the faith, and pierced themselves through with many sorrows"* (1 Tim. 6:10). God wants us to be in love with Him and give from that motive.

God gives to us from a motive of love and wants us to imitate Him. *"For God so loved the world, that he gave"* (Jn. 3:16). Love motivated God to give His best, His Son. Love should motivate us to give our best to the Lord, our firstfruits. This type of giving gives honor to the Lord. *"Honor the Lord with thy substance, and with the firstfruits of all thy increase"* (Prov. 3:9).

The Pharisees gave out of self interest, not love toward God and compassion toward people. This motive caused them to give large amounts to impress people or to remove a feeling of guilt for not truly obeying the Word of God.

Make your own giving count. Let every penny you give come from your love for God and His people. Your gift will advance the kingdom of God and you will receive a reward for being a cheerful giver. *(Written by Bob Yandian)*

SEPTEMBER 18
PERSONAL LIABILITY
1 SAMUEL 3:11-18

1 Samuel 3:13 "For I have told him that I will judge his house for ever for the iniquity which he knoweth; because his sons made themselves vile, and he restrained them not."

Eli's sons, Hophni and Phinehas, were very wicked. They perverted the priest's office by despising the Lord's sacrifices and lording it over God's people (1 Sam. 2:12-17). They also committed fornication with the women who came to the tabernacle (1 Sam. 2:22). It's understandable why God judged them, but why did Eli come under judgment?

Some would say it was because he was their father and was therefore responsible for their actions. But that's not what the Lord said. In this verse, the Lord said He was judging Eli because he knew what his sons were doing and he restrained them not. Eli wasn't judged for what his sons did. He was judged by God because he didn't use his authority to restrain them.

Eli did rebuke his sons. In 1 Samuel 2:22-25, Eli told his sons that what they were doing was wrong and that they would be judged by God, but he didn't restrain them from doing those things. He was the high priest. He could have removed them from the priesthood. But he didn't. He preferred his sons over the Lord (1 Sam. 2:29). Talk isn't enough. There has to be consequences attached to actions. Eli didn't act.

Satan often condemns us over the actions of others, especially our children. But God holds us accountable for our own actions, not those of others. God believes in and practices personal liability. Apply this truth in your own life and business today. You are the only one you have absolute authority over and responsibility for. *(Written by Andrew Wommack)*

SEPTEMBER 19
ABUNDANT LIFE
JOHN 10:10

John 10:10 "The thief does not come except to steal, and to kill, and to destroy. I have come that they may have life, and that they may have it more abundantly."

Jesus said in John 10:10, *"I have come that they might have life, and . . . more abundantly."* You can't have abundant life unless you know Him. Paul said in Philippians 3:10, *"That I might know Him."* My good friend, Walter Olson, from Kenya said, "My best friend is God!" Wow, that's my prayer!

The big deception in the garden with Adam and Eve was that Satan was trying to get them to eat of the fruit so that they could be like God, when in reality, they were already like God. They walked and talked with God.

The devil is still using the same kind of deception on us today in that he is trying to get us to be like God. The real truth is that when we accept Jesus we become like Jesus through His blood and our position with God has been renewed through the New Covenant just like Adam and Eve before they sinned. Thank you, Jesus!

When a person is born of God and becomes a real Christian, he is made a Christman. If the world wants to see Jesus, it must look upon the Christian. The secret of Christianity is not in doing, but in being. Real Christianity is in being in possession of the nature of Jesus Christ.

You are built for connection. Something on the inside of you draws you to God. You are the temple of God's presence.

God wants you to succeed (Psalm 84:11). You are engineered for success. You are God's number one interest. Calvary revealed the intensity of His love. He loved us to death.

Decide your dream (Philippians 4:13). Make up your mind what you want. The best way to predict your future is to create it. Be specific. Write down your dreams and desires in a life notebook. Does it line up with what He wants? Relate it to eternity. All great achievements require time and tenacity. Ninety percent of all failures result from people quitting too soon. The Lord will pull you through if you can stand the pull. The road to success runs uphill, so don't expect to break any speed records. *(Written by Dave Duell)*

SEPTEMBER 20
MIRACLES THROUGH FAITHFULNESS
2 KINGS 4:13

2 Kings 4:13 "Behold, thou hast been careful for us with all this care; what is to be done for thee? . . . ."

Faithfulness is one of the most powerful forces in the universe. Its influence on the human existence is both internal and external. It will do an increasingly invasive work in the heart that strips away other motives for the good things we do. As it wends its way into every nook and cranny of life, it plumbs the depths of the nature of God resident in man. Faithfulness is part of God's very character and when it is wielded in the earth it gives expression to His holy passion. Externally, God saw the Shunammite's faithfulness as a steward of the resources He had given her. She used them in service to Elisha. She recognized the power and influence she possessed and chose to use them to further the kingdom of God.

The Shunammite's expression of faithfulness and generosity got the attention of heaven. She was, unwittingly, placed in a position where God could meet the deepest desire of her heart (see 2 Kings 4:13, 16). In spite of her husband's age, she miraculously conceived and gave birth to a son. We can never outgive God! May the Lord drill deeper into the mother lode of His nature within you and release a flow of faithfulness that will enrich your life and the lives of those around you. *(Written by Mike Fehlauer)*

SEPTEMBER 21
SUPERNATURAL PROTECTION
MALACHI 3:11

Malachi 3:11 "And I will rebuke the devourer for your sakes, and he shall not destroy the fruits of your ground; neither shall your vine cast her fruit before the time in the field, saith the LORD of hosts."

We are entering the days where it will take more than a home security system to protect us. We need the hand of God Almighty on our lives. Here is the testimony of Alexander H. Kerr, founder of the Kerr Glass Manufacturing Company, a company still known for its quality fruit jars. Mr. Kerr was born again in the meetings of Dwight L. Moody. After his conversion, Mr. Kerr earnestly desired to see if tithing was still applicable in modern times. He covenanted with God to set aside ten percent of his income for the kingdom of God. At the time, he was deep in debt but knew that if it was a principle of God, putting it into practice would bless him and honor God. Almost immediately, Mr. Kerr started to reap the harvest on his seed sown.

It was during that first year of tithing that he started the fruit jar company. The company was located in San Francisco and was in operation at the time of the famous San Francisco Earthquake. One of the tragic results of the earthquake was terrible fires that destroyed almost everything in their path. The Kerr Glass Manufacturing Company was right in the heart of where the fires were. And, his company was probably the most flammable building in the area. People told Mr. Kerr that he would be totally devastated and he responded by saying that if that were true, then God's Word was a lie. He stood on Malachi 3:11 knowing that God promised to rebuke the devourer and He would be true to His Word.

Mr. Kerr received a telegram telling him that his business was "somehow" miraculously saved. He went to investigate and found that while it was true that the surrounding area was completely destroyed, not one item of his company was touched—not even the wooden fence that surrounded his property. The flames burned everything around it, and even leaped over his property, but his business was untouched. After this, Mr. Kerr went on to publish several leaflets or tracts (the first one was titled "God's Cure for Poverty") and distributed them in every case of jars that he shipped. By the time he went on to be with the Lord, over five million of these tracts were circulated. What a testimony!

Mr. Kerr's testimony is not an isolated case. The same principles that protected him and brought him from poverty to being a millionaire (for the glory of God) will work for you and me. God is faithful to His promises. When we are faithful to tithe, He will be faithful to rebuke the devourer for our sakes. *(Written by Bob Nichols)*

SEPTEMBER 22
INDIVIDUAL MASTERPIECES
EPHESIANS 2:10

Ephesians 2:10 "For we are His workmanship, created in Christ Jesus for good works, which God prepared beforehand that we should walk in them"
(New King James).

Grace changes us. It changes how we view ourselves and others. Grace can change our entire perspective on life itself and how it should be managed. The influence of God's grace upon our lives will direct us into the will of God. Our lives, then and only then, become testimonies to His glory. Again, as we come to understand the grace deposited in us we begin to see ourselves as God views us. We begin to know deep down that we are who we are by the grace of God. His grace on our lives alone is sufficient to identify us.

I talk to so many people who are so distressed, even depressed, over how they see themselves. They are dear people who are constantly comparing themselves with others—a practice the Bible condemns as unwise. Young and old alike are struggling for some certainty about who they are and where they belong in the overall scheme of things. I want so much for them all to find the relief that can only come by drawing near to Jesus and letting His grace flood into their souls.

His grace has made us unique; we are all individual masterpieces by God's design. To hope for anything else is to become just a cheap ten cent copy of someone else. You dress like them, you talk like them, but you can never be them. It's terribly frustrating and everyone gets cheated. Next time you look into the mirror, remind yourself that you are who you are by God's grace and spend a little time thanking Him for it. *(Written by Marshall Townsley)*

SEPTEMBER 23
MONEY IS NECESSARY FOR SPREADING THE GOSPEL
ROMANS 10:15

Romans 10:15 "And how shall they preach, except they be sent . . . . "
God is not the only One who sends people to preach: people also send people.
With the call of God comes a call on many others to prayerfully and financially support the one being sent. When God sends, He supports. When people send, they also support.

People never stand alone. A man called to pastor has to have many others called to support him. Ushers, Sunday school teachers, and youth directors are only a few who sense the call of God on their lives to hold up the hands of the one called by God. Behind one calling is the calling of many.

Like God, churches send people to preach: *"Now when the apostles which were at Jerusalem heard that Samaria had received the word of God, they sent unto them Peter and John"* (Acts 8:14). I'm sure the Holy Spirit must have spoken to the hearts of Peter and John to go, but the church also sent them. *"Then tidings of these things came unto the ears of the church which was in Jerusalem: and they sent forth Barnabas, that he should go as far as Antioch"* (Acts 11:22). Throughout the book of Acts, churches cooperated with the call of God and confirmed the call by sending out a person or group. This was done by the laying on of hands: *"And when they had fasted and prayed, and laid their hands on them, they sent them away"* (Acts 13:3).

This sending forth must have been done with the giving of finances also. When Paul ran out of money in Corinth, the call of God came to the saints of Macedonia to give and assist Paul. They sent out ministers to bring the money to Paul and free him from his tent-making occupation to preach the Gospel again without financial restraints.

Every time you send money to a minister of God, you are assisting the call of God on his life. God has sent you to hold up the hands of many who are called and sent into the fields of harvest. *(Written by Bob Yandian)*

SEPTEMBER 24
THE POWER OF GOD'S WORD
1 SAMUEL 5:1-12

1 Samuel 5:4 "Dagon was fallen upon his face to the ground before the ark of the
LORD; and the head of Dagon and both the palms of his hands were cut
off upon the threshold; only the stump of Dagon was left to him."
The ark of the covenant contained the two tables of stone with the ten commandments written on them that the Lord gave to Moses (Dt. 10:2-5). It also contained all the writings of Moses, or the first five books of the Bible (Dt. 31:24-26). So, the ark contained God's Word.

Israel had been defeated in battle (1 Sam. 4), and the ark had been captured by the Philistines. They brought the ark as a trophy into the temple of their fish god Dagon. But the next morning, they found the image of Dagon laying face down, prostrate before the ark of the covenant. Hoping this was a coincidence, they set the statue back up in its place. However, the next morning, the same thing happened, except this time the head and both palms of the hands were cut off and placed on the threshold of the temple.

This graphically illustrates the power of God's Word. Neither Satan, nor any of his demons can stand before it. Only the stump of what the devil was is left to remind us of our defeated foe. He is defeated!

Jesus used God's Word to defeat the devil (Mt. 4; Lk. 4). Anything Jesus said would have been scripture since He is God. Yet He quoted the same written Word of God that we have because He couldn't come up with anything more powerful. God's Word is powerful! The written Word of God that we have is infinitely more powerful than most of us realize. We have that same power that made Dagon fall prostrate before the ark. Put God's Word on the inside of you today and watch your problems bow down. *(Written by Andrew Wommack)*

SEPTEMBER 25
MORE GOOD NEWS
HEBREW 8:6

Hebrews 8:6 "But now He (Jesus) has obtained a more excellent ministry, inasmuch as He is also Mediator of a better covenant, which was established on better promises."

Under the Old Covenant, if a person fell short of the Law in any way, he would rightfully look for the curse of the Law on his life. He had a covenant with God that was based on his performance. The promises of that covenant were contingent upon a person's ability to obey. The promises were for those who obeyed and the curses were for those who did not.

The New Covenant is different. It is a better covenant. Hebrews 8:6 says, *"But now He (Jesus) has obtained a more excellent ministry, inasmuch as He is also Mediator of a better covenant, which was established on better promises."* We have a better covenant with better promises. Yet, unbelief in the New Covenant makes us continually look back to the Old Covenant.

We follow Satan's method of reasoning and before long, we have fallen from a place where the Covenant is working in our lives. It is hard to believe it can be this good! It is hard to believe God is this good. Yet, He is. The question is, do we believe that?

In the New Covenant God did not make a covenant with us individually. He made a covenant with Jesus. Galatians 3:16 says, *"Now to Abraham and his Seed were the promises made. He does not say, 'And to seeds,' as of many, but as of one. 'And to your seed,' who is Christ."*

The Old Covenant was based on each individual's ability to uphold his side of the Covenant. The New Covenant, however, is based on ONE man's ability to uphold the Covenant. That man is Jesus! He fulfilled all the righteous requirements of the Law. He made the Covenant sure. It has been sealed by His death. It cannot be changed.

God does not, therefore, uphold his Covenant with us based on our ability to always perform properly. We are in Christ. He has received the New Covenant. Because we are in Him, we receive along with Him. *(Written by Dave Duell)*

SEPTEMBER 26
A DIFFERENT KIND OF PROSPERITY
ISAIAH 50:4

Isaiah 50:4 "That I should know how to speak a word in season to him that is weary . . . . "

God desires that we *"prosper and be in health, just as our soul prospers"* (3 John 2). Our scripture from Isaiah, chapter 50, shows a different kind of prosperity—receiving the instruction and wisdom of God in an abundant fashion. Morning by morning, constantly and regularly, God gives us the ability to hear His words of life. This knowledge can become so pervasive that it overflows in our conversations. *"The Lord God has given me the tongue of the learned . . ." (Isaiah 50:4)*. What a monumental benefit this godly wisdom has for the recipients! They are able to deal wisely and shrewdly in the affairs of life, avoiding traps along the way. But it doesn't stop there. The true purpose of this abundance is so that we have a timely word of encouragement and strength to give to another person who may be thinking of throwing in the towel. We all have seasons of pressure, discouragement, and fatigue. During those difficult times, it is a breath of fresh air to hear words of faith and truth from a friend. God's desire is that each one of us becomes a bearer of the Good News, bringing warmth to a brother's long, cold winter. As you're seeking the Lord for prosperity in your life, don't forget to show up to his Wisdom 101 class. *(Written by Mike Fehlauer)*

SEPTEMBER 27
TITHING IS NOT GOD COMING AFTER YOUR MONEY, IT'S GOD COMING AFTER YOUR POVERTY
MALACHI 3:10-12

Malachi 3:10 "Bring ye all the tithes into the storehouse, that there may be meat in mine house, and prove me now herewith, saith the LORD of hosts, if I will not open you the windows of heaven, and pour you out a blessing, that there shall not be room enough to receive it."

I recently read a testimony of a man named Oswald J. Smith who pastored a church in Toronto, Canada, during the Great Depression. As you can imagine, there were many, many people who were destitute during that time and would come to the church for assistance. That's where people should be able to go—to church. Through the tithes and gifts of believers, the church should be able to provide for the needs of people. That is exactly how the early church did things. Pastor Smith was responsible for sowing hundreds of dollars into the lives of needy people who had nowhere else to turn, but to God. During that time he observed something very interesting. He asked each person or family that he helped a question: were they tithing? The response from every single person he asked was no. Not one person had been faithful to tithe. It was confirmation to him that if God's people would be faithful to tithe, God would be faithful to supply their needs.

Tithing is not God coming after your money, it's God coming after your poverty. God can not supply a harvest to you unless you plant the seed. If you don't sow anything, He has nothing to increase. If you would like to see abundance in your life, do it God's way. Tithe and give offerings above your tithe. Poverty cannot stay when God is being glorified by your giving. *(Written by Bob Nichols)*

SEPTEMBER 28
CLOTHED WITH GOD'S ABILITY
I SAMUEL 17:37

I Samuel 17:37 "The Lord, who delivered me from the paw of the lion and from the paw of the bear, He will deliver me from the hand of this Philistine."

The story of young David as he stood before the champion of the Philistines is a convincing example of how grace makes the weak strong.

Goliath stood threatening the men of Israel. The Bible says that they were all afraid at the sight of him and the sound of his voice. But David, seeing him and hearing him, had a completely different response altogether.

When David persisted that something be done to silence the giant, he was finally brought before King Saul. The king bluntly told him, *"you're not able to go against this Philistine"* (1 Sam. 17:33). Now, this is the king talking—the highest authority in the land. But David was not deterred. He didn't see his youth and limited ability as an issue. David knew that God would give him grace and he expected to be clothed with God's ability as he stood before Goliath in battle.

I really enjoy the picture that the scripture paints next. Saul attempts to arm David and clothe him with the very best that he had for battle. But David refused Saul saying, *"I cannot go with these, for I have not proved them" (I Sam. 17:39)*. This is a picture to me of putting off the best our flesh has to offer and choosing to go with God's grace and power which is far superior. Again, the Bible exhorts us to be strong in the Lord and in the power of His might (Eph. 6:10).

David took his staff, which speaks of God's authority and five smooth stones, five being the biblical number for grace, and slew the giant. The message is that it is out of the supply of God's grace and His authority to act that the threatening giants of fear, inadequacy, intimidation and condemnation are defeated. There's grace for every single human weakness. Be clothed with it before you go out to fight. You're more than a conqueror through Christ, and His victory has become yours. *(Written by Marshall Townsley)*

SEPTEMBER 29
WE SHOULD GIVE THE LORD OUR BEST AND MOST COSTLY
2 SAMUEL 24:24

2 Samuel 24:24 "And the king said unto Araunah, Nay; but I will surely buy it of thee at a price: neither will I offer burnt offerings unto the LORD my God of that which doth cost me nothing. So David bought the threshingfloor . . . . "

David the king looked at every circumstance as an opportunity to sow seed. He also wanted to sow quality seed. David gave generously and blessed the person he was dealing with. In this story he purchased the threshingfloor which would be the altar for the ark of the covenant to rest beside, and the future altar of the temple of God.

God gave His best for us. He did not give an angel to die for us, but His only Son. Jesus is God's finest—His firstfruits.

Another title for our gift to God is firstfruits. It is not called this just because it is given off the top, but because it is the best of the crop. The choicest of the crop produces the best when planted. Any farmer knows to look for the best of the seed to plant. You do not eat the best, but sow it. Poor quality seed produces a poor quality harvest. A harvest of excellence comes from excellent seed.

I have seen many Christians give gifts of poor quality to the Lord. Cars have been given that needed repair, clothing that was old and torn and appliances that did not work. Why give someone else your headaches? Mountains are to be removed into the sea, not into someone else's backyard. Would you like someone else's problems? Why then would they want yours?

What you sow, you reap. How would you like a hundred fold return on the junk you have sown? Wouldn't it be better to receive a great harvest of good quality merchandise back into your life? Repair what you are about to give and make it a gift of quality. Bring it up to a standard that would bless you if someone gave it into your life. It is good to give what you would just as soon keep. It can then be a blessing in the life of the one you are giving it to, just as it would be in yours. *(Written by Bob Yandian)*

SEPTEMBER 30
THINGS TO COME
1 SAMUEL 9:15-10:13

1 Samuel 10:9 "And it was so, that when he had turned his back to go from Samuel, God gave him another heart: and all those signs came to pass that day."

Contemplate for a moment how miraculous Samuel's words of knowledge were. The Lord told him he would meet the king-to-be the next day. When Samuel saw Saul, the Lord spoke that this was the one. In Samuel's comments to Saul, Samuel told Saul that the asses he had lost three days before had been found. Saul hadn't mentioned that to Samuel. This was a powerful word of knowledge.

In 1 Samuel 10:2-6, Samuel told Saul that he would meet two men at Rachel's tomb who would tell him the asses had been found. He went on to prophesy that three men would meet Saul in an exact location and he told Saul exactly what they would be carrying. Then Samuel said they would give him two loaves of bread. How specific can you get? He also prophesied that at the hill of God a company of prophets would meet him and Saul would join in and prophesy with them. Every one of these things came to pass that same day. This is one of the most awesome displays of the word of knowledge in all the Word of God.

Jesus said that when the Holy Spirit came, He would show us things to come (Jn. 16:13). The New Testament also reveals that what we have in Christ is so much better than what any Old Testament saints had; there is no comparison (2 Cor. 3:6-11). God's Word says that the Old Testament saints longed for what we have now (1 Pet. 1:10-12). The very least saint in the kingdom of God has a greater salvation than what Samuel had (Mt. 11:11). Yet look at how God used him!

It suffices to say that none of us have realized our full potential. Today, let the Lord challenge you to flow in His supernatural ability more than ever before. *(Written by Andrew Wommack)*

OCTOBER 1
GRACE NUGGETS PART 1
EPHESIANS 2:8

Ephesians 2:8 "For by grace you have been saved through faith, and that not of your-selves; it is a gift of God."
I want to share a few nuggets from God's Word on grace. The foundational definition of grace is fourfold.
1. Grace is unmerited love from God, unearned divine favor. *"For by grace you have been saved through faith, and that not of yourselves; it is the gift of God, not of works, lest anyone should boast."* (Ephesians 2:8-9)
2. Grace is divinely imparted ability. *"But by the grace of God I am what I am, and His grace toward me was not in vain; but I labored more abundantly than they all, yet not I, but the grace of God which was with me."* (I Corinthians 15:10)
3. Grace is the sum total of the activity of God in our lives. *"And God is able to make all grace abound toward you, that you, always having all sufficiency in all things, may have an abundance for every good work."* (2 Corinthians 9:8)
4. Grace is the abundant generosity of God toward us. *"And God is able to make all grace abound toward you, that you, always having all sufficiency in all things, may have an abundance for every good work."* (2 Corinthians 9:8)
G.R.A.C.E. is God's Riches at Christ's Expense. Grace is inseparably tied to the cross, for it was at "Christ's expense" that we are partakers of all that God is and all that God has.
Grace is acquired three main ways: 1. By faith - *"For by grace are you saved through faith; and that not of yourselves: it is the gift of God . . . ."* (Ephesians 2:8); 2. By humility - *" . . . For God resists the proud, but gives grace to the humble"* (I Peter 5:5); 3. By sincerity - *"Grace be with all them that love our Lord Jesus Christ in sincerity"* (Ephesians 6:24). John 1:17 states that *"The law was given by Moses, but grace and truth came by Jesus Christ."* The truth was so much a part of Jesus He could legally declare, *"I am . . . the truth . . . "* (John 14:6). *(Written by Dave Duell)*

OCTOBER 2
GRACE NUGGETS PART 2
JOHN 1:17

John 1:17 "For the law was given through Moses, but grace and truth came through Jesus Christ."
In like manner, because He was the very incarnation of grace itself, He could have easily confessed, "I am the grace of God." To know Jesus is to know grace. But even though grace was graciously introduced by the Son of God, and even though His very coming ushered in a new era entitled the Age of Grace, it is somewhat amazing and ironic that Jesus never directly alluded to the subject Himself.
Later on, in the Pauline epistles, the doctrine of grace became a major scriptural emphasis. But Jesus never mentioned the word. He never explained what grace was. Instead, He revealed it. He demonstrated it. He proved its reality. Defending one caught in the act of adultery. Eating with publicans and sinners. Sharing the deep mysteries of God with the woman at the well. Healing His own enemy in the garden. Praying forgiveness for the very ones who crucified Him. In all these things and more, Jesus became the absolute expression of grace, so rich and so full that thousands have since been left awestruck.
We can grow in grace in four main ways:
First, grace is multiplied unto us *"through the knowledge of God, and of Jesus our Lord"* (II Peter 1:2). Usually this knowledge comes to us by the Word and through the Spirit.
Second, we grow in grace by the influence of other grace-filled individuals and the transfer of their "gift." Paul said in Philippians 1:7 *"Ye are all partakers of my grace."*
Third, we grow in grace by more deeply consecrating ourselves to God.
Fourth, we grow in grace by giving away to others the mercy, love, strength, knowledge and abilities that God has graciously given to us.
The more grace we give away, the more grace we attract; for God is far more apt to bless channels than cisterns. *(Written by Dave Duell)*

OCTOBER 3
ONLY A SYMPTOM
MALACHI 3:16

Malachi 3:16 "Therefore take heed to your spirit, and let none deal treacherously . . . . "

The book of Malachi is probably most recognized for its passage on tithing, and subsequently, receiving the blessings of God. A comprehensive study of the book reveals additional factors in obtaining a prosperous life. The people of Malachi's day were distant and passive in their relationship with God. Their worship had become a mere formality. Lack of tithing is the commonly taught symptom of their spiritual disease. Looking further, we see that the impact of their decaying spiritual condition was also seen profoundly in their family relationships. Marriages were crumbling. Fathers were hardening their hearts against their children. Children were hating their fathers.

Within God's call for repentance and restoration of His people, is the admonition to *"take heed to your spirit, and let none deal treacherously . . . . "* This reveals an undeniable connection between the health of our relationship with God and the health of our relationships with our family. If we have allowed our hearts to grow cold and hard toward God, it will translate into indifference and lack of passion in our marriages and relationships with our children. We cut ourselves off from the blessings that can only come through healthy, intimate relationships. As God reaches out to His people in mercy, He touches the depths of our human poverty—lack of a shared love, security and tenderness in our homes. The abiding promise is, *"And he shall turn the heart of the fathers to the children, and the heart of the children to their fathers . . . "* (Malachi 4:6). *(Written by Mike Fehlauer)*

OCTOBER 4
THE SEED THAT LEAVES YOUR HAND WILL NEVER LEAVE YOUR FUTURE
2 KINGS 8:1-6

2 Kings 8:6 "And when the king asked the woman, she told him. So the king appointed unto her a certain officer, saying, Restore all that was her's, and all the fruits of the field since the day that she left the land, even until now."

Many of us are familiar with the passage of the Bible where Isaac reaped even in famine (see Genesis 26:1 & 12), but that is not the only example. Do you remember the Shunammite woman in 2 Kings 4:1-37? She and her husband built a prophet's chamber to house Elisha when he was in their area. They planted a seed. They sowed into Elisha's life and then when their son died, Elisha prayed and the boy was raised from the dead.

But, as if that wasn't enough, her reaping didn't stop there. Look at 2 Kings 8:1-2, *"Then spake Elisha unto the woman, whose son he had restored to life, saying, Arise, and go thou and thine household, and sojourn wheresoever thou canst sojourn: for the LORD hath called for a famine; and it shall also come upon the land seven years. And the woman arose, and did after the saying of the man of God: and she went with her household, and sojourned in the land of the Philistines seven years."* God warned her about the famine ahead of time. When the famine was over, she came back to beg the king to give her back the land that she had deserted for seven years.

Just look how God set it all up: divine connections and divine appointments. It "just so happened" that the king was talking with Gehazi, Elisha's servant, wanting to know about the great things that Elisha had done. And, it "just so happened" that Gehazi told him about the Shunammite woman and how her son was raised from the dead. While Gehazi was telling the king about this miracle, in walks the very woman. Coincidence? Not at all. God set it up. The king was obviously hungry to hear about the things of God. He was stirred. The woman told the king of her situation and not only did he restore her land to her, but everything that the land produced while she was gone was restored to her, as well. Did you catch that? *Her land was still producing fruit even in famine!* Oh, when we serve God and follow His way of doing things, He will provide for us! He is faithful! We will reap even in famine! The seed that leaves your hand will never leave your future! *(Written by Bob Nichols)*

OCTOBER 5
DISTINCTIVELY CHRISTIAN
PSALM 112:4

Psalm 112:4 "Unto the upright there arises light in the darkness; He is gracious, and full of compassion, and righteous" (New King James).
Being gracious means possessing and exercising the ability to see worth and value in people beyond what they deserve, despite their unattractive qualities and irrespective of what they can do for us. Operative grace lifts us out of our own extremely selfish, narrow sited point of view to see and treat people as Christ would. It relieves us and those we give it to—those we share it with.

Grace goes beyond addressing the sin problems to solving them. It goes beyond teaching us to abstain from all forms of ungodliness. It is the transforming power of God that enables us to live holy and acceptable lives unto God and grace-like lives, toward all others.

Do you realize how important that is? People need Jesus. They need to know His love which is well beyond mere human love. They need a living revelation of His character served up to them. If Jesus is lifted up, the Bible says, He will draw man to Himself. And if they come, their lives can be changed for all eternity.

In short, being gracious means living a distinctively Christian life that daily revels in the power of God's grace while also allowing it to inform and thus transform, our ordinary ways of living. Christians should be distinctively grace-like. If we minimize grace, we lose our distinctiveness as Christians. *(Written by Marshall Townsley)*

OCTOBER 6
WHOM DOES GOD PROSPER?
PSALM 35:27

Psalm 35:27 "Let them shout for joy, and be glad, that favour my righteous cause: yea, let them say continually, Let the LORD be magnified, which hath pleasure in the prosperity of his servant."
This verse should give you a reason to shout. God delights and has great pleasure when you prosper. I think this verse is trying to wake up most Christians. God is more anxious for you to prosper than you are. Instead of feeling guilty about prospering, you can actually sense God's pleasure over you.

But whom does God delight in prospering? Those who favor His righteous cause. What is God's righteous cause? It is souls. When winning the lost is your highest priority, you share God's highest priority. As you give into God's work, sowing tithes and offerings to Him, imagine God's delight as He searches for ways to bring social, family, business and financial prosperity to you. His rejoicing then becomes your rejoicing. His joy becomes yours. This verse says you can shout for joy and be glad.

The rejoicing of the Lord then comes through your own mouth. Your lips begin to continually bless the Lord. What should your continual confession be? *"Let the Lord be magnified, which hath pleasure in my prosperity."* When you put God's desires above your own, God's promise is, *"Wealth and riches shall be in his house: and his righteousness endureth for ever"* (Ps. 112:3). Your rejoicing can also be continual because God gives the joy of the Holy Spirit with His prosperity. *"The blessing of the Lord, it maketh rich, and he addeth no sorrow with it"* (Prov. 10:22).

Finally, your prosperity and joy become a witness to the lost. Prosperity is promised to those who will follow after the commandments of the Lord. One result is, *"And all people of the earth shall see that thou art called by the name of the LORD and they shall be afraid of (fear) thee"* (Dt. 28:10). Your prosperity is a witness even when your mouth is silent. *(Written by Bob Yandian)*

OCTOBER 7
COMMITMENT, NOT CONVENIENCE
1 SAMUEL 13:1-14

1 Samuel 13:13 "And Samuel said to Saul, Thou hast done foolishly: thou hast not kept the commandment of the LORD thy God, which he commanded thee: for now would the LORD have established thy kingdom upon Israel for ever."

Many people think that whatever the Lord wills to happen, happens regardless of what we do. This verse proves that wrong. The Lord had plans to establish Saul's kingdom over Israel forever. If Saul would have obeyed, then we would be talking about the sure mercies of Saul instead of the sure mercies of David (Isa. 55:3; Acts 13:34). David was not God's first choice. Saul was. Yet, he didn't accomplish all of God's plans for him because of his disobedience.

Saul's disobedience wasn't hatred for God. Saul had an arrangement with Samuel to wait seven days for him to come and offer a sacrifice before he joined battle with the Philistines. Samuel didn't show in the allotted time so Saul offered the sacrifice himself.

He wasn't eager to disobey God. He did wait the amount of time that Samuel said. But circumstances "forced" him to disobey God, or so Saul reasoned. The truth is that those who obey the Lord only when it is convenient will never have God entrust true leadership to them.

The kingdom of God is going uphill while Satan's kingdom is headed downhill. That is to say that following God is never the easy thing to do. Those who don't commit themselves to obeying God at all costs will always find a reason to do otherwise. Obedience is based in commitment, not convenience.

God has great plans for your life (Jer. 29:11). But you need to cooperate by following Him at all costs. Commitment is the key. *(Written by Andrew Wommack)*

OCTOBER 8
CHIP OFF THE OLD BLOCK
ISAIAH 51:1

Isaiah 51:1 "Hearken to me, ye that follow after righteousness, ye that seek the LORD: look unto the rock whence ye are hewn, and to the hole of the pit whence ye are digged."

Jesus is the cornerstone of our salvation. He is the firm foundation on which we may build our lives. More than that, we are made from the same stuff. We have the same Father as Jesus. *"God hath sent forth the Spirit of his Son into your hearts"* (Gal 4:6). We have *"the same spirit of faith"* (2 Cor. 4:13) as Jesus. We have the same spiritual position: *"(He) hath raised us up together, and made us sit together in heavenly places in Christ Jesus"* (Eph. 2:6).

Jesus was also the stone that the builders rejected. He suffered ridicule and shame at the hands of ungodly men. People were blinded to his inestimable value. Why are we so surprised when it happens to us? No matter what pit we may find ourselves in, God sees our intrinsic worth. He digs us out, slinging the muck and mire aside.

As we seek after Him and all of His benefits, we will do well to regularly focus our attention on two things: We will be humbled when we look at where we came from. We will be encouraged when we look at who we are and where we are going. *(Written by Mike Fehlauer)*

OCTOBER 9
TRAMPLED BY UNBELIEF
2 KINGS 7:1-20

2 Kings 7:19 "And that lord answered the man of God, and said, Now, behold, if the LORD should make windows in heaven, might such a thing be? And he said, Behold, thou shalt see it with thine eyes, but shalt not eat thereof."
Some people are their own worst enemy. In 2 Kings 6:25 it tells us that there was a great famine in Samaria because it was besieged by the king of Syria. During that time food was scarce, prices were ridiculously high, and people were doing desperate things just to stay alive. Have you ever fallen upon desperate times? God can turn it around in a day! Elisha came in and announced that the Lord declared that by the very next day, prices for food would fall to practically nothing. That would set anyone to dancing and shouting, or would it? The officer assisting the king was a man full of doubt and unbelief. He said, "That couldn't happen even if the Lord opened the windows of heaven!" That unbelief cost him his life. Elisha told him, *"Behold, thou shalt see it with thine eyes, but shalt not eat thereof."*
In a miraculous move, God caused the Syrian army to hear the clatter of speeding chariots and galloping horses, as if a great army was approaching. They became so scared that they ran away and left everything behind. Four lepers discovered the riches that were there for the taking and reported it back to gatekeepers of Israel, and it got back to the king. The king's scouts confirmed it, and that ignited a mad dash of people plundering the deserted Syrian camp. The king's official, who said that there was no way that God could turn it around in a day, had been assigned to guard the city gate. During the human stampede to plunder the Syrians, the official was trampled to death by the rush of people.
The same God that miraculously provided for the Israelites in this account, is the same God that is faithful to provide for us today. It is our job to be faithful to Him and believe that His Word is true. Let us never be guilty of being trampled by unbelief. *(Written by Bob Nichols)*

OCTOBER 10
THE RICH YOUNG RULER
MATTHEW 19:16-17, 21-22

Matthew 19:16-17, 21-22 "'Teacher, what good thing must I do to get eternal life?' 'Why do you ask me about what is good?' Jesus replied. 'There is only One who is good. If you want to enter life, obey the commandments . . . If you want to be perfect, go, sell your possessions and give to the poor, and you will have treasure in heaven. Then come, follow me.' When the young man heard this, he went away sad, because he had great wealth" (NIV).
This of course, is Matthew's account of the rich young ruler's encounter with Jesus. If you asked the average Christian the meaning of this somewhat well-known incident, the answer would probably be something like: "Well this man just had his priorities messed up. He loved money more than God." Or, more simply, "You know it's the money. Money is just the root of all evil. More than once I've seen it destroy a young life."
I'll ask you, was it the money? Was it the love of riches that was this young man's real problem? No, not really. It appears that something is going on here that might point to a problem much closer to home for most of us, regardless of how much money we have.
So, what is it that Jesus is getting at here? I'm convinced what He is addressing in this parable is that can-do, without-any-help, work-your-way-to-heaven attitude. The rich young ruler's problem was that he viewed salvation as a business transaction—you work for God, He pays you a wage in the form of salvation.
If it's "hard" for the rich to enter the kingdom of God, it's more because of the self-reliant spirit that seems to typify them than that they have great possessions.
What's really ironic about this parable is that which the young man sought in way of an answer was already present in the form of his question to Jesus. He said, "What must I *do* to *inherit* eternal life?" Well, everyone knows that what we inherit is not based on what *we* do. An inheritance is representative of the work of another normally left to us at their death; it's not of our works but the works of another. The only appropriate answer to his question was: "only believe." *(Written by Marshall Townsley)*

OCTOBER 11
BIGGER CUP
PSALM 23:5

Psalm 23:5 "My cup runneth over."

When the manna fell in the wilderness for the Israelites to eat, we are told that everyone gathered and ate " *according to his eating"* (Ex.16:16).

This meant every person gathered and ate according to his capacity. Skinny people gathered and ate a little and heavy people gathered and ate much. They collected what they could eat. Anyone who gathered too much saw the heavenly bread spoil.

This Old Testament story is used as an example of New Testament financial prosperity: *"As it is written, He that had gathered much had nothing over; and he that had gathered little had no lack"* (2 Corinthians 8:15). The meaning is simple. If you want to be able to handle more prosperity, you have to increase your capacity. God gives more to those who can handle it. If your cup is running over and you are losing what God is giving, build a bigger cup.

You may think that is easier said than done, but it is really simple. Your cup is your understanding of God's Word. Knowledge and application of God's Word is the key to handling more of God's divine provision. God wants us to *"prosper and be in health, as our soul prospers"* (3 Jn. 2).

A line from a movie says, "If you build it they will come." God tells us if we will build a bigger cup, the prosperity will come. It is not up to us to find more prosperity. That is God's job. Our responsibility is to enlarge our capacity to handle God's blessings. Once this is accomplished, the additional prosperity will come.

You do not give a child a thousand dollars. You may give that child an allowance, of just a few dollars. Maturity is needed to receive more. With more money comes a greater degree of responsibility. Building a bigger cup, enlarging your capacity to handle prosperity, is just another term for growing up spiritually. *(Written by Bob Yandian)*

OCTOBER 12
YOU AND GOD ARE A MAJORITY
1 SAMUEL 14:1-23

1 Samuel 14:6 "And Jonathan said to the young man that bare his armour, Come, and let us go over unto the garrison of these uncircumcised: it may be that the LORD will work for us: for there is no restraint to the LORD to save by many or by few."

The Israelites were at war with the Philistines. The Philistines had 30,000 chariots, 6,000 horsemen and soldiers as numerous as the sand on the sea shore (1 Sam. 13:5). The Israelites had a total of 600 men (1 Sam. 14:2). It looked hopeless. The 600 Israelites were hiding wherever they could. But God had a man.

Jonathan, the son of Saul, had faith in God. He made a tremendous statement that God wasn't limited. He could save by many or by few. And he was willing to back his faith up with actions. If it didn't work, he would be dead.

He went over to the Philistines and with his armor bearer, started fighting. He only killed about 20 men in a space of half an acre, but it was enough. God caused fear to come on the Philistines so much that their trembling caused an earthquake (1 Sam. 14:15). The multitude didn't flee because of two men with one sword. They fled because of the fear that God put in their hearts. But it all started with one man who believed God could do anything.

You may say, "Well that was war. That's different than my situation." I'm sure that Jonathan would have been glad to swap his situation for yours. Nothing is impossible with God. The only thing that limits Him is the lack of people who will take that step of faith.

Jonathan didn't have to defeat the whole army. He only beat 20 men. You don't have to do it all. Just do what you can, and let God do the rest. *(Written by Andrew Wommack)*

OCTCBER 13
BLESSED TO BE A BLESSING
GALATIANS 3:13-14

Galatians 3:13-14 "Christ hath redeemed us from the curse of the law, being made a curse for us, for it is written, Cursed is every one that hangeth on a tree: that the blessings of Abraham might come on the Gentiles through Jesus Christ."

Here's how to walk in the blessings of God. It is God's will for you to walk in His blessings and provision. You must develop a life of faith and obedience so that you can appropriate God's best, spiritually, mentally, and physically.

You must develop a Blessing mentality. You must come to believe that God's will is for you to be blessed so that you can be a blessing to others. Galatians 3:13-14 says, *"Christ hath redeemed us from the curse of the law, being made a curse for us, for it is written, Cursed is every one that hangeth on a tree' that the blessings of Abraham might come on the Gentiles through Jesus Christ."*

The blessings of God are legally yours by the blood of Christ. They are promised blessings and provision that cover every area spiritually, mentality, and physically. *"According as his divine power hath given unto us all things pertaining unto life and godliness . . . "* (2 Peter 1:3).

Forgiveness, Righteousness, Mental Peace, Divine Guidance, Protection, Healing, Finances, Strength beyond our own. All these are ours as we have revelation from God's word and we appropriate them for ourselves.

You will only be able to help others on a permanent basis with the blessing and provision of God. That is why you must learn to walk in God's blessing so that God can use you to bless others. God gave Abraham this eternal principal: "I WILL BLESS THEE, and make thy name great; AND THOU SHALT BE A BLESSING." Some Christians talk as if it is wrong to want God's blessings. Maybe they don't want to help others. But I want God's rich blessings so that I can enjoy life and be greatly used to bless others. *(Written by Dave Duell)*

OCTOBER 14
PLENTY OF MERCY
PSALM 103:8

Psalm 103:8 "The Lord is merciful and gracious, slow to anger, and plenteous in mercy."

Even under the Old Covenant, David and others who really knew the character of God understood that He was tight with His anger and judgment, but generous with His love and mercy. If we read through the Old Testament, we will see, over and over again, that when it came time to bring people to task for their ungodly deeds, mercy was also overwhelmingly present. "But, if you will repent, then . . ." and "Nevertheless, if you will turn, I will . . ." are repeated phrases. We have a good God who has an abundant supply of patience and compassion for us. He wants us to live in His daily flow of forgiveness and renewal. He desires that we allow it to flood our lives to the point that it spills out on our family, friends, brothers and sisters in Christ, and our community. True godly prosperity? How about a deluge of the kindness and tenderness of God? *(Written by Mike Fehlauer)*

OCTOBER 15
THE PROCESS OF PROSPERITY
MARK 4:26-29

Mark 4:27 "And should sleep, and rise night and day, and the seed should spring and grow up, he knoweth not how."

It is a basic truth that you go where you sow, because where you sow your seed, is where you put your emphasis. We must target our seed. There is a process to reaping a harvest from a seed we have sown. It is a process of time. It's a process of planting your seed faithfully and consistently—planting in faith believing. We sow seeds in our tithes and offerings, but we also sow seeds by our lives. We sow seeds of kindness and mercy. You need to sow mercy wherever and whenever you can, because you never know when you'll need to reap mercy.

One of the greatest deceptions for people is this: Have it all, have it all now. There is a process of time. We have seen people with tremendous anointings and people doing great things for God. The devil will try to tempt some young ministers to take shortcuts—shortcuts in character, or shortcuts in the way they receive offerings by using manipulation. Some will yield to the temptation to take a little shortcut to get to where someone else is or have what they see someone else have. Let's not succumb to that. It's a process of time. Just keep sowing seed and let God bring the harvest. Keep doing what is right because it is right.

Often times our gifts can take us to where our character can't keep us. What you compromise to obtain, you will ultimately lose. We may not understand how, we may not understand when, but God is responsible. If you will sow seed in faith, He will take you to the place you need to be. There is a process to prosperity. *(Written by Bob Nichols)*

OCTOBER 16
OUR GENEROUS FATHER
ROMANS 6:23

Romans 6:23 "The wages of sin is death, but the gift of God is eternal life . . . . "
(King James).

Let's say that you agreed at the beginning of this day to work all day for a certain wage—say $250. Toward the end of the day someone else shows up and the boss hires him to work what's left of the day with you. When you go to collect your paycheck, the man who hired you issues a check to both you and the other guy for the same amount—$250. What would your reaction be?

The owner of a vineyard is pressed hard by a harvest deadline and so employs workers throughout the day to get the job done on time. At four different hours throughout the workday the man hires workers and sends them out into the field. When the day is ended and everyone lines up to receive their pay, all are surprised to receive the same amount, one full day's pay! Some of the workers get angry and begin to murmur and complain. When the owner hears about it, his reply is simple, "I can pay whatever I want to whomever I want. I promised you a full day's wages and you're getting it. If I decide to pay a full day's wage to the others, so what? I'm a generous man; I can do whatever I like!"

This parable, like others, magnifies the wonders of His grace while downplaying the merit of works. The work we do is wonderful and most often necessary, but it is not the basis on which we are "paid." It is by grace that we are saved, not by works. We are saved, once and for all, for no reason in particular other than because the master is generous.

To say grace and anything else, or plus anything else, saves, would be as crazy as saying that something was free for one dollar—yours absolutely free for your "gift" of one dollar. None of us can merit a gift, or it never was a gift in the first place. *(Written by Marshall Townsley)*

OCTOBER 17
THE MAN WITH THE WATERPOT
MARK 14:13

Mark 14:13 "And he sendeth forth two of his disciples, and saith unto them, Go ye
into the city, and there shall meet you a man bearing
a pitcher of water: follow him."

Jesus was about to celebrate the last supper with his disciples and needed an upper room to hold the feast. It would take a big room to accommodate Jesus and 12 disciples. When the disciples had exhausted their list of available rooms, they asked Jesus where they should look. Jesus gave them these instructions: They would find the upper room by following a man with a water pot. What timing God has! Think of the divine arrangement God had to make to have the disciples arrive at a particular intersection at the same time the man arrived with the pot of water. This man would be a sign and a guide from God.

How many of us can look back on our lives and give God the glory for the men with waterpots that have been there at the right time for us? Finances, healing and divine wisdom are only a few of the needs we have had when a servant of God met us and helped steer us in the right direction. Thank God for His many supernatural appointments.

Is there anything better than meeting a man with a waterpot? Yes, being the man with the waterpot! There was probably a day when this man had need of a helper with a waterpot to guide him.

After that wonderful encounter, he probably told God, "If I can ever carry a waterpot and lead others, please allow me to repay the debt of gratitude I owe." Since that day, the Holy Spirit had used him on more than one occasion to lead others into the will of God, including the disciples of the Messiah.

God helps us so we can help others. *"Who comforteth us in all our tribulation, that we may be able to comfort them which are in any trouble, by the comfort wherewith we ourselves are comforted of God"* (2 Cor. 1:4). Get your waterpot. *(Written by Bob Yandian)*

OCTOBER 18
WHAT RANK ARE YOU?
1 SAMUEL 15:1-29

1 Samuel 15:22 "And Samuel said, Hath the LORD as great delight in burnt
offerings and sacrifices, as in obeying the voice of the LORD? Behold,
to obey is better than sacrifice, and to hearken than the fat of rams."

God commanded Saul to make war with the Amalekites. His instructions were to kill every living thing, man and beast. Saul didn't do it. As Samuel came to the battle, Saul greeted Samuel with the statement that he had fulfilled God's command. Samuel then asked him why then all the animals were still alive which should have been killed. Saul reasoned that he had saved the best to sacrifice to the Lord. Then Samuel gave the tremendous truth that obedience is better than sacrifice.

My experience in the military was of the old school. We had no rights. We were GIs (government issues). In basic training, much of what we experienced was designed to break us of our individuality. We were taught to obey, not to think.

I once asked why they did this, and a drill sergeant, in a rare moment of candor, explained it to me. In battle, a commander doesn't have time to explain his orders. The commander has access to information that the normal troops don't. The lives of his troops depend on them trusting him and following his orders without question, immediately. The individual soldier doesn't see the big picture. Logistics demand that some people command and others follow.

God is our Commander-in-Chief. When He gives orders, we are not supposed to interpret or change them. There is a reason for His commands and He shouldn't have to explain Himself. It all comes down to a matter of rank. Subordinates obey their superiors. By his actions, Saul ranked himself higher than God. I pray that we will not make the same mistake. *(Written by Andrew Wommack)*

OCTOBER 19
FAITH AND PATIENCE
HEBREWS 6:12

Hebrews 6:12 "That you do not become sluggish, but imitate those who through faith and patience inherit the promises."

In the King James Hebrews 6:12 says, *"That ye be not slothful, but followers of them who through FAITH and PATIENCE inherit the promises."* Walking in God's blessings is definitely not a "get-rich-quick" scheme. But it is an "ETERNAL-RICHES" system! It will demand that you grow up spiritually and be transformed by the renewing of your mind. These are the true riches. All this comes by faith, patience, and prayer.

Faith is believing what God has said is true. Faith is the lifestyle for the New Covenant believer. Faith is what makes life full of adventure and excitement. Faith is seeing God's promises come to pass. Faith believes the impossible and the incredible. Faith will cause you to speak what the average man would not say. I have found that the bolder I speak, the greater miracles I see.

Patience is truly a blessing from God. Years ago God spoke to me and told me that patience will pay. How would you like to work and wait for 45 years for a vision to come to pass? God showed me a vision when I was 16 and it is now happening in my life. It was worth all of the hard work, training, and patience that it took for me to find myself in this position. When you win, you forget the hurts.

Why is it so hard for Christians to talk about money? I believe the reason people have such a hard time with money is that they are so self centered they forget what Jesus told us to do. I can hardly believe how much money is involved in Jesus' two words, "Go ye." This is my definition of prosperity: To have enough of God's supply to accomplish God's instructions. We are on the verge of great breakthroughs. We are standing with you for yours so receive this word "I WILL BLESS YOU AND YOU SHALL BE A BLESSING" (Genesis 12:2). *(Written by Dave Duell)*

OCTOBER 20
THE GREATEST REVENGE
ISAIAH 61:3

Isaiah 61:3 "That they may be called trees of righteousness; the planting of the Lord that He might be glorified."

Isaiah 61 is the passage that Jesus stood up and read in the temple at the onset of his ministry. After reading it from the scroll, he gave an unqualified declaration that He was its fulfillment. His ministry was to preach good news to the poor, to bind up the brokenhearted, to proclaim liberty to the captives, and to comfort those who mourn. He came to give people beauty in place of ashes, the oil of joy instead of mourning, and a garment of praise instead of a cloak of heaviness. His ministry continues today.

The culmination of this comprehensive redemption and restoration is expressed in our featured verse: *"That they may be called trees of righteousness."* Through this word picture we see that God's work is so pervasive that it transforms a devastated, unstable, unproductive and undesirable life into one that is securely and deeply planted in the ground of His love, grace and truth. A supernatural life-flow is tapped and this person becomes a healthy tree, spreading its branches, producing buds and flowers, and burgeoning with fruit. I can see the Lord surveying his orchard of trees, his heart swelling with holy pride. Our success at His expense is what brings Him glory and is the greatest revenge against our enemy. *(Written by Mike Fehlauer)*

OCTOBER 21
SOME PEOPLE BELIEVE FOR NOTHING AND
THEY ARE GETTING ALL THEY BELIEVE FOR
HEBREWS 11:6

Hebrews 11:6 "But without faith it is impossible to please him: for he that cometh to God must believe that he is, and that he is a rewarder of them that diligently seek him."

Everything in the Word of God is based on faith. Not just faith in faith, but faith in God. From Genesis to Revelation, it is all faith. "By faith Abraham; By faith Abel; By faith Noah; the just shall live by faith." It even clearly tells us that without faith, it is impossible to please God.

We must mix faith with our giving. A farmer doesn't just go out and plant a bunch of miscellaneous seeds and expect to get a good crop of corn. He plants corn seeds. It's the same for us. We must target our sowing. At our church, every time we take an offering we speak, in faith believing, over our giving. We declare, out loud, that we are believing for jobs and better jobs; raises and bonuses; benefits; sales and commissions; settlements; estates and inheritances; interest and income; rebates and returns; checks in the mail; gifts and surprises; finding money; bills paid off; debts demolished; houses paid for; cars paid for; royalties received; multiplication; new businesses. All of this so that we can finance God's end time harvest, and properly support the needs of our church, our families and ourselves. As a result, we have been receiving so many wonderful testimonies of these things happening in the lives of the people who are standing in faith for them.

We don't just throw our money, we sow our money. What are you believing God for? Are you speaking the Word of God over that seed? Some people believe for nothing and they are getting all that they believe for! *(Written by Bob Nichols)*

OCTOBER 22
DESTINED FOR GREATNESS
JEREMIAH 29:11

Jeremiah 29:11 "For I know the thoughts and plans that I have for you . . . thoughts and plans for welfare and peace and not for evil, to give you hope in your final outcome" (Amplified Bible).

I am convinced that all who are in Christ Jesus are destined for greatness by His grace. Certainly *not* greatness as the world might define greatness, but greatness nonetheless. The Lord has predestined you to be a spiritual champion and to run the race of life expecting to win! And because both the opportunity and power to run the race are supplied by His grace, the victory won is to His glory.

Let me encourage you not to give up or stop short of fulfilling God's plan for your life. Speaking of the continual grace that God supplies, the scripture says that God is faithful, having begun a good work in you, to complete it.

God is the Alpha and the Omega; the Beginning and the End—the First and the Last. The Word of God teaches us that even when we find ourselves in unbelief that He (God) abides faithful. "Faithful is He who calls you Who also will do it," the Word declares in 1 Thessalonians 5:24. Oftentimes, as we endeavor to do the will of God, we tend to underestimate, even forget altogether, the strength of God's commitment to help us succeed. A good friend of mine once said something to me that I have never forgotten. He said, "Taking into consideration all that God has begun in you and wants to complete in you, Marshall, you must forever remember, it's always too soon to quit." *(Written by Marshall Townsley)*

OCTOBER 23
LIFT UP YOUR EYES
JOHN 4:35

John 4:35 "Lift up your eyes, and look on the fields; for they are white already to harvest."

This phrase, "lift up your eyes" was used many times in the ministry of Jesus. Before the feeding of the five thousand with five loaves and two fishes, Jesus "lifted up his eyes." Before Jesus raised Lazrus from the dead He stood before an empty tomb and an unbelieving crowd and "lifted up his eyes." We are told that when Jesus taught or prayed before the multitudes, He "lifted up his eyes."

This means more than just looking toward heaven with your physical eyes. It is a redirecting of your attention from this natural world and its circumstances to the realm of the Holy Spirit. We sometimes think of God sitting on His throne in heaven, when He is actually closer than that; an ever present help in the time of need. If we will acknowledge His presence, look to Him for help, we will be delivered.

To receive divine healing, the Israelites were commanded to look at the brazen serpent. The serpent represented Jesus on the cross, bearing our curse. The natural look did not heal, but seeing the image through the eyes of faith would bring divine deliverance. The look of faith for us will bring supernatural help, wisdom and guidance from the Holy Spirit.

Many times Christians want to spend long periods of time in prayer before fighting a spiritual battle. Before laying hands on the sick or counseling another believer, they believe hours of intercession are needed. What did Jesus do as He went through His day? Needs came at Him so fast; He did not have time to go into His prayer closet. In one day He spoke at the synagogue, healed a man let down through the roof, cured Peter's mother-in-law, healed the woman with the issue of blood and raised Jairus' daughter from the dead. Jesus knew the power of God was ever present, one glance away. He "looked up."

Are you faced with a need? Get your attention off yourself. Help is a look away.
(Written by Bob Yandian)

OCTOBER 24
FILL YOUR HORN AND GO
1 SAMUEL 16:1-13

1 Samuel 16:1 "Fill your horn with oil, and go . . . ."

Samuel is the one who anointed Saul to be king over Israel. He had seen him mature from the frightened boy who hid at his inauguration (1 Sam. 10:22), to a warrior king. He also saw Saul reject the Lord and the Lord reject Saul. Samuel, as God's representative, had refused to see Saul, but he still mourned for him (1 Sam. 15:35). This must have hurt him deeply.

In the first verse of chapter 16, God is saying to Samuel, "Get over it! Quit looking back and look forward! My plan *b* will be better than my plan *a*." God wasn't mourning or sulking. Why should Samuel? God told him to fill his horn with oil (symbolic of the Holy Spirit) and go anoint a new and better king.

People often become captives of the past and what might have been. If we aren't careful, that attitude will cause us to miss what God is doing now. The Lord is never at a loss. Regardless of what men do, God has another way to accomplish His purposes.

Some of you have sorrow because of personal failures. Others are mourning because of loved one's failures. Regardless of how you arrived where you are, God has somewhere better for you to go. The world has never seen anyone manifest all God had for him except Jesus. There is more for each of us.

But we have to fill ourselves with the Holy Spirit and go on with what God has called us to do. The only way any of us can fail is if we fail to fill ourselves and go. *(Written by Andrew Wommack)*

OCTOBER 25
LOOKING UNTO JESUS
HEBREWS 12:2

Hebrews 12:2 "Looking unto Jesus, the author and finisher of our faith, who for the joy that was set before Him endured the cross, despising the shame, and has sat down at the right hand of the throne of God."

Hebrews 12:2 says, *"Looking unto Jesus, the author and finisher of our faith."* The word "looking" means "having eyes for no one but Jesus." Jesus is our prototype. He came to earth and showed us how to live the Christian life.

You have to see yourself as a Jesus person. Jesus thinks through your mind. Jesus loves through your heart. Jesus helps through your hands. Jesus listens through your ears. Jesus speaks through your voice.

Jesus words come to me when He said, "Do unto others as you would have them do unto you" (Matt. 7:12). This is the way to live the life. See yourself as God's representative in the world of people around you. Comprehend that living is giving. Realize to help another is to help yourself. When you sow a seed, it never leaves your life, it simply enters into your future where it multiplies.

Knowing that Jesus lives in you with His unlimited power and His unconditional love at work through you, is happiness. You perceive that you are a people person. A witness of the life of Jesus. You are a loving embodiment of Jesus in the flesh, touching and helping people. You are learning to activate the Holy Spirit in you. It's wonderful to be born again and baptized in the Holy Spirit. But then we must learn how to release the power and gifts of the Holy Spirit that are in us.

God is a Spirit, and you are His flesh. As Jesus was God in the flesh when He walked on this earth, now you are God's expression in this world. Happiness is knowing that nothing is impossible for you and God as a team. Jesus saw this world as one big problem, but He knew that He was the answer to all of the world's problems. That is the way you have to see yourself. *(Written by Dave Duell)*

OCTOBER 26
PROSPERITY WITH A PURPOSE
ISAIAH 61:6

Isaiah 61:6 "Ye shall eat the riches of the Gentiles and in their glory shall ye boast yourselves."

This promise is clear. Monetary wealth is part of God's blessing in our lives. The word "glory" can be interpreted as wealth or substance. As we grow in God, it is His will that we increase in the financial area of our lives. God makes His purpose for our prosperity clear in verse four of Isaiah, chapter 61: *"And they shall build the old wastes, they shall raise up the former desolations, and they shall repair the waste cities, the desolations of many generations."* When God's restoration invades our lives, we are then equipped to be promoters of other people. We can lift up those who are downtrodden and devoid of hope. We can be instruments of healing for hurting relationships. We can also rebuild family structures and social structures that have fallen into ruin. The resources it takes to accomplish this task are propelled in our direction by this promise. If we reach a place of personal wholeness that causes us to lift our eyes off of ourselves to reach out to the hurting world around us, God will give us a plan and provide every hammer, nail and 2x4 that we need to get the job done. *(Written by Mike Fehlauer)*

OCTOBER 27
GOD ONLY ASKS YOU TO GIVE WHAT HE WANTS YOU TO HAVE MORE OF
MATTHEW 25:15-30

Matthew 25:20-21 "And so he that had received five talents came and brought other five talents, saying, Lord, thou deliveredst unto me five talents: behold, I have gained beside them five talents more. His lord said unto him, Well done, thou good and faithful servant: thou hast been faithful over a few things, I will make thee ruler over many things: enter thou into the joy of thy lord."

There was a couple in our church who were faithful in serving and giving. They were big on sowing. They asked me to come over to dedicate their new house. I don't very often get to do things like that anymore, but this time I was able to go. When I arrived I saw that it was a very beautiful home. With grins from ear to ear they told me, "God gave us this house." I thought, *God gave it to them? They probably mean that God worked out the financing or gave them a super deal on the home.* They reiterated, "No, Pastor. You don't understand. God *gave* us this house." It was theirs—free and clear.

I know of a young man in our church who was believing God for the money to pay his tuition to go to school. As he was sitting in the service, he felt the Lord prompting him to give the twenty-dollar bill he had in his wallet. At first he thought, *Lord, you know I can't give that twenty. I need it to go toward my tuition!* Within a brief amount of time, the young man obeyed God and put the money into the offering. After the service, a business man in the church walked up to the young man and said, "Son, the Lord put it on my heart to give you this." It was a large sum of money—just the thing the young man needed. It makes me think, what would have happened had the young man not been obedient to give that twenty? It can never be stressed too much, God only asks you to give what He wants you to have more of. *(Written by Bob Nichols)*

OCTOBER 28
FRUIT-BEARING LIVES
JOHN 15:16, 8

John 15:16, 8 "You have not chosen Me but I have chosen you—I have appointed you, [I have planted you], that you might go and bear fruit and keep on bearing, that your fruit may be lasting [that it may remain, abide]. When you bare (produce) much fruit, My Father is honored and glorified and you show and prove yourselves to be true followers of Mine" (Amplified).

Know for certain that it's by grace that we stand or endure and that it's by His grace that we succeed or bear fruit. Just as sap serves the healthy growing plant or tree, so grace, working in us, moves us forward toward a life well-pleasing and acceptable to God. As I've said so often, it is the transforming power of His grace that makes the difference. His grace in us works to fill every weakness. It is His grace at work that keeps us supple and yielded, shaping and forming us to be the fruit-bearing lives that Jesus spoke about.

It's absurd to think that the divine call on our lives, that upward call that the Apostle Paul referred to in one of his letters, could ever be fulfilled in mere human strength and ability. To love as He loves takes divine strength; to forgive on every occasion as we have been forgiven—divine intervention. To bring healing to the wounded and salvation to the lost can't possibly be accomplished apart from the grace that He supplies. To be Christ-like takes Christ living through us by His Spirit; to be grace-like means having our souls flooded with His grace.

No command from God should ever be understood to be a challenge to our own weakened flesh or abilities. We should rather view each one as an invitation to trust and to receive a full and overflowing supply of His grace to finish what we start. Our God is more than enough. *(Written by Marshall Townsley)*

OCTOBER 29
RESURRECTION
PHILIPPIANS 3:10

Philippians 3:10 "That I may know him, and the power of his resurrection . . . . "

It seems like we have made Christianity into a religion centered around the cross where Jesus died. We have crosses on our churches and pulpits. We even have them hanging on our wrists and necks, made into bracelets and necklaces. I am glad our crosses are empty, because Jesus is no longer there. But is the empty cross what the New Testament believers centered their lives around? No it is not.

The cross is where our problems, sin, sickness and poverty were removed. The Old Covenant, the law, was crucified with Jesus, nailed to His cross and removed once and for all. It is wonderful for our problems to be removed, but more necessary and exciting for the answers to be given.

It was the empty cross that solved our problems, but the empty tomb brought our answers. Death was conquered at the cross, but life was given at the resurrection. Sickness was destroyed at the cross, but healing came through the resurrection. Jesus became our poverty on the cross, but our prosperity came through resurrection power.

The focal point of Christianity is the empty tomb, not the empty cross. For three days, while the cross was empty, Jesus was still dead.

This would make us no different than any religion on the earth. All the founders are dead. But only Jesus came back from the dead.

To be born again, we do not confess the cross, but the fact that Jesus was raised from the dead by the power of God the Father. Our daily prayer, like Paul's, should be to know Jesus in the power of His resurrection.

Perhaps the emblem of Christianity should not be an empty cross around our neck, but a rock with a hole in it. Jesus is no longer in the grave, He is risen from the dead.

(Written by Bob Yandian)

OCTOBER 30
HOW'S YOUR HEART?
1 SAMUEL 16:1-13

1 Samuel 16:7 "But the LORD said unto Samuel, Look not on his countenance, or on the height of his stature; because I have refused him: for the LORD seeth not as man seeth; for man looketh on the outward appearance, but the LORD looketh on the heart."

Samuel came to Jesse's home to anoint one of his sons to be king. The first king of Israel, Saul, was a head and shoulder taller than anyone else in the nation (1 Sam. 9:2). He was the choicest of all the men in the land. Samuel supposed that the next king of Israel would be similar. As Samuel looked on Jesse's oldest son, Eliab, he thought this was the one. Eliab must have been an impressive looking man.

But the Lord had someone else in mind. David was the youngest son of Jesse and verse 12 says, *"he had reddish hair and fair skin, beautiful eyes, and was fine looking"* (Amp.). David wasn't what you would consider king material. He kept sheep, played the harp, and sang and wrote music. But God sees us differently than others see us and even how we see ourselves.

Our modern society has put a premium on the outward appearance. People abuse their bodies to achieve the perfect shape. Some people actually kill others to have the right standard of living and to be in the proper social group. All that is vanity. All that will fade with age if nothing else. The true qualities that are valued in the sight of the Lord are the qualities of the heart.

How's your heart? And how is the heart of the person you work with or live with? You may be passing by another King David just because of the earth suit he is living in. The real person is on the inside. *(Written by Andrew Wommack)*

OCTOBER 31
POWER OVER THE ENEMY
LUKE 10:19

Luke 10:19 "Behold, I give you the authority to trample on serpents, and scorpions, and over all the power of the enemy, and nothing shall by any means hurt you."

Happiness is releasing Him for action through you. Jesus said, *"I give you power to tread on serpents and scorpions and over all the power of the enemy and nothing shall by any means harm you."*

1. Practice the art of doing for others what you want them to do for you.
2. Recognize and value the unique person you are.
3. Accept responsibility for your own life. Your life is what you make it through the power of choice and action.
4. Absorb the fact that failure is never final. Keep trying and don't give up.
5. Realize that whatever is worth doing is worth doing the very best you can.
6. Understand that true happiness is having hope and experiencing love and taking action for the betterment of the people.
7. Assimilate the irreversible law that you are the tangible reality of your very own thoughts.
8. Grasp the winning criteria that what you know, discover, learn and prove becomes the only power that you can utilize in this world.
9. Actualize the power within you by accepting your own uniqueness. Be calm, confident and happy. Know that your goals are good for God, for people and yourself, then go forward with God.

It's only "forever!" We have one life to live and we should make it count for Jesus. We are always learning and applying what we know. We always make decisions on the knowledge we have at the moment. But Praise God we are learning and receiving new knowledge each day. We are so controlled by our minds that it is hard to follow the Holy Spirit when He speaks to us sometimes different than what we are used to doing. We play life too safe, always trying to preserve ourselves. When we get to heaven, I don't want Jesus to show me what I could have done if I would have trusted Him. Let's go for life with all that Jesus has given to us and make a difference. *(Written by Dave Duell)*

NOVEMBER 1
GIVING OUR BEST
MARK 12:43

Mark 12:43 "So he called the disciples to Himself and said to them, 'Assuredly, I say to you that this poor widow has put in more than all those who have given in the treasury.'"

In these verses we see hundreds of people filing by the treasury, putting in their offering. Jesus is standing there, watching silently—until a widow woman places two mites into the offering. That is when we hear heaven speak. Jesus knew she had given all she had. The others had given out of their abundance. Their offering didn't cost them anything. It didn't require any faith. You see, it wasn't the amount, but the attitude of the heart that mattered to Jesus. That is what always matters to Him. The others saw their offering as an obligation they needed to meet. The widow woman saw it as an opportunity to sacrifice, to worship. It cost her something. But what she gained was far greater than what it cost her. Her small sacrificial offering caught the attention of the God of the universe.

If you want your life to matter, it is going to cost you something. It is going to cost you—you. If you want your offering to matter, then it must be a sacrifice. Giving is more than an obligation that needs to be met. It is an opportunity to worship. It is an opportunity to express our love to the One who has redeemed us. It is an expression of faith and trust in Him. This applies not only with money, but also with our lives. Dare to give Him your best today. The best of your efforts, the best of your best time, the best of your heart. *(Written by Mike Fehlauer)*

NOVEMBER 2
SUBSTANCE ABUSE
PROVERBS 3:9

Proverbs 3:9 "Honour the LORD with thy substance, and with the firstfruits of all thine increase."

Many people in the church today have a problem with substance abuse. You can't hardly pick up a newspaper or watch TV without hearing about some famous movie star or athlete who got into trouble because of substance abuse. Just as often you'll hear about folks checking into a substance abuse treatment program. There are many programs offering help, saying that we must follow a certain number of steps or do this routine to straighten out our lives. That's not the kind of substance abuse I mean here. I'm referring to the abuse of the money and possessions we have.

The word translated in Proverbs 3:9 "substance" is the Hebrew word "hown" which means wealth, riches, price, high value, enough, or sufficiency. While certainly it is a problem for a professing Christian to selfishly rack up money and possessions while neglecting anyone else, it is just as grave of a sin as to say a simple "no" when God tells you to give something small. I heard a woman minister talk about how the Lord dealt with her on obedience by telling her to give someone her favorite pair of earrings. Although she ultimately gave the earrings, it was after much debating and arguing with God. That is an example of substance abuse. Spending money on things that a believer has no business buying is also an example. And for a youth, using your tithe money "just this once" for a new CD you've been wanting is another example.

The Bible doesn't give us a five, ten or twelve step program to follow. God laid it out plain and simple, "Honour the LORD with thy substance, and with the firstfruits of all thine increase." Firstfruits means the first, beginning, best, chief or choicest part. Doctor Jesus is the answer to every malady we may have! Have you been guilty of substance abuse? Why not check into Jesus' treatment program. Every problem, including substance abuse, can be wiped away in the presence of God.

(Written by Bob Nichols)

NOVEMBER 3
POSITIONED TO RECEIVE
JAMES 1:5-7

James 1:5-7 "If any of you lacks wisdom, let him ask of God, who gives to all liberally, and without reproach, and it will be given to him. But let him ask in faith, with no doubting, for he who doubts is like a wave of the sea driven and tossed by the wind. For let not that man suppose that he will receive anything from the Lord" (New King James).

Apart from a special act of sovereign grace on God's part, we must have faith or trust in God to receive from Him.

Nowhere is this spiritual principle made clearer than right here within these verses of scripture. This truth is of extreme importance. James works hard in this letter to communicate God's greatness, His dependability, and His love. But just as important, he goes on to share this vital truth. That is, that the doubting man should not expect to receive anything from the Lord. Unbelief shuts God out. Unbelief cuts me off from receiving the divine supply so faithfully made by God. We are told in Mark 6:5 that when Jesus went to His hometown of Nazareth shortly after His wilderness temptation, *"He could there do no mighty work, save that He laid His hands upon a few sick folk, and healed them" (King James).* Why was Jesus unable to do any "mighty work" in Nazareth? Matthew, relating the same incident, states it clearly, *"And He did not many mighty works there because of their unbelief" (Matthew 13:58, King James).*

When Mark says that Jesus could not do any mighty work in Nazareth, he was not intending to imply any inability in Jesus. Rather, he was showing how unbelief fails to receive the divine supply. It closed the door on the operation of Christ's power. Jesus was both able and willing to do mighty works of healing and deliverance on their behalf, as He had been doing for others, but His ministry was actually limited by the unbelief of the people. The entire failure of Israel in the Old Testament is summarized in these words: *"they limited the Holy One of Israel."* Those words are taken from Psalms 78:41. Study will show that it was unbelief that caused the limitation of God on their behalf in Old Testament times. Now this is what James is saying. He lays down this spiritual principle with regard to the one who doubts, *"Let not that man think that he shall receive anything from the Lord."* *(Written by Marshall Townsley)*

NOVEMBER 4
CAN YOU PASS THE TEST?
MARK 4:35

Mark 4:35 "And the same day, when the even was come, he saith unto them, Let us pass over unto the other side."

What "same day" was this verse referring to when Jesus told his disciples to sail to the other side of the Sea of Galilee? It was the same day Jesus had taught the multitudes and the disciples, the parable of the good and bad ground, the sower and the seed. Why is this important to know? When Jesus finished teaching this parable, He asked His disciples if they understood." They said, "yes."

Jesus knew what was coming. He knew they would go to the other side of the Sea of Galilee and minister to a man possessed with a legion of demons. He also knew that Satan would try to take their lives on the way across the water. The teaching they had just received would be used within a few hours after hearing it.

The parable teaches about a sower, seed, good ground, bad ground and an enemy who tries to steal the word through persecution and affliction. Jesus would now put the disciples to the test.

Jesus (the Sower) told them, "Let us pass over unto the other side" (the seed is sown). He did not say, "Let's try to go over." He did not say, "Let's go halfway and sink." The promise was given—telling them they would make it. Halfway across the water, a storm erupted (persecution and affliction arose from Satan) to take the word from their hearts. Jesus was so assured they would make it, He went to sleep and rested on His own promise. The disciples were in panic and blamed Jesus for not caring. Jesus woke up, calmed the storm and then rebuked His disciples for their lack of faith. They proved they had not understood the parable. They also proved they were hard ground. Jesus took them safely over, but they failed the test of faith.

Between you and the will of God is a Sea of Trouble. Take hold of a promise and rest in it. The promise will sustain you and you will make it to the other side. *(Written by Bob Yandian)*

NOVEMBER 5
HOW BIG ARE YOU? PART 1
1 SAMUEL 17:1-11

1 Samuel 17:4 "And there went out a champion out of the camp of the Philistines, named Goliath, of Gath, whose height was six cubits and a span."

When I was a teenager I went to a Golden Gloves boxing match where there were thousands of people. I noticed a baldheaded man way down close to the ring who looked like he was standing through the entire match. Then he stood up. This man was a giant! I found out he was called the Corn King Giant and was 9 feet 6 inches tall. I ran down to see if I could get up next to him. My eyes were level with his belt buckle. It was quite an experience.

Goliath was about that size. But David was even smaller than me. Goliath was twice as tall as David. David probably weighed no more than the coat of mail that Goliath wore. But David was bigger on the inside than Goliath was. David was God's anointed king.

We too often evaluate things only in physical terms. Physically, Goliath was a giant, but in trusting God, Goliath was a dwarf. David was the giant in that category, and that's the most important category. Anyone who is strong in believing God is a giant in the spiritual realm and able to do great exploits.

We overestimate and over emphasize the physical problems that confront us. The spiritual realm is where the real power to live life comes from. Everyone who is born of God is a spiritual giant with powers far greater than anything the physical realm can ever confront us with.

Ask God to open your eyes to who you are in the Spirit. You will find that you are the real giant who has been intimidated by dwarfs. *(Written by Andrew Wommack)*

NOVEMBER 6
YOU'RE THE ONE WITH THE COVENANT PART 2
1 SAMUEL 17:12-30

1 Samuel 17:26 "And David spake to the men that stood by him, saying, What shall be done to the man that killeth this Philistine, and taketh away the reproach from Israel? for who is this uncircumcised Philistine, that he should defy the armies of the living God?"

There were a number of keys to David's faith that enabled him to kill Goliath. One of those keys was David's knowledge of and faith in God's covenant with the nation of Israel. The Lord had said that no man would be able to stand before his people (Dt. 11:25). Goliath was just a man. And an uncircumcised man at that! That meant he didn't have a covenant with God. David's faith was in God.

Everyone of the Israelite soldiers had that same covenant, but the covenant is of no effect until it is believed. Hebrews 4:2 says, *"For unto us was the gospel preached, as well as unto them: but the word preached did not profit them, not being mixed with faith in them that heard it."* David believed in God's Word and activated the power of God's Word.

King Saul tried to give David his armor to wear but David wouldn't take it (v. 38). That was just an attempt to change his focus from God to the flesh. His trust was in the covenant and the God of the covenant, not Saul's armor. After all, Saul's armor wasn't doing him any good. He was hiding along with the rest of the soldiers. David's faith was in God alone.

God's covenant to us has promised us total victory in every situation. There is no reason for us to cower before our enemies. We have God's covenant promises. Activate them by faith and watch your giants fall. *(Written by Andrew Wommack)*

NOVEMBER 7
PERSECUTION IS JEALOUSY PART 3
1 SAMUEL 17:28-30

1 Samuel 17:28 "Eliab his eldest brother heard when he spake unto the men; and Eliab's anger was kindled against David, and he said, Why camest thou down hither? and with whom hast thou left those few sheep in the wilderness? I know thy pride, and the naughtiness of thine heart; for thou art come down that thou mightest see the battle."

There was more to Eliab's anger than just care for his father's sheep. Eliab was there when Samuel anointed David to be king (1 Sam. 16:13). God had passed over Eliab and chosen his younger brother, David, to be king. Eliab was jealous of David.

Proverbs 13:10 says, *"Only by pride cometh contention . . . ."* It was Eliab's love for himself that caused him to lash out at his younger brother. And it was also fear. Fear that if David was right, and Goliath was no match for a man in covenant with God, then Eliab was a coward. He had to condemn David's words or they would condemn him.

This is the root of all persecution. If you throw a rock into a pack of dogs, the one that yelps the loudest is the one that got hit. So it is with persecution. The ones who protest the loudest are the ones who are feeling the pressure of conviction.

Before you can defeat the giants in your life, you have to withstand the critical remarks of others, even if they are family. If David hadn't overcome his older brother's criticism, he would never have overcome Goliath. Understanding that persecution is actually a defensive act of a person under conviction will help you keep your focus and fight the real battles. *(Written by Andrew Wommack)*

NOVEMBER 8
WHEN NO ONE IS LOOKING PART 4
1 SAMUEL 17:31-47

1 Samuel 17:36 "Thy servant slew both the lion and the bear: and this uncircumcised Philistine shall be as one of them, seeing he hath defied the armies of the living God."

David had faith that God would enable him to kill Goliath and win the war. But no one else did. King Saul, the biggest and most powerful man in all of Israel, openly mocked David, saying that David wasn't up to the fight. That would have deterred most people, but David wasn't like most people.

Prior to this, David had kept his father's sheep. A lion and a bear had come after the sheep and he killed both of them. This was on the backside of the desert. No one was around to see his valiant fight. Probably, no one would have blamed him for running away.

But it was David's victory over the lion and the bear that gave him the assurance and faith that he would be able to conquer Goliath as he had them. If David hadn't been faithful in the smaller things, he wouldn't have had the confidence to fight in this big thing.

Many people dream of slaying some giant of a problem or doing some great exploit. But they aren't faithful in life's everyday trials. They are waiting for the grandstands to be full before they give it all they have. But those who don't win the local trials never make it to the Olympics. David's faithfulness in the relatively small things was what enabled him to be ruler over much (Lk. 16:10).

Be faithful in the things you face today and you will strengthen your faith so you will be able to win when the big tests come your way. *(Written by Andrew Wommack)*

NOVEMBER 9
MAKE SURE THEY'RE DEAD PART 5
1 SAMUEL 17:48-58

1 Samuel 17:51 "Therefore David ran, and stood upon the Philistine, and took his sword, and drew it out of the sheath thereof, and slew him, and cut off his head therewith. And when the Philistines saw their champion was dead, they fled."

We fight giants every day. But a mistake that is often made is that we quit before the battle is complete. We don't destroy our enemies. We just chase them out of sight and leave them to return and fight another day. In Psalm 18:37, David said, "*I have pursued mine enemies, and overtaken them: neither did I turn again till they were consumed.*" Never was that illustrated in the life of David more than when he fought Goliath.

David had a holy hatred for his enemy. He wasn't just trying to scare him off. He was out to kill him. David ran towards Goliath. He wasn't tentative. He was bold. He slung the stone and God made sure it hit its mark. Goliath, the giant of Gath, fell on his face before David.

But David wasn't through yet. The scriptures don't say that Goliath was dead. He may have been, but he may not have been. Certainly, the Philistines who were on the mountains watching couldn't tell for sure the fate of their champion. However, David left no doubt. He climbed up on top of the giant, drew Goliath's own sword, and cut off his head. Once David held Goliath's head in his hand, there was no doubt in anyone, who had won. Goliath would never fight again.

We don't know the exact reason why David chose five smooth stones from the brook (v. 40), but there were four other giants in Gath (1 Ch. 20:4-8), one of which was the brother of Goliath. David was ready to take on all of them.

If you have fought and obtained some relief, don't quit until the victory is complete. Chase the devil out of every corner of your life. *(Written by Andrew Wommack)*

NOVEMBER 10
GREAT POWER, GREAT GRACE! PART 1
ACTS 4:33

Acts 4:33 "And with great power the apostles gave witness to the resurrection of the Lord Jesus. And great grace was upon them all."

We will be centering in on Acts 4:33, *"And with great power the apostles gave witness to the resurrection of the Lord Jesus. And great grace was upon them all."* We see this verse as a fulfillment of Acts 1:8 where Jesus said we would receive power from the Holy Spirit when we received the Baptism of the Holy Spirit.

Power comes from the Greek word "dunamis" and means, energy, power, might, great force, great ability, to strengthen. We are talking about normal Christianity. We must learn to use what God has given to us. This requires faith in the Holy Spirit and in yourself that you know His voice.

The purpose of the outpouring of the Holy Spirit is to empower the church for ministry and world evangelism. He convinces us to go or to support those who are going and to serve as servants to one another and to the body of Christ. It takes power to establish His church locally and globally.

The book of Acts is the acts of the Holy Spirit through men and women who know Him. There is a relationship in the Gospels and Acts. Both the public ministry of Jesus and the ministry of the Church are the same and begin with the life-changing work of the Holy Spirit. After Jesus received the Baptism of the Holy Spirit, His ministry started, and He began to teach, preach, and heal the sick—a power ministry.

The same Spirit in Acts chapter two gave the same authority to the disciples. Jesus is the prototype of the Spirit-filled, Spirit-empowered life. Acts 10:38, *"How God anointed Jesus of Nazareth with the Holy Spirit and with power, who went about doing good and healing all who were oppressed by the devil, for God was with Him."* The book of Acts is the story of the disciples receiving what Jesus received in order to do what Jesus did. *(Written by Dave Duell)*

NOVEMBER 11
GREAT POWER, GREAT GRACE! PART 2
ACTS 4:33

Acts 4:33 And with great power the apostles gave witness to the resurrection of the Lord Jesus. And great grace was upon them all."

To witness means to demonstrate what you believe with proof, evidence and proclamation of personal experience, reaching the world with the supernatural. We have many stories that prove this point. Read my second book, *Faith, What a Deal!* We have reached thousands of people with signs, wonders, and miracles. The world needs some demonstration, not just information. Don't go see the sights, be the sights.

Grace is the unmerited favor of God. Ephesians 2:8 states, "For by grace you have been saved through faith, and that not of yourselves, it is the gift of God." God in His mercy saves us by His grace, so that grace is manifested in the great dynamic of the Holy Spirit at work in power in our lives. Great grace comes from Zechariah 4:7 when the prophet instructed Zerubbabel to speak "grace" to the mountain to become a plain—the hindrance he faced in the trying task of rebuilding God's temple.

Speaking grace to obstacles we face is an action of faith, drawing on the operations of God's great power. We only speak and the work is entirely His, by His gracious power and for His great glory. He only needs someone to speak. And they were told in this story to shout, "Grace to it."

We have many opportunities each day to speak to the mountains that come into our lives. It is wonderful to know that we are not in these situations by ourselves, but God has given us the Holy Spirit to help us in our daily lives.

When we receive salvation, we receive it only through the power of His grace. We can trust that this same grace will operate in us and through us as it has been shown to us—as with the early disciples; great authority and power flowed through them. As we call upon the Name of Jesus, speaking His grace into the face of our mountainous impossibilities, we have reason to expect great power and great grace today. *(Written by Dave Duell)*

NOVEMBER 12
THE INFLUENCE OF UNRIGHTEOUS MAMMON
LUKE 16:8

Luke 16:8 "For the sons of this world are more shrewd in their generation than the sons of light."

Within this story we have a man who was a steward of his master's accounts. We also know that this steward had not been faithful over the accounts and is losing his job. He only has a certain amount of time before he no longer has access to his master's accounts. So what he begins to do is reduce the debt of the master's debtors. This not only brought in immediate cash for the master, but it also helped this steward make some much needed friends.

What was so shrewd of the steward is that he understood the influence he had for a limited time. He used the influence he had to establish his future. There is a tangible influence, or power that comes with earthly wealth. I am sure that you have heard the old adage, "The golden rule is, he who has the gold, makes the rules." To a great degree, that is true. Jesus wants us to understand and recognize the influence attached to money. It is His desire that we wield that influence for the sake of the kingdom. Just like the widow woman who gave all she had. She recognized and honored what she had. What impressed Jesus was not how much she gave, but HOW she gave.

The same is true for you and me. Whatever we have has been given to us from God. It is all His, we are simply stewards. A faithful steward will recognize the value of what he has. A wise steward will recognize the power that is attached to whatever resources he has. How do we release that power for the sake of the kingdom? By giving. You have an opportunity today to be a wise steward. Look for a way to give. Release the power of your finances by giving to the poor. Sow seed into the soil of others. *(Written by Mike Fehlauer)*

NOVEMBER 13
SMALL SEEDS CAN MEET TALL NEEDS
LUKE 13:19

Luke 13:19 "It is like a grain of mustard seed, which a man took, and cast into his garden; and it grew, and waxed a great tree; and the fowls of the air lodged in the branches of it."

The seed in your purse or your pocketbook is never going to help the kingdom of God. It is the seed that you take out and sow that is going to grow. You can keep seeds in a package. I remember hearing about how they opened up some pyramids over in the Middle East and found seeds from thousands of years ago. The seeds were still there, but they haven't helped anyone. Good intentions will never grow a crop. Seeds can only grow when you plant them.

Some might think that their seed is too small to plant. No seed is too small! When the small seed is sown, it becomes tall and great and blesses others. Small seeds can meet tall needs. Take a tiny little mustard seed. It could even fall out of your hand, but you come back a few years later and that mustard seed has become a big tree. Big trees offer big shade. The Bible said that even the birds, the fowls of the air, fly and lodge in the limbs of that tree.

We've seen that in our lives. I've lost count of how many hotel bills we have paid over the years for ministers that were burned-out, tired and discouraged. We told them, "If you can get here, we'll give you a hotel room for a few days." They would come into our morning prayer services, and to the regular services and be a part of what God was doing. Before long, they were going home, rekindled by the fire of God. They could then go out and help the lives of others. The planting of the seed of the hotel room, the planting of the seed of a missionary, the planting of the seed of a van, a lunch, or even a smile—our seeds may be small, but we can meet tall needs because we plant those seeds. *(Written by Bob Nichols)*

NOVEMBER 14
GRACE TO FULFILL HIS CALL
PHILIPPIANS 1:6

Philippians 1:6 "Being confident of this very thing, that He who has begun a good work in you will complete it until the day of Jesus Christ" (New King James).

God will never call you to something without giving the grace to see it fulfilled. The will of God won't lead you where the grace of God can't keep you.

The Apostle Paul came to a place in his own life where he was able to finally see and accept that who he was and what he had to do in this life was founded in the grace of God. Grace identifies us and qualifies us. Then it enables us to live out our divine destiny; if we abide in it, grace will keep us until the dream is fulfilled and God's will is done.

Grace 1) *identifies* us; 2) *qualifies* us; 3) *enables* or *empowers* us; and 4) *keeps* us unto destiny's fulfillment.

Through a revelation of His grace, Paul came to know that he was chosen. God chose him to preach to the Gentiles before he was ever born. That has to be grace. He had no works to qualify him.

The same happens to be true of you and me. God has a plan for our lives. We, too, have been called before the foundations of the earth by His grace and equipped with His grace to fulfill that call. It's in knowing God, our Father, discovering the grace upon our lives and then drawing from the endless supply of that grace to see His will fulfilled. And if we live by His grace, then we will also live to His glory because all reason for boasting is set aside. *(Written by Marshall Townsley)*

NOVEMBER 15
THE PAST IS PAST
PHILIPPIANS 3:13

Philippians 3:13 "Forgetting those things which are behind, and reaching forth unto those things which are before."

Paul had just come to a place in his life where he was ready to put his past behind him. Although his past had sins and mistakes, it was also filled with many triumphs and victories. The Greek word for "forgetting" means, to assign to oblivion. There comes a time in our lives when we need to break loose from the past—our successes as well as our sins, and reach toward the plans and goals God has for us.

Paul talked about laying aside every "weight and the sin which doth so easily beset us" (Heb.12:1). Sins will beset us when we do not forgive ourselves. God is always "faithful and just to forgive us," but it is quite something else to forgive ourselves. We actually set ourselves up as greater than God when we do not forgive ourselves after God has forgiven us. Unforgiveness toward ourselves is really a manifestation of arrogance. We think we have committed a sin bigger than God can forgive.

We also need to forget the successes of the past. They are the "weights" mentioned in Hebrews 12:1. Many Christians end up in a daily competition with their own past victories. The former blessings of God seem so great. How can God ever outdo Himself? Many church denominations build a monument to the past revivals and end up living in the glory of days gone by. Thank God for what He did in the past, but thank God even more for what He can do today. His mercies are new every morning.

The new blessings God wants to give are what is "before" us. Join Paul in turning aside from the past and looking forward with great anticipation to the blessings yet to be reached. There is a "high calling" waiting for you. *(Written by Bob Yandian)*

NOVEMBER 16
THE WAY OF DILIGENCE LEADS TO THE WAY OF ABUNDANCE
HEBREWS 6:11

Hebrews 6:11 "And we desire that each one of you show the same diligence to the full assurance of hope until the end."

There is a godliness to being thorough. Very few have the ability to follow through to the end of a project. Even fewer go through the diligence of thinking through problems. Most merely guess, speculate or theorize their way through life. Diligence involves taking the time and effort in doing a project right the first time. This always leads to abundance. It is the man who follows through, and is thorough that gets the raise in salary. While others are gathered around the water cooler sharing the latest gossip, or criticizing their boss, it is the man or woman at his or her desk getting the job done who will receive the next promotion. You can tithe faithfully, but if you are lazy at work prosperity will allude you. You can give offerings, but if you continue to spend more than you earn, poverty will be your companion.

Cultivate the habit of diligence. Be the one person who thinks and works through every problem that comes up. Your boss can always get people to do what he tells them to do. He is looking for someone who has the ability to understand the problem and is able to instruct others on *how* to complete a project. Drive yourself. Don't let up. See laziness as an enemy to your purpose in life. Attack laziness with diligence and show it no mercy. *(Written by Mike Fehlauer)*

NOVEMBER 17
DO NOT DESPISE SMALL BEGINNINGS
ZECHARIAH 4:10

Zechariah 4:10 "For who hath despised the day of small things? for they shall rejoice, and shall see the plummet in the hand of Zerubbabel with those seven; they are the eyes of the LORD, which run to and fro through the whole earth."

My family and I are tremendously blessed, but we didn't start out where we are today. If you will take faithful steps, you will see increase in every area of your life, as well. Do not despise the day of small beginnings. Sow what you have. It is amazing the ways the enemy tries to deceive church people. Some have the concept that when they can sow 100 dollars or 1,000 dollars, then they will sow, but they won't turn loose of the nickel or the dime, or the five dollars or the ten that is in their pocket right now. Even if you consider it to be a baby step, sow seed somewhere in the ministry, your local church, or somebody else's life.

There was a single woman in our church who was coming out of some bad past relationships that hurt her financially. She didn't make a whole lot of money, but after she gave her life to the Lord, she began to tithe and give offerings as she could. God was faithful to see that her rent and all of her bills were paid on time. She was paid every other week. One Sunday immediately after payday, a minister in the church was taking an offering for a special men's ministry event to provide scholarships to men who didn't have the money to attend otherwise. The Lord nudged the woman to give everything that was left in her checking account. It wasn't much, only ten dollars, but it was all she had left until the next payday. The Lord told her to tell the minister who was collecting the money, "This is for my husband." It was odd, because she wasn't looking to get married. After she gave, she didn't give it another thought. There was also an announcement on the radio that the same event needed volunteers to work there. Three weeks later, at the conference, the woman sowed her time, as well. It was there that she met the man who is now her husband. She had totally forgotten about the donation she made until a friend brought it to her remembrance. Guess how her husband, a missionary man, was able to come to the conference. That's right, on a scholarship. You go where you sow! The couple now lives in a beautiful house and are prospering: spirit, soul and body. As a matter of fact, she was able to leave her job to prepare their house for the family and ministry God has laid on their hearts.

This woman is an example of someone in the process of God's increase. From having ten dollars to last her for two weeks, to having a wonderful marriage and home. Do not despise the day of small beginnings. Be faithful to sow what you do have, and God will provide the increase in every area of your life. *(Written by Bob Nichols)*

NOVEMBER 18
CALLING AND SEPARATION
GALATIANS 1:15-16

Galatians 1:15-16 "But when it pleased God, who separated me from my mother's womb and called me by His grace, to reveal His Son in me, that I might preach Him among the heathen; immediately I conferred not with flesh and blood" (King James).

I want you to consider some important things that the Apostle Paul had to say in his letter to the Galatians and how they might apply to you. Take note here, that Paul says he was called and separated, or set apart, unto God for service before he was ever born and that by grace. Well, if God chose Paul before he was ever born, that has to be grace because Paul had no works being in his mother's womb. He wasn't born; he had no opportunity to work. Remember, grace is unmerited favor from God. In this account, that favor came in the form of Paul's calling and separation to God's service. Paul didn't always know, nor did he probably always accept what he's sharing here with the church in Galatia. That is, that grace makes us, first, who we are and then second, empowers us to live up to our potential.

In numerous other places, in just as many different ways, Paul indicates that he is who he is and does all he does by the grace of God. And I, particularly, like that he does it without apology. I don't think even Paul knew at the time this revelation became real to him, how often he would be called upon to qualify himself or prove his value to those to whom he ministered. How often he must have been thankful for the grace upon his own life. Constantly criticized and almost always harassed everywhere he went, Paul seemed to find a way to allow God's grace to speak for him. And grace will speak. The gift will become evident in time if we trust. That's not to say that everyone will love you or what you've become, but in the end, God will be glorified and that's all that counts anyway!

(Written by Marshall Townsley)

NOVEMBER 19
A PERFECT CHURCH?
ACTS 6:1

Acts 6:1 "And in those days, when the number of the disciples was multiplied, there arose a murmuring of the Grecians against the Hebrews . . . ."

Many think that the early converts of Acts attended a perfect church. Some congregations are returning to the means and structure of the church services recorded in this book, trying to find a church without problems. I am sorry to shatter your dreams, but even the early church that began after the day of Pentecost had problems. This verse says there was murmuring as the church grew. The previous chapter told of members lying to the Holy Spirit and to the church leadership.

There is no perfect church. All churches have problems. The reason being, all churches are run by people striving to hear from the Holy Spirit. Even if you could find a perfect church, why would they want you?

A lady informed me after church one Sunday that she was looking for a perfect church. I told her I would shoot her and she would find it. The perfect church is in heaven. If you are looking for the perfect pastor, you will meet Him when the trumpet sounds. His name is Jesus. In the meantime, you, like the saints in Acts, are asked to attend imperfect churches with imperfect pastors, imperfect music directors and imperfect youth leaders.

You are to be committed to a church and not float around to many churches in a city or area. Many who "float" from one church to another think they are mature and "given" to more than one local church. Ephesians 4:14 tells us that babies are tossed to and fro, carried about by every wind of doctrine. It takes a mature believer to settle down in a church, call it home and become committed.

Why would God call you to an imperfect church? So He can take your gifts and talents and offer them to the church. Walking in love together, we will come a little more into spiritual maturity, striving to become the perfect church. *(Written by Bob Yandian)*

NOVEMBER 20
GRACE PART 1
ROMANS 6:14

Romans 6:14 "For sin shall not have dominion over you: for you are not under the law, but under grace."

I want to share some thoughts with you on "grace." It is a disaster to become a Christian, to give your life to Jesus and then remain powerless. We need the power of the Holy Spirit to work in our lives, transforming our lives into Jesus' image. People are born-again but can't conquer their thoughts, habits, fears and those life-dominating sins. They are paralyzed by themselves and condemnation, and they never overcome or receive deliverance. *"For sin shall not have dominion over you: for you are not under the law, but under grace"* (Romans 6:14).

The greatest change that ever came into anyone's life was at the moment of salvation. In an instant everything changed. That change came about by simply believing. The moment we believed God, His grace came into us and we changed. If the greatest change came about because we believed, why not continue in that same simple way of believing? Or as Paul said in Galatians 3:3, *"Are you so foolish? Having begun in the Spirit, are you now made perfect by the flesh?"*

In other words, when you came into this salvation, the Spirit of God did a work in you. Do you think that now that you are saved, you will finish this work by your own ability? No! Just as sure as you could not get yourself saved by your own efforts, you cannot bring about change by your efforts. You are NOT saved by grace and then brought into righteousness by works.

When you came to Jesus, God gave you a new heart and a new spirit. *"A new heart also will I give you, and a new spirit will I put within you; and I will take away the stony heart out of your flesh, and I will give you an heart of flesh"* (Ezekiel 36:26). Your spirit was not only made new, it was made righteous, perfect and complete. Your spirit was not made a little baby that had to grow up. God did a perfect work in you. Your spirit is as whole, clean, righteous and perfect as it will ever be. The need is NOT for you to become righteous. The need is for you to get that which is in your spirit to become a reality in your life. *(Written by Dave Duell)*

NOVEMBER 21
GRACE PART 2
ROMANS 6:14

Romans 6:14 "For sin shall not have dominion over you, for you are not under law but under grace."

While your spirit man can only be changed by God, your heart can be changed by your thinking. What you think, what you expose yourself to, the beliefs you adopt, all affect and influence your heart. The early Galatian church started in faith and grace and then Paul said to them, "Who has bewitched you" or what have you taken in? They started listening to the Judaizers, the law men, and stopped operating in faith. They put law with their faith.

The devil does not want you to be free and neither do the religious folks, so they tell you that you must put works with your salvation. If you pray long enough you can get God to move—Works and not faith. Fast long enough. Take the promises and turn them into law. We start in faith and go back into works for our salvation. You can take New Testament truth and turn it back into law.

All faith does is accept the promise and grace comes into your life. You are saved by grace and that's how you get faith. When you received salvation, you stopped trying to be saved. What happens is that you are born-again, and then you slowly slide back into works and don't believe the promise.

Everything comes to us through grace by faith. The Bible says that there is the manifold, many-sided grace of God: Born-again grace; overcoming sin grace; ministry grace; etc. Everything you do in your Christian life should be a work of grace. And in this way we can enter into His rest, which is not in our strength, but in His.

Remember that Jesus came and brought grace and truth. Grace—God's riches at Christ's expense, unmerited favor, or God's ability in our lives. Our ultimate goal is not what we can do for God but what we can become in God. *(Written by Dave Duell)*

NOVEMBER 22
YOUR LITTLE AND HIS MUCH
2 CORINTHIANS 12:9

2 Corinthians 12:9 "And He said to me, 'My Grace is sufficient for you, for My strength is made perfect in weakness . . . .'"

Many times we are tempted to give into the thought pattern of the victim of circumstance. This mentality says, "If things were different, then I could become something in life." Or, "If only I had grown up differently. If I had different parents. If I had the right friends, or more money." This is a pathetic way to live. The challenge is to do something with our lives the way that they are now.

The great violinist, Nicolo Pagini was performing one night to a sold-out theater. In the middle of his most dramatic and difficult piece, one of his strings broke. He continued to play. Then moments later, a second string broke. Difficult as it was, Pagini continued to play. Seconds later, as Nicolo was finishing the song, to the shock of the crowd, a third string broke. This left the great violinist with one string. With an attitude of triumph, Pagini raised his violin to the crowd and announced, "Nicolo and one string!" Then he proceeded to play the entire piece again *on just one string.*

You may feel like all you have left to your life is one string. You may look at those around you and see them holding perfectly strung violins. You may be tempted to feel slighted. You may feel that life isn't fair. Well, life isn't fair and it never will be. God is glorified not through our perfection, but through our weakness. You must get rid of the paralyzing word "if." Commit your life, your inabilities to Him. He is the Master creator. He takes what little we have, then He creates more to add to it, bringing glory to His name. *(Written by Mike Fehlauer)*

NOVEMBER 23
SEEING THINGS GOD'S WAY
HABAKKUK 1:1-5

Habakkuk 1:5 "Behold ye among the heathen, and regard, and wonder marvellously: for I will work a work in your days, which ye will not believe, though it be told you."

Life is not always what we perceive it to be. That is why we need to pray for the Lord to open the eyes of our understanding. Habakkuk was concerned about the plight of seemingly unanswered prayer. He was also worried about the bloodshed of the violence. You open the newspapers today and you read about who has gone crazy overnight this time. You look out at the world around you, and you see bloodshed. You see violence. We can look at our own cities and see all the craziness. There is precious little, if anything, that children can watch on television. We need to really be diligent about our children and our grandchildren in that area. Habakkuk saw sin on the increase. So many people seem to be mad about something, and then justice falls in the streets. It seems there is no justice, the law is a joke and "wrong judgment proceedeth." All of this was in Habakkuk 1:1-4. But, God's word and God's answer to this is found in verse five. God was saying, "Open your eyes and see it like I see it, Habakkuk."

It is the same today. You can focus on the negative, or you can focus on the positive. You can focus on all the people who are dying, or focus on all the people who are living. Elijah was a prophet of God who complained that he thought he was the only one left who loved God. But God told him, "Hey, I have 7,000 people who have never bowed their knee to Baal. You think you're the only one" (1 Kings 19:18).

Worry and burdens will sap the very life out of your time, your energy, your health, and your finances. It is impossible to see through the eyes of discouragement and still prosper. God is saying, "See it from My point of view." Because when we see it like He sees it, then we get God's vision, His plan. He is saying, "I'm working a good work in your days. I have a good plan to give a hope and a future (Jer. 29:11). The best is yet to come." Are you going to believe it? If you believe it, you will be a part of it. That is what it really comes down to. I don't want to be a doubter, do you? Let's pray to God today, "Lord, I know that you desire for me to prosper because your Word says that you have pleasure in the prosperity of your people. Help me to see things your way today so that I can fulfill the good plan you have for my life." *(Written by Bob Nichols)*

NOVEMBER 24
THE BETTER DISH
LUKE 10:42

Luke 10:42 "Mary hath chosen that good part . . . . "

Jesus made this statement to Martha, the sister of Mary. The Greek for "good part" means the "better dish." This must have been a hard statement for Martha to accept.

Martha had been working all day to prepare the meal for Jesus and his disciples. The opening of this story tells us she was "cumbered" or weighed down by the preparation of the food, drinks and table settings. She must have wanted each table setting to be perfect, each disciple to have enough of her prize winning dishes and each drinking glass to stay filled.

Martha was also angry at her sister, Mary. Instead of helping serve food, Mary was sitting at Jesus' feet, listening to His every word. Finally Martha shouted at Jesus, "Don't you care that Mary has left me alone to serve? Tell her to help me." Jesus did not tell Martha that working and serving were wrong, but she had become too worried and overtaken by her work. Mary had chosen the better dish—sitting and learning at Jesus' feet.

We often get caught up serving the Lord, working in the church, and forget about the greatest dish of all—learning God's Word. It is through the word that Jesus fellowships with us. The true power for service comes through God's promises and fellowship with Jesus. This is where our hearts become truly committed to the Lord. Out of a heart of commitment and love for Jesus, we should serve the Lord.

This is what was missing in the heart of Martha. She thought by working, she would find favor with the Lord. She worked hard to impress Jesus and the disciples. Mary found the true way to the heart of God. She put communion with Jesus number one in her life. Her works would then count for the Lord. We are saved "unto good works." We do not work to be saved. *(Written by Bob Yandian)*

NOVEMBER 25
THANKSGIVING
I THESSALONIANS 5:18

1 Thessalonians 5:18 "Thank God in . . . (all) circumstances, for this is God's will for you in Christ Jesus . . . . "

Thanksgiving, to be truly thanksgiving, is first thanks and then giving. Relationship with God should fill us with thanksgiving. I believe those who know God are always thankful. 1 Thessalonians 5:18 says *" Thank God in . . . (all) circumstances, for this is God's will for you in Christ Jesus . . . . "* Thanksgiving is a duty before a feeling. Gratitude is a choice.

Jesus is our example. He gave thanks before feeding the multitude. Even at the last supper he gave thanks, broke the bread and told us it was His body. I Corinthians 10:16 calls it the cup of thanksgiving. Communion is a thanksgiving. How can you remember Jesus and not explode with gratitude?

As members in the kingdom of God, giving thanks produces practical benefits:

1. Cleanses our food - I Timothy 4:3 *"Foods which God created to be received with thanksgiving by those who believe and know the truth."*

2. Strengthens our faith - Colossians 2:7 *" Rooted and built up in Him and established in the faith, as you have been taught, abounding in it with thanksgiving."*

3. Reduces our anxiety - Philippians 4:6 *"Be anxious for nothing, but in everything by prayer and supplication, with thanksgiving, let your requests be made known to God."*

4. Makes every day God's - Romans 14:6 *"He who observes the day, observes it to the Lord . . . . "*

5. Keeps peace - Colossians 3:15 *"And let the peace of God rule in your hearts, to which also you were called in one body; and be thankful."*

6. Gives access to God - Colossians 3:17 *"Do all in the name of the Lord Jesus, giving thanks to God the Father through Him."*

Thanksgiving reaps such benefits as these; focuses attention on God Himself and causes us to imitate Jesus. It causes overflow and greatly improves us, so what is left for me to say? Thanksgiving is good, but "thanksliving" is better! *(Written by Dave Duell)*

NOVEMBER 26
FACING LIFE AS IT IS
HEBREWS 6:11

Hebrews 6:11 "And we desire that each one of you show the same diligence to the full assurance of hope until the end."
My son, Josiah, just returned form a three-week mission trip to India. He loved it and wants to go back. There were a few disciplines they had to follow as a team. One of the things they were not allowed to do was to say the word "can't." If they did, they had to do a certain number of push-ups. We do allow that word to invade our thinking too often. I know that there are some things that are literally impossible, but too often, we use the word can't as an excuse from trying and putting forth an effort in life.

There is a story I read about a young man who discovered a vein of gold high up on a mountain. He struggled for some time trying to develop a mine to harvest the gold. After weeks he was no further along than when he started. It seemed too difficult. Then he realized that he needed more knowledge about mining. He went to town and found a mining department in the university near the city. He met with the head of the department. Then he met with a mining engineer. This young man and the engineer went back to the mine. It took about a week to get there. The engineer told him that there were millions there. He had two choices. He could go through the work of developing it, or he could sell it off. If he sold it off, he could have enough cash immediately to live comfortably for the rest of his life. If he developed it, he would be one of the richest men in America, as well as establish wealth for his children. The young man decided to develop it. It took a year of hard training, study and preparation. When spring came he was ready. That mine made him millions over.

The trouble with too many people is that they want it easy. Prosperity always involves hard work. It is the man who does more than what he is paid to do, who gets the raise. Some of you have a gold mine in you. A gold mine in the form of an idea. A gold mine of gifts and talents. Are you willing to take the time and work to develop it? *(Written by Mike Fehlauer)*

NOVEMBER 27
LOOK ON THE FIELDS
JOHN 4:35-38

John 4:35 "Say not ye, There are yet four months, and then cometh harvest? behold, I say unto you, Lift up your eyes, and look on the fields; for they are white already to harvest."
Part of sowing seed to reap our harvest is helping God reap His harvest. His harvest is souls. The Word of God says to look on the fields. It is amazing how many people come to church and never look on the fields. They hear the songs, they hear the message, they do the things that people do in church, but they leave and never take a look on the fields. God wants us to look out at the needs of others. When your stomach is full, don't forget that there are those who do not have sufficient food. When your home is comfortable, never forget that there is someone else that does not have a comfortable dwelling.

Can we do everything for everyone? No. But God wants us to look for opportunities to do what we can. Look for people who need Jesus. Look for those who will respond to the gospel of Jesus Christ. Live alert and don't live selfishly. Live with your eyes open. This is not to bring condemnation or pressure on us, but let's look for opportunities where we can make a difference. One single church or one single person can not respond to every need in the world today, or even in our city. I realize that. I can not respond to every need that is presented to me. But, *if we will look*, we can respond to those needs that we see, and then we can happily do something about it.

Behold, look on the fields. Look at the people you work with. Study the needs of people's lives and do what you can. Tell them about Jesus. Don't lose your vision of the fields. A church that loses the vision of the fields that surround even their own church, is a church that is in the process of dying and they really don't even realize it. I want to live alert. Yes, I want to be blessed, but I want to be one that when God needs someone to do something on this earth, He can use me to be a blessing. By sowing into their lives, God will multiply it back to your own life. *(Written by Bob Nichols)*

NOVEMBER 28
WHAT TO FORGET—WHAT TO REMEMBER
PHILIPPIANS 3:13

Philippians 3:13 "Forgetting those things which are behind, and reaching forth unto those things which are before."

God's Word tells us many things we are to remember. We are not to forget God's benefits of forgiveness, healing, strength and mercy (Ps. 103:1-4). We are commanded to remember our former days and the fight of faith we endured (Heb. 10:32). God commands us to remember many other of His works.

So why does Paul command us as believers to forget the things that are behind? This is not only telling us to forget the sins, but also the blessings and triumphs of the past. How does this verse fit in with the many commandments to remember the good times and the bad? What are we to forget, and what are we to remember?

First, we are to forget anything that hinders us from advancing. In the Christian life we are either advancing or retreating. We never stand still. God wants us to advance and any hindrance should be removed, including our past.

Second, we are to forget yesterday when it is at the forefront of our minds. God promises to keep us in perfect peace as our minds are stayed on Him. When the past overshadows our ability to have our minds stayed on the Lord, we are to forget the past, assign it to oblivion and advance in our spiritual growth.

Third, we are to forget the past when it is a stronghold. We are to cast down imaginations and high thoughts that exalt themselves against the knowledge of God. When the past exalts itself in our minds against the power of God's Word, we need to take authority over Satan's power in Jesus' name.

Ask yourself a question: Do you control your memories, or do they control you? If you can control them, they can be a blessing. Past successes can bring great anticipation of future blessings. Past sins can teach the strategies of Satan so you won't fall for them again. Yesterday is to be remembered when you are ready. *(Written by Bob Yandian)*

NOVEMBER 29
WHERE'S THE FRUIT?
NUMBERS 17:1-11

Numbers 17:8 "And it came to pass, that on the morrow Moses went into the tabernacle of witness; and, behold, the rod of Aaron for the house of Levi was budded, and brought forth buds, and bloomed blossoms, and yielded almonds."

Lack of respect for authority is one of the most common problems in our world today. We see it in the home, in the church and in the attitudes people have towards government. It's everywhere. And it's not just a new problem of our modern times.

The people of Israel questioned Moses and Aaron's authority to govern the nation. In Numbers, chapter 16, Korah slandered Moses' character and authority; Korah and all those in association with him, were swallowed up by the earth. Then another 14 thousand, who criticized Moses for the way he had handled Korah, died by a plague of the Lord. Moses' authority was under attack.

To resolve the issue, the Lord had Moses command the leaders of each tribe to take their rods, which symbolized authority, and write their names on them. Then all the rods were placed in the Holy Place overnight. When they came in the next morning, Aaron's rod had budded, blossomed and produced almonds. The other rods were still just sticks. This forever settled the issue of whom God had chosen to rule the nation. The fruit made the difference.

There are many people who proclaim their own authority today and seek to exercise it over us in various ways. But we can always tell those who have God-given authority by the fruit they produce. Threats, boastings, and publicity don't prove authority. We can tell godly leaders by their fruit (Mt. 7:20). Those who are great in the kingdom of God are servants, not lords (Mk. 10:44). *(Written by Andrew Wommack)*

NOVEMBER 30
THE HITCHHIKER
HEBREWS 6:12

Hebrews 6:12 "That you do not become sluggish, but imitate those who through faith and patience inherit the promises."
There is a mental attitude that marks our society today. That attitude is to get something without giving. So many want the best wages with as little work possible. I call these people hitchhikers. They want to get somewhere, but they want to get there in someone else's vehicle. They want someone else to pay for the gas and the car. It is impossible to prosper with that attitude. The road that leads to a good bank account is an uphill road, and most of us have to build the road ourselves to get there!

Are you a hitchhiker? Or are you the one who is willing to bear the burden, do the work, and pay the taxes? If you are going to be a success, you will have to bear the burden. I heard someone say that success is the willingness to bear the pain and the burden. Many bear pain *unwillingly.* The key is having the attitude that is willing to do the work and carry the responsibility to succeed. The path of least resistance always leads to poverty. Abundance starts with seeing yourself as one who helps others, instead as the one in need. Instead of always borrowing a car, begin to sow, work, and buy your own car. God wants you to prosper. He has provided you all things necessary to do so. But you must combine the natural with the super to get the supernatural. *(Written by Mike Fehlauer)*

DECEMBER 1
GOD DOESN'T GIVE A HOLY HOOT
ISAIAH 55:9

Isaiah 55:9 "For as the heavens are higher than the earth, so are my ways higher than your ways, and my thoughts than your thoughts."
God doesn't give a holy hoot about some of the things that we get so uptight about on this earth. We need to let the main thing continue to be the main thing. I enjoy nice things and good things as much as anyone, but somehow those things just don't mean what they used to mean. Just let me reach some more people for Jesus. Let's bless another missionary. Let's reach out and do something to see more souls come to Jesus. One time when my wife and I visited the island of Grenada, we had quite an experience. We flew into San Juan and there was no electricity. They had over 18 inches of rain in one day and over one million people were without electricity, but we were able to check into the hotel. After searching around in the dark, we finally found the door to our room and went in. The room was so dark that when my wife set her purse down, she couldn't even find it. When we woke up the next morning, we could finally see because the sun was up. Joy and I got to laughing. I said, "You know honey, Americans are so spoiled. Thank God we have a decent bed to sleep in." I mean it is inconvenient when a woman can't find her purse, but she finally found it. Some people don't realize how blessed they are. In a third world nation everything is delayed, if it happens at all.

After Grenada, we flew to Georgetown, Guiana. I'll never fuss about a rough road again. To me, the whole world looked like the old beat up Toyota we were in. And there were cows in the road—it was something else. It was nighttime and I was glad that the taxi driver could see better than I could. I was saying "God give him x-ray vision." And some of the food I've seen in other countries! They were thankful just to have food!

God does not see things the same way we see them. He doesn't accept someone based on the label in his clothes or the kind of car he drives. He looks at the heart. Are you concerned about the same things He's concerned about? Are you doing what you know to do with all that He's given you? You can count the seeds in the apple, but you can't count the apples that come out of a seed. God will cause you to prosper so that you can be a blessing. He will prosper you so that you can help provide for the end time harvest. That's what it's all about. *(Written by Bob Nichols)*

DECEMBER 2
OFFENSES
MARK 4:17

Mark 4:17 "Afterward, when affliction or persecution ariseth for the word's sake, immediately they are offended."
As a pastor, I can tell you that offenses are the number one reason why people leave the Word of God, their walk with Jesus and the church. Affliction and persecution come to every Christian, but some handle them better than others. They are designed by Satan to steal the Word from your heart. It is not you Satan hates, it is the Word in your heart. The Word believed and spoken will overthrow Satan's hold on you and others.

An offense is a mole hill that becomes magnified into a mountain. Offenses are never major issues, but are only minor. They can be disagreements over carpet colors in the church, wall colors or pews versus chairs. Many become offended because the music is too loud or not loud enough; the room is too cold or too hot or we stand too long for worship. I have even had people become offended because I did not say "hi" to them in the halls. Many times I did not see them.

Eventually, offenses are like glasses. When you put them on, you see the whole world through your offenses. You judge the preaching through your offenses, the music and others in positions of leadership. When you leave the church, Satan has you right where he wants you.

An offense is a side issue to take you away from the real issue—the Word of God. What does it matter if you have a chair or pew to sit on? Many around the world sit on the ground to hear the Word. The temperature and volume are again nothing more than side issues. I have spoken in churches that had no sound system, heat or air conditioning. The people attended because they only wanted to hear the Word.

This verse comes from the parable of the sower and the seed. All that is needed for spiritual growth and victory over Satan is a sower (minister), seed (the Word) and ground (the hearts of people). Anything else should be treated as a blessing, not as an opportunity for offense. *(Written by Bob Yandian)*

DECEMBER 3
WHERE'S YOUR EBENEZER?
1 SAMUEL 7:3-13

1 Samuel 7:12 "Then Samuel took a stone, and set it between Mizpeh and Shen, and called the name of it Ebenezer, saying, Hitherto hath the LORD helped us."
God had just won a great victory for the Israelites. As they assembled to pray and repent as a nation, the Philistines attacked them. The people cried out to God for help and the Lord was violently agitated and irritated with the Philistines. That's what the word "thundered" in verse ten means. God routed the Philistines before the Israelites.

Samuel placed a large stone at the site of the battle and called it Ebenezer. The Hebrew word "Ebenezer" means "stone of the help." Samuel was placing a visual reminder for everyone present and generations to come that God was the one who had helped the people of Israel defeat their enemies.

The Lord commanded the observance of many feasts to remind His people of things He had done. He also commanded us to reverence the landmarks of others by not removing them (Deut. 19:14; 27:17; Prov. 22:28; 23:10). All this stresses the importance of having markers that remind us of the faithfulness of God.

Psalm 103:2 says, *"forget not all his benefits."* The reason we are commanded not to forget is because we will forget if we don't make an effort to remember. That's what the stone Ebenezer was for.

Do you have Ebenezers in your life? Each one of us has many instances where God has been faithful, but whether or not you've marked that spot is a different thing. Let the Lord direct your memory back to His faithfulness and put a marker there in your mind. Then visit that place often. *(Written by Andrew Wommack)*

DECEMBER 4
STAND FAST
GALATIANS 5:1

Galatians 5:1 "Stand fast therefore in the liberty by which Christ has made us free, and do not be entangled again with a yoke of bondage."

Galatians 5:1 says to *"Stand fast therefore in the liberty by which Christ has made us free, and do not be entangled again with a yoke of bondage."* Stand fast is a military term meaning to hold one's ground. Paul is telling these people that once they have gained ground in their spiritual life, they are to hold fast to it and not allow the enemy to wrestle it from them.

Liberty is freedom, but freedom is not free. It doesn't come easy, nor does a person remain free without effort. Just as it takes courage and commitment to hold on to political freedom, so it requires dedicated effort to preserve spiritual liberty. In both cases we have an enemy who will destroy and enslave us if we are not continually on our guard. Paul is warning us about our enemy without and within.

Paul is warning us against religion, and man made systems of laws and regulations. Religion gives the appearance of godliness and devotion by imposed restraints, but it does not have the power to bless, heal and to set free. It is a system of bondage.

If God's children cannot be set free to think, speak, and act as they choose, if they must be chained by a system of "do's and don't's," then the new birth is not better than the life of sin; it's one bondage to another.

Grace is not a license to sin but to serve, which binds us with love. God is not a dictator, but a liberator. He looses our bonds and frees us as captives. He sets us free, praise God! Free to worship, love and to serve Him. Then look at verse 13: *"For you, brethren, have been called to liberty; only do not use liberty as an opportunity for the flesh, but through love serve one another."* (Written by Dave Duell)

DECEMBER 5
BE WORTH MORE THAN WHAT YOU ARE PAID
LUKE 6:38

Luke 6:38 "Give, and it shall be given unto you; good measure, pressed down, and shaken together, and running over, shall men give into your bosom. For with the same measure that ye mete withal it shall be measured to you again."

Those who have made the greatest contribution to the world have put the world in debt to them. They have lived their lives as contributors. Givers and not takers. Make the world a better place because you live in it. Look for a way to deposit life and love into others. Show your appreciation to someone today. Take a moment and think about those who have blessed and impacted you. Then, do something to show your appreciation.

Don't wait for your boss to tell you what needs to be done. Find out what needs to be done and then do it. Do more than what they are paying you to do. That will be as great a testimony to the reality of Jesus as your preaching and prayers. Selfishness cramps ability.

I remember when I was out of the ministry for a season. I sold vacuum cleaners door to door. I sold men's clothing. I also sold hearing aids. The man I worked for when I sold hearing aids is a solid Christian man. He was not Spirit-filled. What I mean, is that it was not his custom to operate in the gifts of the Spirit. He was not subject to dreams or visions. I had been doing my best to do more than what he asked of me. One day he came to my office. He said that the Lord woke him at 3:00 a.m. and told him to increase the percentage I would receive from each sale. For 30 years this man had a system for what percentage his sales people would receive. Thirty years! Yet God woke him in the early morning hours and told him to give me a raise. As we live as givers, as we choose to believe God, as we offer ourselves in service to Him, we will receive all the good things God has for us. (Written by Mike Fehlauer)

DECEMBER 6
IS YOUR HEART STILL BEATING?
HEBREWS 12:12-13

Hebrews 12:12-13 "Wherefore lift up the hands which hang down, and the feeble knees; And make straight paths for your feet, lest that which is lame be turned out of the way; but let it rather be healed."

This verse describes a person after he has been through the discipline of the Lord. The hands are hanging down and the knees are weak because this person is feeling sorry for himself. Like a child after being disciplined, the pouting needs to end. It is time to live again.

Does this sound like you? Have you been disciplined by the Lord, but find it hard to forgive yourself? Have you asked yourself, "How could I have ever let myself become so foolish? How could I have disappointed the Lord so much?"

The good news is, there is restoration after forgiveness. Many Christians will try to tell you that God may forgive you, but you can never rise to a level of usefulness with God again. You can be forgiven, but you cannot be restored. A popular phrase is, "A bird with a broken wing can never fly as high." This may be true in nature, but it is not true in grace.

King David flew higher than he had ever flown before. He became a greater king than ever. It took time and much healing, but not only was he forgiven, but restored by the power of God.

If you think you have failed so miserably that God can never forgive or use you again, take this test. Put you hand on your heart. If it is still beating, God is not through with you. The only time God cannot forgive or restore you is when you are dead. Until that time, God has a plan for your life and you need to accept it.

Go ahead. Lift up your hands hanging down and your weak knees. Straighten out the path ahead of you and get back into the race. Heroes are not people who never make mistakes. They are people who get up afterwards. *(Written by Bob Yandian)*

DECEMBER 7
GOD HAS A PLAN FOR YOU
JEREMIAH 1:4-10

Jeremiah 1:5 "Before I formed thee in the belly I knew thee; and before thou camest forth out of the womb I sanctified thee, and I ordained thee a prophet unto the nations."

The Lord spoke to Jeremiah that he was called, sanctified and ordained before he was born. This wasn't unique to Jeremiah either. John the Baptist (Lk. 1:15-16), Jesus (Isa. 49:1-5), and Paul were the same (Gal. 1:15). You are too!

Psalm 139:13-16 says that God possessed us in our mother's womb. God knew exactly what we would look like before we were born. Before we were formed, all our parts were written in His book. You didn't just happen. You didn't evolve. You were created by a God who had a purpose in your creation. God created you with special giftings to fulfill His purposes for your life. God has a plan for you and your life.

Your greatest opportunity for happiness and success is in fulfilling God's purposes for your life. You may be able to use God's talents to accomplish other things, but you will not experience God's anointing and blessings on other efforts as you will if those abilities are devoted to God.

You may wonder and say, "How do I know what God wants me to do?" The answer comes in giving yourself completely to God. When you make a total surrender to Him, He begins working circumstances in a manner that lead you into His perfect plan for your life. Your part is to surrender. His part is to reveal. You do your part and He will do His part. And you will experience a new fulfillment and joy that only those who are in the center of His will can know. *(Written by Andrew Wommack)*

DECEMBER 8
WORRY IS ALWAYS FUTURE
EXODUS 17:3

Exodus 17:3 "Why is it you have you brought us up out of Egypt, to kill us and our children and our livestock with thirst?"

When we are facing a tragedy or trial, we usually lose sight of all God's blessings, that brought us to this point. The children of Israel had only been in the wilderness a few days when they came to a place where there was no water to drink. They began to complain to Moses calling the situation his fault. They also now had God's plan figured out. God brought them to this spot to kill them.

Let's look at the stupidity of this argument. The Israelites had been in captivity for 400 years in Egypt. Even with the oppression, they continued to increase in population. When Moses arrived, God spared the Jewish people through ten plagues. While the Egyptians suffered and even died, the Israelites were protected by God from the plagues and death. God then parted the Red Sea for them to travel across safely and even drowned the Egyptian army behind them. God did all of this to bring them to this one spot and kill them?

You have done the same thing. You have looked at your bills, your lack of food in the cupboard and your overdue mortgage bill and cried, "I'm going to die right here." Stop and think about what you have just said. God saved you years ago, filled you with His Holy Spirit, healed your body, performed miracles for you and your family many times and supplied all of your needs on more than one occasion. He has done all of these wonderful things to bring you to this spot and watch you die?

Worry is always future. God has taken care of you every moment of every day, but somehow, tomorrow, this will all fail. God's grace will run out today. Of course this is blasphemous. The God who has taken care of you always, will not fail you tomorrow, next week or next year. He will continue to walk with you and provide until Jesus comes. David said, *"I have been young, and now am old; yet have I not seen the righteous forsaken, nor his seed begging bread"* (Ps. 37:25). *(Written by Bob Yandian)*

DECEMBER 9
YOU NEVER PUT GOD FIRST AND COME IN SECOND
1 KINGS 17:9-16

1 Kings 17:13, "And Elijah said unto her, Fear not; go and do as thou hast said: but make me thereof a little cake first, and bring it unto me, and after make for thee and for thy son."

Here was a desperate situation, but there was a man of faith, and a woman of faith, who were willing to do whatever it took for breakthrough. In many circles today, Elijah would have been criticized for saying, "Go make *me* a little cake first." There was only enough meal and enough oil for this widow woman to make something for her son and herself and then they thought they would die. And here walks up a man of God and says in 1 Kings 17:13, *" Fear not; go and do as thou hast said: but make me thereof a little cake first, and bring it unto me, and after make for thee and for thy son."* But Elijah, how could you take advantage of a poor widow like that? He wasn't taking advantage of her. He was giving her an opportunity to be blessed with a miracle. He knew that God was a "sure thing." Elijah said in 1 Kings 17:14, *"For thus saith the LORD God of Israel, The barrel of meal shall not waste, neither shall the cruse of oil fail, until the day that the LORD sendeth rain upon the earth."*

1 Kings 17:15-16 says, *"And she went and did according to the saying of Elijah: and she, and he, and her house, did eat many days. And the barrel of meal wasted not, neither did the cruse of oil fail, according to the word of the LORD, which he spake by Elijah."* By putting the man of God first, the widow woman was really putting God first. What happened as a result of that offering? A miracle. And what was that miracle? She and her family were sustained until the drought broke. This woman knew the principle: You will never go wrong by putting God first. And it paid off.

As believers, we are not supposed to be worried about what we're going to wear or what we're going to eat. God promised to take care of all our needs. Matthew 6:33 spells it out very plainly, *"But seek ye first the kingdom of God, and his righteousness; and all these things shall be added unto you."* Paul wrote in 1 Corinthians 9:24, *"Know ye not that they which run in a race run all, but one receiveth the prize? So run, that ye may obtain."* When you put God first, you will never come in second. *(Written by Bob Nichols)*

DECEMBER 10
WHAT'S YOUR EXCUSE?
JEREMIAH 1:4-10

Jeremiah 1:6 "Then said I, Ah, Lord GOD! behold, I cannot speak: for I am a child."
God had just revealed to Jeremiah that He had created him for a specific purpose. He had sanctified and ordained him to be a prophet to the nation of Israel. What wonderful news! How awesome to know that God had a special purpose when He created you. You aren't an accident. You were created on purpose to accomplish a specific purpose.

But Jeremiah wasn't blessed by the news. He was intimidated. He wanted out of God's plan for his life. He thought this was greater than what he could do. As my good friend Dave Duell says, "If what you feel called to do isn't greater than what you think you can do, then I doubt if it's God." God is a big God and He calls us to big things. Man thinks small. God thinks big.

Jeremiah protested that he was only a child and couldn't speak. In truth, he was a grown man at this time. He was referring to his belief that he was inadequate for the task. Moses tried this same line on God (Ex. 4:10). We've all tried it. But the Lord commanded Jeremiah never again to say he was incompetent.

The truth is that none of us are capable of accomplishing God's will on our own. But it is also true that none of us are on our own when we submit to God's will. The Lord gives us special anointings and gifts to accomplish His will. All we have to do is yield. God does the rest.

Do you know what God's will for your life is? Are you lacking what it takes to get it done? You're in good company. But don't try to fulfill the task in your own strength. Don't ever again refer to your weakness. Go in His might. *(Written by Andrew Wommack)*

DECEMBER 11
WHEN PRAYER GOES UP, GOD COMES DOWN
HABAKKUK 2:1-4

Habakkuk 2:1 "I will stand upon my watch, and set me upon the tower, and will watch to see what he will say unto me, and what I shall answer when I am reproved."
In Habakkuk chapter one, God told a discouraged prophet to open his eyes and to see the way He looked at things. Habakkuk made a decision in chapter two. Faith is a decision. When trouble knocks on the door, you have to make a quality faith decision. I know it literally says, "I will stand," but what Habakkuk was saying was, "I will pray." He said, "I am going to pray, watch and see what God will say." That's kind of strange, isn't it? To *watch and see* what God will *say.* Habakkuk 2:2 says, *"And the LORD answered me, and said."*

For the person who wants to walk in the abundance of God, prayer is not optional. I have heard some preachers say that prayer is works. Yes, prayer sure works for me! The more we pray, the more we see. The more prayer goes up, the more God comes down. You may not always be able to reach a prayer partner on the phone, or be able to run to a prayer meeting, but you can have your own prayer meeting. You can pray in your car or walking in your neighborhood, or in the shower. Many a time, I've been out walking at night just praying in the Spirit. I like praying in the dark, because I like praying in the Spirit and I don't have to be concerned about who is around. I can't count how many times God made things real to me, or would get some cobwebs out of my head while I was praying. Many, many times I would just go along, praying in the Spirit and God would show me something. He will reveal things to you. What does that have to do with prosperity? Well, one Word from God can turn any situation around.

Missionary Wayne Myers said that if all you have is ten minutes a day to talk to God, spend nine minutes of that time praising Him and fellowshipping with Him, and spend one minute asking Him for something. So many times we spend all of our time petitioning and never get around to talking to God. We give the television time, we give the telephone time, and we give people time. The most important thing in your life is God. We cannot say, "Okay, God, you have five minutes to do something, or I'm out of here."

In a difficult time in Habakkuk's life, when nothing made sense—people didn't make sense, circumstances didn't make sense, the world didn't make sense—he said, "I'm going to go talk to God and I'm going to wait and see what He has to say about this." And God answered him. God gave him a vision. It is important to wait, to watch, to see what God will say, because remember, when prayer goes up, God comes down. *(Written by Bob Nichols)*

DECEMBER 12
GOD'S PROSPERITY FOR YOU
ECCLESIASTES 5:19

Ecclesiastes 5:19 "Also every man to whom God has given riches and possessions and power to enjoy them, and to accept his appointed lot and to rejoice in his toil, for this is the gift of God."

Many Christians believe the lie from Satan that their lot in life is to live within the prison of poverty and lack. Or, at best, living from paycheck to paycheck. Yet, according to the Word, your lot is to receive from Him riches and possessions. Not only has God given us riches and wealth, but also the ability to enjoy them. There are two important keys to experiencing this life of abundance that He has provided for us.

Key number one: It is imperative that we believe the integrity of God's Word concerning financial prosperity. We must allow the Word of God to destroy the limitations that society, fear and religion have placed on us. We must, through the Word of God, begin to see ourselves enjoying the wealth and riches God has provided for us. This is what we call a revelation.

Key number two: A lifestyle of giving is vital in receiving God's provisions! Giving is the only proof that we have conquered greed. In 1 Timothy 6:10, we read, *"For the love of money is the root of all kinds of evil."* Jesus said Himself in Mark 10:24 *"Children, how hard it is for those who trust in riches to enter the kingdom of God."* Consistent giving will affect your perspective on money. When we give, it is an outward expression of faith. As you go about your day, look for ways to give: whether it is a smile, a word of encouragement, or a prayer. If you haven't already developed a lifestyle of giving, start today. Trust Him with your finances and demonstrate that trust through the giving of your finances. *(Written by Mike Fehlauer)*

DECEMBER 13
THE BIBLICAL PERSPECTIVE IS THE RIGHT PERSPECTIVE
ISAIAH 55:8-9

Isaiah 55:8 "For my thoughts are not your thoughts, neither are your ways my ways, saith the LORD."

We need to understand some very important things from a biblical perspective. First of all, God wants you blessed. Second, Satan wants you poor. Third, Jesus bore the curse of poverty for all of us. And fourth, God is not the problem—He is the answer!

In 3 John 2 it says, *"Beloved, I wish above all things that thou mayest prosper and be in health, even as thy soul prospereth."* That word "wish" in the verse literally means, "pray." The word "prosper" comes from a compound word meaning to be well off, fare well; and to lead by a direct and easy way, to have a successful, prosperous and expeditious journey. God's will is for us to prosper in every area of our lives, including financially.

John 10:10 says, *"The thief cometh not, but for to steal, and to kill, and to destroy: I am come that they might have life, and that they might have it more abundantly."* Who is the thief? The devil is the thief. And, it is the devil that wants to convince believers that they should be poor. But, hallelujah, Jesus came to give us abundance! Abundance means great plenty, an overflowing quantity, and ample sufficiency. He became poor so that we could be rich (2 Corinthians 8:9). Not so that we could be greedy or selfish, but rich so that we could bless others from the overflow of the blessings He pours on us!

One of the curses of the Law was poverty (see Deuteronomy 28). What good news to know that Jesus bore all those curses for us when He was crucified! Galatians 3:13, *"Christ hath redeemed us from the curse of the law, being made a curse for us: for it is written, Cursed is every one that hangeth on a tree."*

The balance and the key to receiving all that God has for us on this earth is believing the Word of God. I can sit down with you for hours and tell you that God wants you to prosper, but until you believe the Word of God for yourself, it will not be operative in your life. It all comes from the Word of God. Joshua 1:8 says, *"This book of the law shall not depart out of thy mouth; but thou shalt meditate therein day and night, that thou mayest observe to do according to all that is written therein: for then thou shalt make thy way prosperous, and then thou shalt have good success."* Obedience to the Word will bring the blessing to you. What is obedience? It is doing what the Word says, not what we "come up with" in our own minds. If someone tells us something, or we have an opinion about something and it disagrees with what the Bible says, we need to stick with the Bible and throw the other stuff out! Judge all things from the biblical perspective. *(Written by Bob Nichols)*

DECEMBER 14
YOU ARE THE CHRIST
MARK 8:27-30

Mark 8:29 *"And he saith unto them, But whom say ye that I am? And Peter answereth and saith unto him, Thou art the Christ."*

People often think how wonderful it would have been to be one of Jesus' disciples. They speculate that if they had seen Jesus with their own eyes performing all those miracles that it would have been easy to believe. Not so.

I once dreamed that I was one of Jesus' disciples. I witnessed Jesus raising Jairus' daughter from the dead. I saw blind eyes opened and deaf ears unstopped. I was walking down a road with all the disciples and we were talking about the incredible things we had seen when Jesus walked right up to me and said, "But who do you say I am?"

I was torn with emotion. Everything I'd witnessed and all my heart wanted to say, "You are the Christ," but how could I? As I looked at Jesus, He looked like any other man. There was nothing special about His looks. There was no halo as you see in pictures. All my sensory knowledge said He was just a man. I realized just how hard it was for Jesus' disciples to believe.

I finally gave Peter's reply, "You are the Christ," but it took all the faith I could muster. I had to look past His physical body and see who He was on the inside. I now believe it is actually easier for us who are removed from the scene to believe. We can read the Word about all the miraculous things He did and envision Him seated on the throne in heaven. The disciples were constantly having to battle the logic of how God could be in a human body.

You can believe in the Lord just as strongly as those who walked with Jesus during his physical ministry. Choose to believe today and reap the benefits. *(Written by Andrew Wommack)*

DECEMBER 15
SUPERNATURAL BREAKTHROUGH
1 KINGS 18:33-35

1 Kings 18:33-35 "Fill four barrels with water, and pour it on the burnt sacrifice, and on the wood. And he said, Do it the second time. And they did it the second time. And he said, Do it the third time. And they did it the third time. And the water ran round about the altar; and he filled the trench also with water."

There comes a time when enough is enough. The nation of Israel had fallen deep into sin. They were worshipping Baal. God said, "We're going to take care of a lot of things at once here. We are going to see repentance and revival. It's time to have a showdown with this humanistic, demon-worshipping crowd. It's time." There is again going to be a time when God says, "It's time. I've had enough."

The prophets of Baal already had 12 hours worth of jumping around and cutting themselves, trying to get their god to move on their behalf without success. Around noon, it was Elijah's turn and he mocked them saying, "Maybe your god is on vacation." Elijah sent them to pour out four barrels of water on the offering. He sent them three times. That's 12 barrels of water! Remember, they were at the end of three years of drought! Elijah was sowing what was most precious to him at the time. Twelve barrels of water would go a long way when you've had three years of drought! Desperate times call for desperate measures. He sowed, believing God. In verse 41, it says, *"And Elijah said unto Ahab, Get thee up, eat and drink; for there is a sound of abundance of rain."* He saw with the eye of faith what was ahead. Then in verse 45 it says, *"And it came to pass in the mean while, that the heaven was black with clouds and wind, and there was a great rain . . . . "*

It's amazing how some people have a hard time understanding this. Somewhere along the line there is always going to be supernatural sacrifice before there is supernatural receiving. Somebody sacrificed in prayer, somebody sacrificed in giving. Somebody sacrificed in going out to minister. It doesn't always mean that it's a hard thing to do. When your heart is engaged and your heart is in love with Jesus, even a sacrifice isn't the challenge it used to be. Notice carefully, Elijah was willing to sow for his family, so to speak, and toward national revival. He was willing to sow what was most precious and most needed at the time in order to see a breakthrough in every realm of his life. There was revival in Israel. Evil was put away, and, there was rain, hallelujah. The outpouring of the Lord, and, the outpouring of what they naturally needed most—rain. Do you see the key? Only God could supply what they really needed, and He did. Elijah sowed water, and they reaped rain in abundance. In *one day* there was national revival!

We have to get our faith out there. I believe entire cities are going to be won in a day! I believe it's going to come down to testimonies like this. Maybe it will be you in your workplace or in your school—standing up and challenging the evolutionist, the humanist, the satanist. Then God shows Himself strong on your behalf and pours out the flood of His blessing. Lord, we pray, do it again. Let it come in buckets, in waves. Let it overfill the troughs, in Jesus' name. *(Written by Bob Nichols)*

DECEMBER 16
THE LIFE-PRODUCING WORD
LUKE 1:37

Luke 1:37 "For with God nothing is ever impossible and no word from God shall be without power or impossible of fulfillment" (Amplified).
God's Word is purposed to bless you and to impart the life of God to you. Luke wrote in his Gospel, that just as the rain that falls on good ground brings forth an overflowing abundance of life, in the same way, God's Word by its very nature has the power to bring life. God and His Word are one. To trust God's Word is to trust God Himself. Just as surely as the rain from heaven will make you wet, God's Word will produce life. His Word will bring grace and faith for change. First to you and then to your circumstances.

No matter what kind of lack or drought you may be facing today, your greatest need is for God's Word and His glorious presence. So my encouragement to you is not to take the Word of God for granted. Hear it, pray it, meditate it, speak it, declare it, and most of all, treasure it. It will bring grace and life to you and to all that you come into contact with. Allow the Father God to rain down upon you a flood of life-changing grace and mercy. *(Written by Marshall Townsley)*

DECEMBER 17
BREAKING THE CURSE OF POVERTY
MATTHEW 6:25-33

Matthew 6:32 "For your heavenly Father knoweth that ye have need of all these things."
The battle here is in the mind. God has already defeated poverty for us in Christ Jesus. We are blessed because we are in Him. To be able to partake in the blessing that is rightfully yours, you will have to overcome some soul trouble. The soul is the life of the flesh. It is our mind, our will, and our emotions. John said in 3 John 1:2, *"Beloved, I wish above all things that thou mayest prosper and be in health, even as thy soul prospereth."* It seems that we need to get it in our mind—which is part of our soul—before we can get it into our wallets.

You are going to have to change the way you think about your money and stuff. First, you must give up ownership. Ownership is God's part of the relationship. Stewardship describes our part. According to Psalm 24:1-2, the earth belongs to God and so does everything in the earth. Second, tithing is a "must." The tithe is not giving back God His part, because we realize that it *all* belongs to Him. Third, when we get it right with what we already have—meaning we are good stewards—He will allow us to steward over more. Look at James 4:3, *"Ye ask, and receive not, because ye ask amiss, that ye may consume it upon your lusts."* The moment we lose sight of the ownership issue, we have become covetous and thereby cut off the blessing. God wants us to think right about money. Matthew 6:24 says, *"No man can serve two masters: for either he will hate the one, and love the other; or else he will hold to the one, and despise the other. Ye cannot serve God and mammon."* If we fall in love with our money, we will not be able to do what He wants us to do with it.

1 Timothy 6:6-10, *"But godliness with contentment is great gain. For we brought nothing into this world, and it is certain we can carry nothing out. And having food and raiment let us be therewith content. But they that will be rich fall into temptation and a snare, and into many foolish and hurtful lusts, which drown men in destruction and perdition. For the love of money is the root of all evil: which while some coveted after, they have erred from the faith, and pierced themselves through with many sorrows."* It doesn't say that money is the root of all evil. It says the *love of* money is. I heard a minister rightly point out that there are people who don't have a dime that are sinning all the time, so having money isn't the problem.

The next step in the process of getting free from poverty is to fill your soul (mind) with what God's Word says about prosperity and provision. You will need to begin to change your mind with the Word of God. It is called renewing your mind. Prosperity begins on the inside and works its way out. Your soul begins to prosper the moment you believe and act on God's Word. Proverbs 22:9, Psalms 35:27, and Psalms 1:3 are great examples of scriptures you should be speaking and thinking about. Get a concordance, or search through your Bible and get some scriptures on your own. If your thoughts were previously formed with lack, they can now be filled with God's abundance! By appropriating what Jesus already did for you, and acting on the Word of God, you will break the curse of poverty in your life. *(Written by Bob Nichols)*

DECEMBER 18
GOD'S WORD WILL MAKE YOU PROSPEROUS
JOSHUA 1:1-9

Joshua 1:8 "This book of the law shall not depart out of thy mouth; but thou shalt meditate therein day and night, that thou mayest observe to do according to all that is written therein: for then thou shalt make thy way prosperous, and then thou shalt have good success."

Putting God's Word first in our attention and doing as it instructs will produce prosperity in every area of our lives. God is the one Who made us. He knows what makes us tick and how He created this world to function. The Bible is like the owner's manual or the manufacturer's guide for humans. Success comes by following the instruction manual. Failure comes when we do it our way (Jer. 10:23).

The Apostle Peter put it this way, "*his divine power hath given unto us all things that pertain unto life and godliness through the knowledge of him . . . whereby are given unto us exceeding great and precious promises . . .*" (2 Pet. 1:3-4). Everything we need comes through the knowledge of God. That's what His Word is. It's His knowledge recorded for us in black and white. Verse four says that God's knowledge has given us the great and precious promises. That's the Bible.

The world's system says, "The way to abundance is to hoard." God's Word says, "*Give and it shall be given unto you . . .*" (Lk. 6:38). The world says, "The way to happiness is to put self first." Jesus said, "*he that loseth his life for my sake shall find it*" (Mt. 10:39). The world says, 'hurt me and you will die." Jesus said to turn the other cheek (Mt. 5:39).

God's Word is awesome! Put God's Word first in your heart and actions, and watch prosperity come. *(Written by Andrew Wommack)*

DECEMBER 19
FAITH TO RECEIVE
MARK 9:14-24

Mark 9:23-24 "Jesus said unto him, If thou canst believe, all things are possible to him that believeth. And straightway the father of the child cried out, and said with tears, Lord, I believe; help thou mine unbelief."

Your faith is the key to your receiving from God. It is faith in the love, mercy and grace of God Almighty. It is the faith in the atoning sacrifice and resurrection of the Lord Jesus Christ. It is your faith in His promises—that He will do what He said He would do. Actually, He has already done it. We just have to accept it as ours. You are never too young for a miracle. You are never too old. The man in Mark chapter nine wanted desperately to believe. He realized that his faith played an important part in the miracle that was to come forth. He asked the Lord to help him, and He did.

Look at the following examples of receiving on the basis of faith. They apply to healing, but the same principle works for every need. In Matthew 9:22 it was the woman with the issue of blood; in Mark 10:51-52 it was a blind man; in Luke 17:17-19 it was the one leper that returned to give thanks—all these people had one thing in common. Jesus said, "*Thy faith hath made thee whole.*" I believe He clarified the point in Mark 11:22-24, *"And Jesus answering saith unto them, Have faith in God. For verily I say unto you, That whosoever shall say unto this mountain, Be thou removed, and be thou cast into the sea; and shall not doubt in his heart, but shall believe that those things which he saith shall come to pass; he shall have whatsoever he saith. Therefore I say unto you, What things soever ye desire, when ye pray, believe that ye receive them, and ye shall have them."*

If we believe, we receive the things we desire when we pray. When do we get the desire? When we pray. When do we believe? When we pray. When do we receive the things we desire? When we pray. Faith through prayer works for you individually, and it also works corporately. Just as a body of believers has corporate goals, you should have individual goals. And, you should pray about those goals. Faith believes, confesses, works, praises, and rests! The question is not, "Can God?" Yes, God can. The question is, "Can you believe?" "Will you believe?" I say, "Yes God can, and yes I will!" *(Written by Bob Nichols)*

DECEMBER 20
FIGHTING TO WIN AND KEEPING FAITHFUL TO THE END
2 TIMOTHY 4:7

2 Timothy 4:7 "I have fought a good fight, I have finished my course, I have kept the faith:"
Paul says that he has fought the good fight of faith. Do you know why it is a good fight? Because we are promised to win. It is a fight of faith. Prosperity never comes without conflict or adversity. The attitude we have when we face challenges determines the outcome of the fight. I want to share with you a few principles.

First, welcome conflict and warfare. Opposition many times, is a signal that you are making progress. Warfare always surrounds the birth of a miracle. Remember that many infant male children were killed after the birth of Christ.

Second, name your real enemy. Don't waste your energy and time fighting people. Satan is your enemy. Jesus is the Lion of the tribe of Judah. Satan is merely a roaring lion. He is a defeated foe. Third, use spiritual weapons. Our weapons are not carnal, but mighty through God. He has given us His Word. We have His Spirit and we have the name of Jesus.

Fourth, keep your eyes on the spoils of war. Champions always focus more on the spoils of war than on the conflict. Keep focused. You have a reward. You have an inheritance, a promise. Remember, where you are going is greater than what you are going through.

Last, give God time to work. Allow patience to have her perfect work. Allow time to be your friend. It is through faith and patience that we inherit His promises. After having done all to stand, STAND. You are promised the victory. *(Written by Mike Fehlauer)*

DECEMBER 21
TURNAROUND
LUKE 11:37-42

Luke 11:41-42 "But rather give alms of such things as ye have; and, behold, all things are clean unto you. But woe unto you, Pharisees! for ye tithe mint and rue and all manner of herbs, and pass over judgment and the love of God: these ought ye to have done, and not to leave the other undone."
The Pharisee in these passages of scripture was concerned about ritual, but Jesus was concerned about the heart. If cleaning up the inward man was the topic, why do you think Jesus turned to the man's giving? It sounds very similar to what He told the young man in Mark 10:21-23: *"Then Jesus beholding him loved him, and said unto him, One thing thou lackest: go thy way, sell whatsoever thou hast, and give to the poor, and thou shalt have treasure in heaven: and come, take up the cross, and follow me. And he was sad at that saying, and went away grieved: for he had great possessions. And Jesus looked round about, and saith unto his disciples, How hardly shall they that have riches enter into the kingdom of God!"* The man who is whole is a giver, not a hoarder. He looks at an offering as what he can share, not what he can spare. If your income belongs to God, your outcome will be established. The prosperous man determines where his money goes. The poor man has given up that privilege through debt.

The key to turnaround for me was tithing. The tithe forces you to face the issues of surrender and submission. There is liberty in that. It ends the struggle over who will rule—you? Your money? Or God? The non-tithing Christian is saying that he has the faith to trust God for his eternal salvation, but not with ten percent of his money.

The stronghold lies in the thought life. It requires a faith response to activate the power of the Word. Your mind can't figure out God or His ways. We need to pay attention to 2 Corinthians 10:5, *"Casting down imaginations, and every high thing that exalteth itself against the knowledge of God, and bringing into captivity every thought to the obedience of Christ."* Because, your thought life is really where you live! It's not so much what happens to you, as what you *think* about what happens to you that affects you the most. Prosperity has to be an internal reality first. The scorner is a scorner because his thoughts are full of scorn. Someone coined the phrase "Life is rough and then you die." That is not the confession of a believer! I like the way one friend of mine puts it, "Life is great and then we get to go to heaven!" The prosperous man has a prosperous thought life. His soul is prospering because he thinks on the Word of God.

Turnaround takes time. It takes 21 days to form a habit, but an entire year to make it a part of your life. Sure, God can do it in a day, but change begins with a decision right now to do what the Word says, regardless of what the circumstances say. Change takes place when the decision to do what's right, because it's right, has been acted on. Make up your mind to be a tither—not because of the blessing, but because it's God's will. Then the turnaround, and blessing, will come! *(Written by Bob Nichols)*

DECEMBER 22
FREEDOM FROM ARROGANCE
PSALM 131:1

Psalm 131:1 "Lord, my heart is not haughty, nor mine eyes lofty . . . . "
Unlike many leaders today, David was not afraid to share his secrets of success. He did not fear someone taking his insights and becoming more successful than he was. David was completely secure in himself and in the Lord. He wished others success and did not hesitate to share what he had learned in the process of becoming a successful king. One of four secrets described in Psalm 131, is David's freedom from arrogance.

Arrogance is exaggerated self-esteem. It is the source of the original sin of Lucifer (Isa. 14:12-14, Ezek. 28:16), and the source of all personal sins in our lives. This sin puts those who are arrogant into competition with everyone around them. It causes them to condescend to those they consider beneath them, and to be jealous of those who seem better. They are too proud to admit their own weaknesses or recognize anyone else's strengths.

They can tell a woman how to be a better housewife, a businessman how to better manage his company and the computer operator how to access the newest technology. The arrogant can teach others, but cannot be taught themselves. How can you teach someone anything who thinks he knows everything? Arrogance is the only disease that makes everyone sick except the one who has it.

The enemy of the arrogant is the confident. The confident person relies on God's grace and not his own ability. David's security did not come from his position as king, but from his relationship with the Lord.

He could lose his kingdom and not lose his security. If you met with King David, you would walk away saying, "He is still a shepherd; he is just wearing a crown." *(Written by Bob Yandian)*

DECEMBER 23
JESUS WAS THE NEW TESTAMENT PRECEDENT SETTER
LUKE 8:1-3

*Luke 8:3 "And Joanna the wife of Chuza Herod's steward, and Susanna,
and many others, which ministered unto him of their substance."*
Some people complain, saying all a preacher wants is money. We need to be aware of something: Preachers didn't start the concept of New Testament offerings—Jesus did. Jesus received offerings in His earthly ministry. He set the precedent. The practice of receiving offerings is a God idea. Man did not think it up on his own. In Luke 8:3, the word "substance" means possessions, goods, wealth, or property. There was a difference. Jesus didn't need a mailing list. He took His partners with Him! People gave to Jesus—gave Him their substance—because they believed in His ministry. They believed in Him. If you believe in a ministry, get behind it financially. If you believe in your church, get behind it financially. If you don't believe in it, you better find one you do believe in, because giving to your local church is one very major principle to living in prosperity.

Paul received offerings, too. Philippians 4:17: *"Not because I desire a gift: but I desire fruit that may abound to your account."* The motivation is not to get people's money, but first to worship God with our financial increase. Then second, that we may have fruit to abound to our account. The fruit is not all financial; the blessings touch every part of our lives.

It is a biblical principle to supply resources so that the Church will prosper—individually as well as corporately—and to be able to do the work of the Lord. 2 Corinthians 8:13-14: *"For I mean not that other men be eased, and ye burdened: But by an equality, that now at this time your abundance may be a supply for their want, that their abundance also may be a supply for your want: that there may be equality."* I like how the Amplified Bible shows 3 John 7-8: *"For these traveling missionaries have gone out for the Name's sake and are accepting nothing from the Gentiles. So we ourselves ought to support such people—to welcome and provide for them—in order that we may be fellow workers in the Truth (the whole Gospel) and cooperate with its teachers."*

If you are serious about wanting to prosper and have God's abundance for every area of your life, then it's time to get serious about doing it God's way. He set the precedent, we are to follow in His footsteps. *(Written by Bob Nichols)*

DECEMBER 24
HOW FAR ARE YOU WILLING TO GO WITH JESUS?
MARK 8:22-26

Mark 8:23 "And he took the blind man by the hand, and led him out of the town; and when he had spit on his eyes, and put his hands upon him, he asked him if he saw ought."
We usually focus on the miracle that this blind man received. But for a moment, think about the faith that this blind man exhibited.

Jesus took this man by the hand and led him out of the town. Remember that this man was blind. He didn't know where he was going and he was putting himself at risk. If Jesus decided to just leave him, what would he do? He couldn't find his way back on his own. He couldn't see. This man was committed. He was expecting to get healed. He made no other arrangements.

What if as soon as this man discerned that he was getting out of the area that was familiar to him, he decided to stop following Jesus? After all, if he remained blind he would be in trouble. It is probable that thoughts of unbelief like that would have stopped him from receiving his healing. He had to go all the way with Jesus. So do we.

There is no record that the Lord explained where He was taking this man or how far away it was. He was just told to hold on to Jesus' hand and follow Him. Isn't that enough? We often don't know exactly where the Lord is leading us or how things will go if we don't receive our miracle, but as long as we are holding the hand of Jesus, we should feel safe.

How far are you willing to go with Jesus?

The Lord didn't fail this blind man and He won't fail you either. You can feel His hand as you fellowship with Him today. You don't need a plan *b* or plan *c* in case Jesus doesn't work. No backups are necessary. Jesus is enough. *(Written by Andrew Wommack)*

DECEMBER 25
SUPER-NATURAL
PSALMS 119:128

Psalms 119:128 " Therefore I esteem all thy precepts concerning all things to be right; and I hate every false way."
God worked through the natural laws of the universe to bring prosperity to the man who was doing His will. Isaiah 55:10: *"For as the rain cometh down, and the snow from heaven, and returneth not thither, but watereth the earth, and maketh it bring forth and bud, that it may give seed to the sower, and bread to the eater."* What the rain does to bring forth fruit in the earth, the word does to bring forth seed and bread. God uses the natural and blesses it. It is His "super" on our "natural." He blesses the work of our hands so that we will be a blessing to others. Deuteronomy 24:19: *"When thou cuttest down thine harvest in thy field, and hast forgot a sheaf in the field, thou shalt not go again to fetch it: it shall be for the stranger, for the fatherless, and for the widow: that the LORD thy God may bless thee in all the work of thine hands."*

Both faith and natural laws come from the same source—God. God used natural laws to bring increase to the children of Israel. Deuteronomy 28:2: *"And all these blessings shall come on thee, and overtake thee, if thou shalt hearken unto the voice of the LORD thy God."* Abraham's flocks grew by natural means, blessed by God. God didn't just make things appear out of nowhere. He blessed what Abraham had and increased it. Whoever owns something has the right to determine how it is used. Who owns everything? That's right, God. Everything you have should increase godliness in your life in some way. The man who uses what he has, in a godly way, will receive increase. Your greatest increase will come from how you use what you have, not from what you don't have.

God lays out His wisdom, and His law for us. By knowing His ways, we will know how to prosper. Proverbs 10:2-6: *"Treasures of wickedness profit nothing: but righteousness delivereth from death. The LORD will not suffer the soul of the righteous to famish: but he casteth away the substance of the wicked. He becometh poor that dealeth with a slack hand: but the hand of the diligent maketh rich. He that gathereth in summer is a wise son: but he that sleepeth in harvest is a son that causeth shame. Blessings are upon the head of the just: but violence covereth the mouth of the wicked."* The Word gives us the spiritual laws. The spiritual laws describe reality whether people admit it or not. For example, God doesn't want His children to be bogged down with debt. He shows the consequence in Proverbs 22:7: *"The rich ruleth over the poor, and the borrower is servant to the lender."* We must control our lives so that we can live comfortably on what we make. Make use of what you have and God will supply what you lack.

We must be willing to change to be able to receive more from God. Until we are willing to change more, we have received everything we can. God's way is the right way. When we do it His way, we win.
(Written by Bob Nichols)

DECEMBER 26
JUBILEE
LUKE 4:18-19

Luke 4:18-19 "The Spirit of the Lord is upon me, because he hath anointed me to preach the gospel to the poor; he hath sent me to heal the brokenhearted, to preach deliverance to the captives, and recovering of sight to the blind, to set at liberty them that are bruised, To preach the acceptable year of the Lord."

Jesus returned from the Jordan River after being given power by the Holy Spirit. He came into his hometown and spoke in the synagogue as He had done many times before. Today the sermon was different because Jesus was different. He spoke about the anointing of the Lord to heal the sick and deliver the afflicted. He also said He had come to preach the *"acceptable year of the Lord."*

This event was the year of Jubilee that is taught in Leviticus, chapter 25. During this event, which occurs once every 50 years, every possession goes back to its original owner and all slaves are released. It is a legal holiday. The only way a person could miss repossessing lost articles was to be ignorant of the law.

Why did Jesus compare His public ministry to this Old Testament event? Because Jesus was anointed to bring back to us what had been taken by Satan. This is why he called healing from blindness *"recovery of sight to the blind."* During Jubilee, slaves were also freed. Through Jesus we have *"deliverance for the captives."* The Gospel is also preached to the poor. The riches taken by Satan have been given back to the redeemed.

Jesus also told us He would not only give the blessing, but remove the curse. Sight replaces blindness, liberty is for the bruised and healing is for the brokenhearted. Jesus removes blindness and gives sight. Why is this important? Jesus gives us what is rightfully ours and removes what is rightfully someone else's. Everything, good and bad, goes back to its original owner. Jesus took the blessing away from Satan and gave it to its original owner—us. He takes the curse from us and gives it back to its original owner—Satan. This new creation jubilee does not last one year; it is eternal. *(Written by Bob Yandian)*

DECEMBER 27
THERE IS ALWAYS MORE
EPHESIANS 3:20

Ephesians 3:20 "Now unto him that is able to do exceeding abundantly above all that we ask or think, according to the power that worketh in us,"

I have heard a minister say that if our shadows are not healing people, there's more. Yes, there is always more with God. We serve a limitless God. There is nothing that is unobtainable in the Spiritual realm. The only limit on God is the end of your faith—that is, where you stop using your faith. It is God's time to take the limits off! There is always a way with God! Isaiah 54:2-3, *"Enlarge the place of thy tent, and let them stretch forth the curtains of thine habitations: spare not, lengthen thy cords, and strengthen thy stakes; For thou shalt break forth on the right hand and on the left . . . . "*

Isaiah 61:7: *"For your shame ye shall have double; and for confusion they shall rejoice in their portion: therefore in their land they shall possess the double: everlasting joy shall be unto them."* God wants you to have at least twice as much—better marriages, better jobs, more profitable businesses, more revival, and more souls! 2 Corinthians 9:10: *"Now he that ministereth seed to the sower both minister bread for your food, and multiply your seed sown, and increase the fruits of your righteousness."* Enlarge! Expand! Raise the bar! Expand your vision!

Faith receives the promises of God. Faith always finds a way. We are not fear people. We are faith people. Trust God and believe God's Word! The Word is constant. Numbers 23:19: *"God is not a man, that he should lie; neither the son of man, that he should repent: hath he said, and shall he not do it? or hath he spoken, and shall he not make it good?"*

Matthew 24:35: *"Heaven and earth shall pass away, but my words shall not pass away."*

Go beyond what is normal, usual, expected, or necessary. If you are going to receive like you have never received, you are going to have to sow like you have never sown. Wayne Myers said, "I have never received more by sowing less." With God, there is always more! *(Written by Bob Nichols)*

DECEMBER 28
MONEY IS THE LEAST AREA OF FAITHFULNESS
LUKE 16:1-13

Luke 16:10 "He that is faithful in that which is least is faithful also in much: and he that is unjust in the least is unjust also in much."

This is an amazing statement from Jesus that has many applications. But in context, Jesus is speaking about money. The whole parable about the unjust steward is talking about his unfaithfulness with money. In the very next verse Jesus repeats this truth and substitutes the words *"unrighteous mammon"* for *"that which is least,"* leaving no doubt that money is the lowest level of stewardship.

This brings up some serious questions. If money is least, and yet we can't trust God with our finances, then how can we trust Him in greater things, like our eternal destiny? How can a person say, "O yes, I know I'm going to heaven, but I can't trust God to tithe." If we don't have enough faith to trust God to give, then how can that faith get us to heaven?

Jesus used this same reasoning to minister to the rich young ruler in Mark, chapter 10. This man had an outward show of devotion and he professed that he had done everything right. But Jesus saw his heart. Therefore, he told him to sell everything he had and give it to the poor. Jesus would be able to tell by his response to this command about money, how he really felt about God in his heart.

Our use of money says volumes about our faith in other areas. No one can profess true faithfulness to God who isn't faithful with his money. Money is the entry level of faithfulness. Financial stewardship is the very least state of faithfulness. It's like the bottom rung on a ladder. We can't go any higher if we don't take that step. Be faithful with your giving and God will move you up the ladder to greater things.   *(Written by Andrew Wommack)*

DECEMBER 29
RELATIONSHIPS THAT EMPOWER
1 CORINTHIANS 15:33

1 Corinthians 15:33 "Be not deceived: evil communications corrupt good manners."

If we are going to live a life of abundance, it is going to require healthy relationships. Anytime God blesses you, He sends someone into your life to be that vehicle of blessing. People around you will either increase you or decrease you. In Hebrews 12:1 the Apostle Paul encourages us to lay aside every weight and sin that does easily beset us. The idea is that our environment, which our relationships make up a large part, helps determine the outcome of our lives. For us to experience God's abundance in our lives, it is important that we guard our environment which includes our relationships.

God's Word many times commands us to abandon abusive relationships and pursue godly relationships. For example, in Romans 16:17, the Apostle Paul urges us that if we are around those who sow strife and division, we are to mark them. We are to make a mental note to avoid consistent contact with them. Many Christians have difficulty in recognizing unhealthy relationships as well as how to develop healthy relationships. The following are some characteristics of people who help create ungodly relationships:

  · People who are more critical than they are encouraging
  · People who belittle and laugh at your God-given dreams
  · People who embarrass and humiliate you
  · People who drain your energy and time through useless talk
  · People who demonstrate an attitude of criticism toward others

Being with people who do the following things are signs of a healthy relationship:

  · Speak words of faith around you
  · Build your faith in God
  · Are excited about your potential
  · Display mercy and love toward others

I hope you will examine the relationships you have today. Do they decrease you or increase you? If they decrease you, find some new friends.   *(Written by Mike Fehlauer)*

DECEMBER 30
GIVING BUILDS A MEMORIAL BEFORE GOD
ACTS 10:4

Acts 10:4 "And when he looked on him, he was afraid, and said, What is it, Lord? And he said unto him, Thy prayers and thine alms are come up for a memorial before God."

There was a man named Cornelius who was, according to 10:2, *"A devout man, and one that feared God with all his house, which gave much alms to the people, and prayed to God alway."* Here was a Gentile who was "doing the stuff." He was a man who loved God, was a big giver and was always praying. It doesn't seem like Cornelius was doing any of these things to try to "buy" God, but Cornelius was planting seeds the whole time. It was obvious that he wasn't giving to selfishly get, because when the angel appeared to him, it surprised him. His prayers and his generosity were building a memorial before a loving, all sustaining God. Proverbs 19:17 says, *"He that hath pity upon the poor lendeth unto the LORD; and that which he hath given will he pay him again."* If you put your money in a bank, it will gain only a small amount of interest. When you are generous to help those in need, God will repay you far more than any bank could!

Because he put God first with his heart, life and substance, God sent him a divine connection—a divine appointment. This man, Cornelius, went on to be part of the first New Testament Gentile revival! He and the others that were with him heard the glorious Gospel, were saved and filled with the Holy Ghost. Hallelujah!

Every time you are generous to give, every time you humble yourself, every time you honor the Lord with everything you have, you are sowing seed for revival in your life and in the lives of everyone around you. You are raising up a memorial to the Almighty God. Just as He did for Cornelius, when you honor God with a right heart, He will prosper you. *(Written by Bob Nichols)*

DECEMBER 31
NEW YEAR'S RESOLUTIONS
PHILIPPIANS 3:13

Philippians 3:13 "Brethren, I do not count myself to have apprehended; but one thing I do, forgetting those things which are behind and reaching forward to those things which are ahead . . . . "

Let me give you some great New Year's resolutions or for any time you want to start over in the year.

I resolve to be...

Like Enoch, to walk in daily fellowship with my heavenly Father;

Like Paul, to forget those things which are behind, and press forward to Christ;

Like David, to lift up my eyes unto the hills from whence comes my help;

Like Jehoshaphat, to prepare my heart to seek God;

Like Moses, to choose rather to suffer affliction than enjoy the pleasure of sin for a season;

Like Daniel: to commune with my God at all times;

Like Job, to be patient under all circumstances;

Like Caleb and Joshua, to refuse to be discouraged because of superior numbers;

Like Joseph, to refuse the seductive advances of this world;

Like Gideon, to advance even though those who are with me are few;

Like Aaron and Hur, to uphold the hands of my spiritual leaders;

Like Isaiah, to consecrate myself to do God's work;

Like Andrew, to strive to lead my brother into a closer walk with Christ;

Like John, to lean upon the bosom of the Master;

Like Stephen, to manifest a forgiving spirit toward all who seek my hurt;

Like Timothy, to study the Word of God;

Like Paul, to preach the gospel to all people everywhere.

We cannot go wrong following the examples of the men in the Bible. Life is based on choices that we make daily.

Let us go forward this year with a new ability to know God's direction for our lives, a new faith to call those things that be not as though they were, a new strength to accomplish all that He has for us to do this year, and a new glory so that we can walk like Jesus walked. This is our year to write history. *(Written by Dave Duell)*